THE UNIT PLAN:

A Plan for Curriculum Organizing and Teaching

by
Earl J. Ogletree, Ed.D.
Patricia Gebauer, MS.Ed.
Vilma E. Ujlaki, Ed.D.

University Press
of America

1/30/8r Beckert Tyler 1 3 75

CONTENTS

PREFACE

The Unit Plan is a method for organizing curriculum
and teaching from it. The unit provides the teacher
with the theoretical and practical background of
knowledge and skills with which he will be dealing in
the classroom. The purpose of this book is to provide
an overview of the unit plan. It answers these questions:
What is a unit? How does the unit relate to the
curriculum? How is it constructed? How is it implemented in teaching? What are lesson plans and how are
they developed? The volume includes a description and
discussion of the different types of units: resource
unit, subject matter unit, broadfield unit, teaching
unit, and different types of lesson plans. Through a
step-by-step process the reader will learn to develop
practical and effective units and lesson plans.
Behavioral objectives are also an integral part of
classroom instruction and unit planning. One chapter
is devoted to the introduction and review of formulating
and writing various kinds of objectives: behavioral,
instructional, conditional and competency objectives.
The strongest point of this volume, is the number of
presented forms, illustrative sample units and lesson
plans throughout the text. Learning by example is one
of the most efficient and effective ways of facilitating
the learning process. Here the student has a direct
and concrete reference to which he can refer as he
writes his unit.

This volume is intended for undergraduate and graduate students as well as in-service teachers, at all levels: Kindergarten-primary, intermediate, and secondary levels. The material in this volume will be especially helpful since writing units and lesson plans is one of the major activities in many pre-student and student teaching courses and in-service curriculum courses. Students and in-service teachers are usually on their own in the preparation of unit plans because it is an individual activity. It is for this reason that this volume is designed to be self-programmed. The student can proceed from section to section on his own. This is of great help to the instructor and curriculum supervisor. It frees them from having to teach the detailed step-by-step procedures involved in unit construction. Here the student or teacher has a ready reference for the development and organization of units and lesson plans to fit his own particular needs.

The idea for <u>The Unit Plan: A Plan for Curriculum Organizing and Teaching</u> developed out of the numerous courses in Principles of Teaching taught by the authors. These included the development of numerous classroom handouts on unit and lesson plan writing. This volume is the culmination of that often repeated but satisfying activity.

CHAPTER I

BACKGROUND OF THE DEVELOPMENT OF THE UNIT

One of the crucial problems which classroom teachers face today is curriculum planning. Whether the teacher is aware of it or not, she is a curriculum planner. She organizes the subject matter content, collects materials and resources, develops teaching strategies and implements them in the classroom. Today, curriculum planning is a much more complex and involved process than it was fifty or so years ago or even a decade ago. The knowledge explosion, the pressures of society and the multi-ethnic cultures, the technical revolution in society and education, the proliferation of resource materials and the many instructional options open to teachers, etc. have substantially increased the teacher's responsibilities Unlike her teaching colleague of the early 1900's, the teacher of today also has the responsibility of meeting the individual needs and interests of her students.

Historically, the curriculum has been organized by subject matter. There was little concern for the experiences and interests of the students. This initial pattern of dividing the curriculum into separate content areas became the basis of curriculum planning until the 1920's. It inevitably led to the atomization of subject-matter, fragmentation of knowledge and a memory-oriented daily recitational approach to teaching. It reduced the role of the

3

teacher to that of a purveyor of information and relegated the student to that of a passive learner. However, it expedited curriculum planning to organization of content by grade level and simplified evaluation procedures. It was assumed that subject-matter not only possessed its own internal logic of prerequisite learnings but an inherent motivational force as well. That is, if a given item of subject-matter impinged upon a student, it would motivate the student to learn. The subject-matter curriculum "was conceived as a body of facts, principles and so on, wholly outside the experience of the learner."[1]

It was during the late 1800's and the early 1900's that the concept of the <u>unit</u> emerged. The term <u>unit</u> connotes unity or wholeness, a deductive approach as opposed to learning isolated facts and subjects. Johann Friedrich Herbart (1776-1841) is credited with giving birth to the unit plan. However, it was Henry C. Morrison (1871-1945) who inaugurated its widespread usage. From 1925 to the late 1930's Morrison's unit plan influenced curriculum development and changed the format of high-school textbooks from chapters into a series of units.[2] As a result of the expanding curriculum offerings and the increase in subject areas to be taught, educators developed new methods of curriculum organization. The daily recitation approach was replaced by long-range curriculum planning, which was more comprehensive

---

[1]Thomas M. Risk, <u>Principles and Practices of Teaching in Secondary Schools</u>. New York: American Book Company, 1958, p. 152.

[2]Ernest E. Bayles and Bruce L. Hood, <u>Growth of American Educational Thought and Practice</u>. New York: Harper, 1966, p. 207.

4

in scope. Subject-matter was organized into different
types of units. One such organizational scheme was
the broad/fields approach in which reading, writing
and spelling were consolidated under the area of
language arts. General science, social studies,
health and safety, fine arts and so on emerged as a
result of this trend. (The different classifications
of units are discussed later in this chapter.)

During the early 1900's and 1920's there was
increased interest in the personal and social growth
in children and to give them "more intellectual
freedom and physical movement in education."[3] This
concern for individual differences in children and the
increased acceptance of Gestalt psychology, which
stressed wholistic and integrated learning, led to
the development and acceptance of the unit as a viable
means of individualizing classroom instruction.

Risk explains:

> Gradual acceptance of the unit as a basis
> for the organization of courses of instruc-
> tion resulted largely from a general recog-
> nition of the fact that learning in units
> can more effectively meet the needs of
> students than the traditional, fragmentary,
> lesson-assigning and lesson-learning
> procedure.[4]

These latter developments facilitated the idea that not
only subject-matter content should be organized and
unified to form the core of the unit plan, but the
experiences and interests of the learner should also
be the focal point of curriculum and, hence, unit
planning. This transition from subject matter to

---

[3]Charles J. Brauner, <u>The American Theory</u>. Englewood Cliffs, NJ, Prentice-Hall, 1964, p. 253.

[4]Risk, <u>op</u>. <u>cit</u>., p. 151.

learner concerns produced a multiplicity of curriculum
schemes and of unit plan types.

Types of Units

A number of different types of units emerged.
Basically they can be divided into two types--the
subject-matter unit and the experience unit. Both of
these types have been briefly discussed; the former
emphasizes the organization of subject matter, while
the latter stresses the learning experiences, interests
and needs of the students. Although both the subject-
matter and experience type unit contain subject-matter
content, their emphasis and application are quite
different. Unit plans identified by different terminology are actually the products of distinct educational philosophies and psychologies. All units
possess the similar characteristics of unity and
wholeness--the presence of some central factor to
which curriculum elements are significantly related,
or some common interest like a problem, project or
event, -- around which learning experiences are centered.
However, it is the philosophy of education and the
theory of learning that determines whether the
unifying element is the organization of subject-matter
content or whether the experiences and needs of the
learner are central factors in the organization of
learning resources.

Let us now examine the different types and
subtypes of unit plans.

Subject Matter-Type Units

Johann F. Herbart and Henry C. Morrison, as indicated, were the innovators and developers of the unit plan.

Herbart, who influenced the thinking of educators during latter parts of the nineteenth and early part of the twentieth century, developed a theory of learning based on the law of apperception and the principles of association and frequency of experiences. He felt if new ideas or experiences are related often enough they become conscious or perceived, thus forming an apperceptive mass of experiences.

Herbart regarded the ultimate goal of education to be the development of morally, well-balanced persons with many-sided interests. The person should become a responsible and contributing member of society by supporting its democratic institutions and laws and advancing the culture and the welfare of others. These attributes could be achieved through the right teaching process.

Although Herbart's curriculum emphasized the study of literature and history because they represented the best of human values and culture, there was nevertheless an attempt to select materials and procedures of teaching, based on his law of apperception in accordance with his conception of child development.

Herbart attempted to find a "method of sound, systematic instruction." In a way, he had attained scientific stature "in the sense that teaching procedures were applications of psychological laws or principles."[5] Out of his apperception mass theory evolved four steps of learning: clearness, association, system and methods. These four steps were later elaborated into the following five-step process by the students of Herbartionism:

1. <u>Preparation</u>. Past ideas and experiences are recalled and related to new ideas being

---

[5]Bayles and Hood, <u>op</u>. <u>cit</u>., p. 159-160.

introduced to bring the student to a state
of interest and readiness for the lesson.

2. _Presentation_. New ideas are defined and
    presented so clearly that the student
    understands completely.

3. _Association_. New ideas are compared and
    contrasted with ideas with which the
    student is already familiar.

4. _Generalization_. A general definition is
    formed on the basis of the combined new
    and old learning.

5. _Application_. Testing the principle with
    appropriate problems and exercises.

All learning was supposed to occur through these
five steps.

Herbart's five-step teaching procedure was widely
used by educators and became the basis of the lesson
plan and more recently, the basis of programmed
instruction.[6] "In the hands of Herbart's followers,
unit teaching tended to degenerate into a very formal
process in which all five steps had to be completed in
each single day's lesson."[7] With the advent of
Thorndike's behavioristic psychology, coupled with the
increasing formalization and rigidity of the Herbartian
teaching procedures, Herbart's soon fell into disrepute
among educators. Although Morrison's teaching procedures were considered to be an adaptation of Herbart's
five-step process, it was Morrison who implemented the
widespread usage of the unit. His theory of learning,
like Herbart's was not specific methods of teaching,
but an analysis of the teaching process.

---

[6]_Ibid._, p. 160.

[7]Ralph L. Pounds and Robert L. Garretson, _Principles
of Modern Education_. New York: Macmillan Co., 1967, p. 245.

Morrison's unit focused upon the process of astery, which is defined as "personality adaptation" o a learning situation. Morrison defines this earning Unit as "...a comprehensive and significant spect of the environment, of an organized science, f an art, or of conduct, which, being learned, results n an adaptation in personality."[8] Adaptation, once astered, included unity and permanence of learning. astery presumed understanding and the ability to emonstrate and apply the learning, rather than the emorization and regurgitation of facts.

Learning does not occur until there is some daptation of the personality. Learning, according to orrison, is expressed as either a change in attitude f the individual or as the acquisition of a special bility as the attainment of some form of skill in anipulating instrumentalities or materials."[9]

Morrison developed three types of units: science-ype, the practical arts-type and the appreciation-ype unit. Unlike the Herbartian unit, Morrison's nit plan required two to five weeks to complete. odified versions of Morrison's theories are still eing used at the secondary level. Morrison's teaching rocedures included in the adaptation unit were:

1. Exploration. Evaluation of what the student learns.
2. Presentation. New ideas are defined and presented understandingly.

---

[8]Henry C. Morrison, The Practice of Teaching in e Secondary School, 2nd ed. Chicago: University of icago Press, 1931, p. 24-25.

[9]Ibid., p. 17

3. <u>Assimilation</u>. Develop new understandings
   of the assimilated material similar to
   Herbart's last three steps of association,
   generalization, and application.
4. <u>Organization</u>. Writing from memory an
   outline of the unit.
5. <u>Recitation</u>. Discuss and write on various
   phases of the unit.

In spite of the rather innovative nature of
Morrison's adaptation unit, pupil progress was
measured by the mastery of the unit. Reorganization
of content was the focal point of the unit, and
mastery was the key to course reorganization, teaching
method and testing. The adaptation unit was a
methodological approach to subject-matter content into
a comprehensive unit plan. Subject-matter type units
took on various organizational structures. Let us
review some of these:

Classification of Subject Matter Units[10]

1. Single Subject Unit:
   Similar to a text; its purpose is to teach specific
   and distinct subject areas, such as history,
   English, and arithmetic. Subject-matter contents
   are not integrated.
2. Correlated Unit:
   Involves the correlation of one subject or topic
   with other related topics at certain points;
   e.g. certain facets of history may be utilized
   in the study of literature; e.g. music, art and
   literature may clarify the development of
   musical styles of different periods.

[10]Ross L. Neagley and N. Dean Evans: <u>Handbook for
Effective Curriculum Development</u>. Englewood Cliffs, NJ,
Prentice-Hall, 1967, pp. 2-5.

3. Cultural-Epoch Unit:
   The organization of single subject areas into a
   series of epochs or historical periods, such as
   "The Colonial Period, Industrial Revolution" or
   "Middle Ages." The epoch unit is a derivation of
   the Herbartian Unit.
4. Broad Fields Unit:
   Several closely related subjects are taught
   together, e.g. general science rather than the
   separate subjects of physics, botany, chemistry,
   zoology, etc.; e.g. social studies rather than
   separate courses in sociology, history,
   geography, etc.
5. Fused Unit:
   Two subject areas, such as English and Social
   Studies--are fused into a single area of study or
   a topic, such as history and literature during
   the Reconstruction or Rennaisance period.
6. Integrated Unit:
   Subject matter lines are totally disregarded,
   approach is through a broad topic such as: a
   study of a particular country; a social problem
   e.g. housing or transportation.

During the closing years of the nineteenth century
new ideas emerged concerning the role of the school in
relation to the needs of society and the nature and
interests of the child in the learning process. The
"center of interest" approach to unit development
evolved in which a systematic organization of content
was adapted to the needs and interests of the learner.
In contrast to the subject matter units, there appeared
the problem solving unit, the project unit, the activity
and the experience unit. Basically the difference
between the units is one of type, emphasis rather
than kind.

11

Development of the Pupil-Centered Units

In the 1920's the developers of the unit approach gave greater emphasis to the needs and processes of development of the child. This essentially was the beginning of experience-oriented units. John Dewey (1859-1952) evolved the problem unit based on the thinking processes. William Kilpatrick (1871-1965), applying the philosophy of Dewey, patterned his project unit on individualized learning, the purposeful activity of each student. Let us examine both Dewey's and Kilpatrick's approach to unit planning.

PROBLEM SOLVING UNIT

Dewey's problem-solving approach to learning in the "complete act of thought" involved students in the problems rather than inert subject-matter courses. Dewey was influenced by Darwin's theory of evolution which postulated an environment in which the organism lives, adjusts, and adapts itself to survive. During the life of the organism it encounters problems and situations which threaten his continued well being and existence. To exist, the man must be able to solve these problems and profit from the experiences. The interaction of man with his environment constitutes experience. Experience builds a social being. The ends of education, for Dewey, were growth leading to still further growth. Growth involved the ability to relate acquired knowledge to new knowledge in a practical way. Knowledge gained through experience in solving problems meant that education and life (being one and the same) were processes of continuous reconstruction of experiences.

12

Dewey's problem solving process included the following
five steps:[11]

1. The Problematic Situation. Perplexity,
   confusion, doubt due to the fact that the
   organism is involved or implicated in an
   incomplete situation whose full character
   is yet to be determined.

2. Definition of the Problem. Tentative
   interpretation of the given elements,
   attributing to them a tendency to affect
   certain consequences.

3. Analysis. Careful survey, examination,
   inspection of all attainable considerations
   which will define and clarify the problem.

4. Hypothetical Resolution. A consequent
   elaboration of the tentative hypothesis
   to make it more precise and consistent.

5. Solution. Taking a stand upon the projected
   hypothesis as a plan of action which is
   applied to the existing state of affairs
   in an effort to bring about resolution of
   the problem.

The problem-solving unit became quite popular because
of its compatibility to the modern technological
advances and the thinking of educators of the time.
To succeed, man must possess skills in the scientific
method and in problem-solving techniques. Like most
educational innovations, it was no **panacea** for
teaching techniques. Not all subjects nor educational
experiences readily adapt themselves to a problem-
solving approach.

---

[11]Outline developed by Dr. Maurice Collins,
Professor of Education, Chicago State University; used
with his permission.

PROJECT UNIT

William Kilpatrick's individual activity-interest
approach was patterned after Dewey's pragmatic
philosophy and scientific method. To Kilpatrick,
education needed a purpose if it was to be meaningful
to the student. Individual projects gave the student
a purposeful activity in which attitudes of cooperation,
participation and democratic ideals would be developed.
Borrowing from Dewey's five steps reflective thinking
process, Kilpatrick conceived of a four-step process
that a student should follow in the development and
completion of a project: have an objective or purpose,
develop a plan, execute or carry out the plan and
evaluate or judge the end product. Kilpatrick had
four types of project units:

Kilpatrick's Four Unit Types[12]

1. The Producer or Creative Project. The
   student formulates a plan or design
   which can be developed and constructed
   (e.g. build a boat, write a letter).

2. The Appreciation or Consumer Project. The
   student learns by means of vicarious
   experiences. He is an observer and a
   consumer of the works of others. He gains
   aesthetic experiences through reading,
   hearing a musical composition or viewing
   the works of artisans.

3. The Problem Project. The student solves
   and analyzes intellectual problems. (The
   problem project is similar to Dewey's
   problem-solving unit.)

---

[12]Bayles, et al., op. cit., p. 235-237.

4. The Drill Project. The student masters
    a skill by repetition and drill such as
    swimming, typing, writing or learning
    the multiplication table.

Not unlike Dewey's problem-solving unit plan,
Kilpatrick's had nearly identical flaws. Not every
subject or educational experience can be learned by
the project-method. "One of the criticisms of the
project method was that although it offered opportunities for physical activity, social contact and
individualized learning, many youngsters might not
progress beyond such activity."[13] Monroe also found
the project method to be incompatible with the
traditional classroom curriculum:

> ...the adoption of the project method...will
> make it impossible to follow a prescribed
> curriculum..A teacher employing the project
> method will seldom, if ever, be able to plan
> in advance the particular projects...he must
> utilize the purposes exhibited by his pupils.[14]

Therefore, teachers either neglected or only did minimal
preplanning of lessons. Brauner explains:

> The emphasis on such indirect learning in getting
> youngsters to plan and to do projects, in turn,
> led to the mistaken view that mastery of
> subject-matter content could be minimized in
> favor of procedures or techniques which were
> part of the general method called "project-
> method."[15]

The project method which was designed for shop and
agricultural subjects, eventually fell into disfavor
with school administrators and classroom teachers.

---

[13]Brauner, op. cit., p. 257-258.

[14]Walter S. Monroe: "Projects and Project Methods,"
University of Illinois Bulletin. Vol. XXIII, No. 30,
March 29, 1926, p. 16.

[15]Brauner, op. cit., p. 263.

Although it grew out of a general reaction against the traditional lecture-recitation approach, it was nevertheless a good example of an overzealous misapplication of a single approach to teaching.

With the increased emphasis on the interest and needs of the learner and the need to broaden the unit of work and to regain control over curriculum activities, the activity unit gained popularity.

ACTIVITY UNIT

The activity unit was a compromise to the problem-solving and project unit in that it also involved activity, experimentation and discovery. The activity unit was based on the principle that children learn best when they are actively involved in what they are learning. However, activity in the context of the activity unit meant overt or demonstrative activity--being physically involved in the learning process. This was one of its drawbacks. It is not always possible to identify the learning process with some type of overt activity. Nor is it always possible to apply motoric activities to all subject areas.

EXPERIENCE UNIT

The Experience Unit is perhaps the most popular and frequently used teaching unit at the elementary school level today. The emphasis is on a wide variety of pupil-related activities and learning experiences. The activities range from the covert-vicarious type to overt-direct type--from thinking to constructing. Activities are devised to bridge the gap between the student's past experiences and his new experiences. New learnings are built upon past learning.

16

In many ways the experience unit incorporates the
st elements of the activity and project units.
thin the framework of a comprehensive experience
it, students will be involved in <u>activities</u> related
general areas of human living and problems related
their own goals, needs and interests. Mehl, Mills
1 Douglas classify <u>activity</u> and <u>project</u> units under
e category of experience-type units.[16]

Risk made a distinction between the unplanned and
unned experience unit.[17] The unplanned experience
t is student-centered "It consists of a series of
sely related experiences or activities employed to
isfy some interest, carry out some purpose, or take
e of some felt need" of the students. Since the
rce of problem, topic or situations are the student's,
perience units cannot be completely planned in
ance..."[18] The planned experience unit involves
selection and adaptation of subject-matter content
learning experiences that students require. "The
mary objectives are the adaptations required to meet
dent needs" in fulfilling the objectives of the
t. The planned experience unit will be referred to
the teaching unit, which will be discussed in detail
Chapter IV.

TH STUDY PLAN
The Depth Study Plan is another name given for the
nned experience unit by Frost and Rowland in

---

[16]Maria A. Mehl, Hubert H. Mills and Harl R. Douglas,
ching in the Elementary School. New York: Ronald
ss, p. 177-178, (1958).

[17]Risk , <u>op</u>. <u>cit</u>., p. 157.

[18]<u>Ibid</u>., p. 161.

17

Curriculum for the Seventies.[19] The difference between
the planned experience unit plan and the Depth Study is
a shift in emphasis from content to planning. The
authors felt the common unit approach was too broad
and too shallow in content. They explain:

> The emphasis in the "Depth Study" is on
> process rather than on content--an approach
> that naturally tends to promote inquiry and
> discovery technique in student response.[20]

The depth study plan is an attempt to synthesize
the processes of self-initiated learning with the
structure of the subject matter, to cover less subject-
matter content but to gain a greater and more in depth
understanding of the subject. The in-depth study unit
is to help assure that topics are dealt with in detail,
and skills are developed through the processes of
inquiry and discovery.

The foregoing types of units--both the subject
matter-type and experience-type are what we will
connote as classroom teaching units in the broad use
of the term. They are units that the teacher would
use with a specific group of students in a classroom.

However, unit teaching requires preplanning. It
entails not only the construction of the classroom
teaching unit, but the planning of the unit and the
gathering of ideas, information and resources. There
is an additional classification of units. Jarolimek
classifies units into two categories--resource units
and teaching units. Therefore, unit planning has two
distinct stages--preparation and teaching. The
preparation stage entails the writing of a Resource

---

[19]Joe L. Frost and G. Thomas Rowland, Curricula
for the Seventies. New York: Houghton Mifflin Co.,
1969, p. 322-323.

[20]Ibid., p. 383.

18

nit. The teaching stage involves the development of
he classroom <u>Teaching</u> <u>Unit</u>.

Resource Unit

A resource unit is a flexible and rich reservoir
f teaching suggestions, resource materials, and
ctivities from which the teaching unit is prepared.

Jarolimek describes the resource unit as a
ollection of suggested teaching materials and
ctivities organized around very broad content topics
uch as "Germany," "Democracy" or "Health and Safety."[21]
he resource unit is applicable to a number of grade
evels. Therefore, it can be used by several teachers
eaching different grades to develop their teaching
nits.

Resource units are considered to be a type of
ourse-of-study unit or curriculum guide unit, because
ll three are to be used as a guide and a reservoir of
uggestions and materials in the implementation of the
eaching unit. (See appendix for additional information
n courses-of-study and curriculum guides.)

The National Association of Secondary School '
rincipals and the National Council for the Social
tudies have defined the Resource Unit as:

> ...a storehouse from which a teacher may draw
> both (1) information and (2) suggested methods
> from which to build a teaching unit for a
> specific class. In all probability, two
> teachers in the same school will prepare
> different teaching units after studying the
> Resource Unit...[22]

---

[21] J. Jarolimek, <u>Social Studies in Elementary</u>
<u>ducation</u>. New York: MacMillan, 1967.

[22] <u>Problems in American Life, Using a Resource Unit</u>,
Teacher's Manual), National Association of Secondary
chool Principals and National Council for Social
tudies, 1942.

(Chapter III explores in detail the development and writing of the resource unit.)

SUMMARY

The classification of a unit is determined by its use. Michaelis defines the unit plan as a curriculum outline of "purpose, content, main ideas, learning experiences and instructional materials."[23] Its definition also depends on the emphasis of the unit and the purpose for which it is being developed. The unit approach is an attempt to replace the fragmented and disjunctive methods of the traditional subject matter curriculum with a more unified and purposeful instructional approach. The modern approach, according to Pounds and Garretson, is an attempt to build a comprehensive study plan focused on and directed toward learning experiences based on a single theme. It usually stresses broad areas of knowledge or skills and the development of desirable attitudes.[24]

Sowards and Scobey define the modern unit of work as:

>...a series of highly related learning experiences of various levels, all focused on some significant aspect of the social or scientific-technological environment, and having as its purpose, the development of understandings, attitudes, values, appreciations and skills that lead to modification of behavior that are important to the children involved and to the wider society.[25]

[23]J. U. Michaelis, Social Studies for Children in a Democracy. Englewood Cliffs, NJ: Prentice-Hall, 1968, p. 203.

[24]Pounds and Garretson, op. cit., p. 238.

[25]Wesley G. Sowards and Mary M. Scobey: The Changing Curriculum and the Elementary Teacher. 2nd Ed. Belmont: Wadsworth Pub., 1968, p. 358.

The modern unit approach is a way of building in opportunities for individualization of instruction in the classroom by the fusion of subject matter with learning experiences and activities of many kinds. The difference between the contrasting types of unit plans is not one of kind, but of degree. In general there are two divergent types of teaching units: the subject-matter unit and the experience unit. Although both unit types include subject matter and learning experiences, the essential difference is one of emphasis. One stresses subject matter and the other learning experiences.

The unit approach is not without its shortcomings. It possesses all the potential liabilities of the textbook--outdated information, subject matter oriented, incompatible with the needs and interest of the students, too uniform and stereotyped--if not properly developed and implemented by the teacher.

A properly developed <u>unit</u> plan should have the following characteristics:

1. It has wholeness and coherence.
2. It utilizes a variety of modern principles of learning.
3. It is experience-based and life-centered.
4. It transcends subject-matter boundary lines and provides for the integration of subject-matter content.
5. It contains short and long-range objectives and learning experiences.
6. It provides a wide range of activities adaptable to individual differences.
7. It is flexible in terms of goal setting, integration of content, and developmental activities and adaptability to individual needs and interests.

21

8. It is informationally contemporary as contrasted with textbooks containing information that may be outdated.

9. It promotes cooperation, democratic planning and social development. It is a total approach in terms of the integration of learning experiences in the cognitive, affective, and psychomotor domains.

The unit approach, being a form of individualized curriculum development, is perhaps one of the most intrinsic and significant teaching procedures, yet developed and is still developing.[26] Gwynn concludes "...one factor is evident, namely, that the unit plan has had and will continue to have significant influence on the curriculum."[27]

When all has been said, it is the teacher who determines whether or not the implementation of the unit will meet with success.

---

[26] J. C. Peel, "The Ubiquitous Unit," _Phi Delta Kappan_, Vol. XXXVII, December 1955, p. 119-121.

[27] Gwynn and Chase, _op. cit._, p. 187.

CHAPTER II

WRITING BEHAVIORAL OBJECTIVES AND ACTIVITIES

Effective classroom teaching requires a sense of
direction, an aim, an objective. Teachers who have
their objectives clearly in mind are able to function
effectively; those who do not, encounter difficulties
in the classroom. Failure to formulate clear, specific
classroom objectives leads to irrelevant learning
activities and ambiguous evaluation procedures. As
a result classroom instruction will lack structure and
continuity.

This chapter will familiarize the reader with the
formulation and writing of behavioral objectives and
activities. If the reader follows the steps outlined,
he will gain skill in the development and writing of
objectives in the cognitive, affective, and psychomotor
areas, learn how to formulate general and specific
objectives (both conditional and competency based) and
understand how to develop learning activities from
specific objectives.

Once the reader has mastered the information, he
should be able to apply his knowledge of objectives and
activities to writing units, lesson plans, programmed
materials, and modules for the modern curriculum.

DEFINITION AND EXAMPLES OF BEHAVIORAL OBJECTIVES

Objectives, whether they be used in education or in
everyday life, are the ends which we intend to achieve
by various appropriate means. An objective is a goal,

an aim, an intent toward completion of a unit of work, a course of study or a culmination point of one's activities. The objective indicates the kinds of changes which will be brought about in an individual as a result of the instructional and learning experiences. Objectives are stated in terms of the learner.

The most practical objectives are those stated in terms which indicate change (behavior) to be brought about in the student and the subject matter or area of life in which this change is operative. For example, objectives stated in terms of behavior only may be stated as follows:

1. To understand
2. To appreciate
3. To construct

These are inadequately stated objectives because they contain only behavior and do not identify the content area to be studied. On the other hand, an objective stated with subject matter may be stated as follows:

1. Equivalent fractions
2. Daily newspaper
3. Three-dimensional paper mache puppet head

The subject matter or topic objectives are inadequate because they do not indicate behavior or changes to be brought about in the learner. Objectives containing both behavior and content are as follows:

1. To understand the concept of equivalent fractions by...
2. To appreciate the importance of the daily newspaper in our lives by...
3. To construct a three-dimensional paper mache puppet head by...

A functional objective must be clearly stated. It
should be definitive. It must define what the student
should be able to do, think or feel. It must define
the subject-matter content to be learned.

DOMAINS OF CATEGORIES OF BEHAVIOR[1]

Man has three ways of expressing himself--thinking,
feeling and willing. These modes of behavior can be
classified in three domains--<u>cognitive</u>, <u>affective</u> and
<u>psychomotor</u>.

Cognitive Domain:[2]

Essentially the cognitive domain deals with
cognition, recall, knowledge, intellectualization,
and the development of abilities and skills in these
areas such as the ability to comprehend, to translate,
to extrapolate, to interpret, to analyze, to complete,
to synthesize, and to judge. General categories of
behaviors are: knowledge, comprehension, analysis,
synthesis, and evaluation.

Behavioral Terms Used In the
Cognitive Domain[3]

...ve	Change	Appraise	Break down	Categorize
...fer	Combine	Compare	Describe	Construct
...dge	Comply	Compute	Estimate	Criticize

---

[1]Grunland, Norman G. <u>Stating Behavioral Objectives
for Classroom Instruction</u>. New York: Macmillan, 1970,
pp. 20-24.

[2]<u>Ibid</u>.

[3]The above and following lists were developed by
Alvin K. Claus, Psychology Department, National College
of Education, Evanston, Ill. Printed by permission from
a paper presented at the annual meeting of the National
Council on Measurement in Education (Chicago: Feb., 1968).

Label	Create	Conclude	Generate	Demonstrate
List	Defend	Contrast	Identify	Differentiate
Match	Define	Convert	Interpret	Discriminate
Name	Design	Diagram	Organize	Distinguish
Plan	Devise	Discover	Point out	Generalize
Show	Example	Explain	Rearrange	Illustrate
Solve	Extend	Justify	Reproduce	Manipulate
Sort	Modify	Operate	Rewrite	Paraphrase
State	Relate	Outline	Separate	Reconstruct
Tell	Revise	Predict	Subdivide	Reorganize
Use	Rewrite	Prepare	Summarize	
Write	Select	Produce	Support	

Affective Domain:

The affective domain includes such behaviors as interest, attitude, values, appreciations and psychological adjustments. General categories are: receiving, responding, valuing, organizing, and characterizing.

Behavioral Terms Used In The Affective Domain

Act	Accept	Attempt	Combine	Advocate
Adopt	Adhere	Arrange	Compare	Annotate
Alter	Answer	Explain	Compile	Challenge
Ask	Assist	Justify	Complete	Differentiate
Erect	Choose	Perform	Conform	Discriminate
Form	Follow	Persist	Consult	Generalize
Give	Modify	Praise	Defend	Initiate
Greet	Seek	Prepare	Describe	Integrate
Help	Select	Promote	Discuss	Investigate
Hold	Serve	Propose	Display	Objects (to an id
Join	Share	Read	Dispute	Organize
Label	Sit	Recite	Evaluate	Participates
Name	Solve	Relate	Explain	Point to

26

	Specify	Reject	Influence	Practice
ey	Study	Reply	Invite	Recommend
fer	Verify	Report	Justify	
der	Visit	Revise	Listen	
st	Work	Subscribe	Locate	
e | Write | Synthesize | Volunteer | |

Psychomotor Domain:

The psychomotor domain includes the development of
manipulative and motor skills. It includes the manipulation and handling of materials, speaking, writing,
and running, all of which require neuromuscular
coordination activities. These behaviors lend themselves to the fields of physical education, technical
courses, trades and practical arts, and activities such
as painting, drawing and diagramming. General categories
are: frequency, energy, and duration.

Behavioral Terms Used In The Psychomotor Domain

	Build	Change	Design	Assemble
x	Clean	Create	Compose	Calibrate
ip	Drill	Design	Connect	Collaborate
at	Make	Grind	Correct	Construct
ok	Mend	Hammer	Fasten	Dismantle
x	Mold	Nail	Follow	Identify
w	Sand	Paint	Locate	Manipulate
t	Stir	Start	Repair	Sketch
w	Tear	Weigh	Sharpen	
w	Wrap	Write	Weight	
e				

These are some of the behavioral terms in each of
the three domains of learning that can be used in
writing objectives. (See the appendix for additional
behavioral terms.) Occasionally behavioral terms appear

in all domains, cognitive, affective, and psychomotor.
They are selected to fit the intent of the objective.

IDENTIFICATION OF BEHAVIOR AND CONTENT OF OBJECTIVES

Let us now look at a few examples of behavioral
objectives and identify the behavior and content.
The behavior is underlined with a single line.
The content is underlined with a double line.

1. To differentiate the roles of people who work on
   a newspaper.
2. To describe the role and duties of the printer.
3. To explain the principles of the lever.
4. To diagram a class one lever.
5. To use appropriate reference materials in obtaining
   information.
6. To locate on a map areas in the Great Lakes Region
   where forests supply paper for newspapers.
7. To list the various kinds of information a newspaper
   reports.
8. To discuss the relationship of oxygen to carbon
   dioxide exchange in the respiration cycle.

EXERCISE:

It is now your turn. Underline that section of the
objectives which describes the behavior with a single
line, and the content with a double line.

1. To develop the ability to apply principles of proper
   nutrition.

28

2. To understand the development of humanism in contemporary French literature by outlining ideas of some writers.
3. To develop an interest to read the works of Russian authors.
4. To comprehend the practical application of stimulus response learning theory by describing an experiment.
5. To achieve communication in the correct use of English grammar in written communications.
6. To know what planet, astroid, comet and galaxy mean by defining each.
7. To gain skill in sharpening a drafting pencil correctly by frequent practice.

ANSWERS:

    1. To develop the ability to apply principles of...

    2. To understand the development of humanism in...

    3. To develop an interest to read other Russian...

    4. To comprehend the practical application of...

    5. To achieve communication in the correct use...

    6. To know what planet, astroid, comet and...

    7. To gain skill in sharpening a drafting...

If you have demonstrated the ability to identify both behavior and content, you are now asked to write your own behavioral objectives, identifying the behavior and the content. Use a single line under behavior and a double line under the content.

EXERCISE:

1.

2.

3.

4.

Each behavioral objective should contain only one
behavior. An example of a verbose objective is one in
which there are two or more behaviors such as: "to
understand and appreciate" or "to read and write."
Check your behavioral objectives.

GENERAL OBJECTIVES
Objectives can be stated on several levels. One
level is the broad aims of education which describe
general educational outcomes. Another level is the
specific objective which describes specific kinds of

30

behavior to be achieved in a particular unit of learning, a subject area, a course or a grade level program.

General objectives are considered to transmit culture, reconstruct society, or provide for the fullest development of the individual (as indicated in the imperative objectives below) or such general social aims as the development of the democratic way of life, civic responsibility, economic self-efficiency, self-actualization, or creativity.

I. GENERAL OBJECTIVES IN NONCONTENT AREAS
   (From National Imperative Objectives)

   A. To make urban life rewarding and satisfactory.
   B. To prepare people for the world of work.
   C. To discover and nurture creative talent.
   D. To strengthen the moral fiber of society.
   E. To deal with psychological tension.

The major reason for stating goals on such general levels is to provide a general orientation to the educational system or program. However, these general goals are too broad for making specific decisions about the development of curriculum and the selection of specific content and learning activities at the school and classroom level. Following are examples of general objectives in content areas.

II. GENERAL OBJECTIVES IN CONTENT AREAS
   A. To understand the principles of the lever.
   B. To be able to interpret data about heredity and genetics.
   C. To develop broad interest in the biological sciences.

31

D. To analyze the marketing processes.

E. To understand how fractions became part of
    our number system.

Objectives can be stated in either general or
specific terms. General objectives have the advantage
of giving one the long range or overall view of what
is to be accomplished, whereas specific objectives give
the short range view. Although the difference between
the general and specific objectives can be relative,
the distinction is in the specificity of the behavior
and the content.

DEVELOPING SPECIFIC OBJECTIVES FROM GENERAL OBJECTIVES

Specific objectives, which are also called instructional objectives, are developed out of the general
objectives. Following are two examples:

General Objective:
    To understand that gathering of news and printing
    of the newspaper required the work of many people.

(Any number of specific or instructional objectives can
be developed from the general objective.)

Specific Objectives:
1. To be able to list the major workers on a newspaper
    staff.
2. To know the duties of each of the major workers on
    the newspaper staff.
3. To understand the process of news gathering from the
    event of reporting to printing.
4. To be able to describe the kinds of information in
    the newspaper.

To be able to demonstrate the process of assembling
the newspaper.

To know how newspapers are counted, wrapped and
bundled for distribution to newsstands and agencies.

General Objectives:

To gain an understanding of simple chemical
equations--synthesis and decomposition.

Specific Objectives:

To be able to define an atom, molecule, and compound.
To be able to differentiate between atoms, molecules
and compounds.
To be able to demonstrate a synthesis reaction.
To be able to explain decomposition reactions.
To be able to diagram an atom, molecule and compound.

The above examples show how specific objectives are
delineated from general objectives. The specific
instructional objective behavior is more demonstrative
and concrete; the content is delimited and specific.

Write three specific objectives from the following
general objective.

General Objective:

To understand the use of common fractions.

Specific Objectives (state in three domains):

EXERCISE:

33

2.

3.

After this task is finished review the specific
objectives and determine if they:
1. Cover the general objective adequately.
2. Contain one specific behavior.
3. Contain specific content.
4. Are stated in the three domains--cognitive, affective
   and/or psychomotor.

WRITING OBJECTIVES IN PROPER FORM
Let us examine behavioral objectives more closely.
Objectives can be stated verbosely or succinctly. The
general rule for a properly stated behavioral objective
is that it should contain a single behavior and a
delimited segment of content.

General Objective:
To understand the respiration cycle.

Specific Objective:
To be able to draw a diagram of the respiration cycle.

To give an oral explanation of sequential processes
of the respiration cycle.

The above are well stated general and specific
objectives. They contain one behavior and specific
content.

The following objectives are poorly stated because
they contain too many behavioral elements and too much
content.

neral Objective:
To possess abilities and interest in observing,
defining, analyzing facts, and solving problems
related to respiration. (Eliminate all but one
behavior.)

ecific Objectives:
To demonstrate the respiratory cycle on the chalk
board and define the terminology. (Too many
behaviors.)
To draw a diagram of the interchange of oxygen and
carbon dioxide and explain the entire oxygen cycle
in the vascular system. (Too many behaviors and
too much content.)

CTICE IDENTIFYING OBJECTIVES
Following is an exercise in identifying well
ted (W) and poorly stated (P) objectives. (Circle
r W.) Rewrite the poorly stated objectives in their
per form.

W   1. To develop skills in using hand and power
         tools.

     1a _____

P W   2. To gain skills in independent project
           activities.

       2a _____

P W   3. To be able to define the functions involved
           in the digestive system.

       3a _____

P W   4. To develop desirable habits, traits and
           attitudes in oral communications.

       4a _____

P W   5. To gain essential skills in preparing the
           balance sheet and to understand the function
           of the ledger.

       5a _____
           _____

ANSWERS:

1. __P__   To develop skills in using (either) hand
            tools or power tools. (Too much content
            to be covered. These are two separate
            objectives, not one.)

2. __W__
3. __W__
4. __P__   To develop desirable (either) habits or
            traits or attitudes in oral communication.

5. __P__   To gain essential skills in preparing the
            balance sheet or to understand the function
            of the ledger.

CONDITIONAL STATED OBJECTIVES

Frequently instructional objectives can be clarified
if materials, data, time and other elements are specified
as being "given" or "withheld." It makes the objective
more specific and clearer. A statement of conditions
is not always needed, but if applicable, as in the

objectives listed below, they help fulfill the first
requirement of a good objective--clear communication.
The conditions are underlined:
1. Given a motion picture script of the "Egg and I,"
    students will memorize their parts.
2. Learners will draw and complete the geometric forms
    presented on the creativity test.
3. Given a German-English dictionary and a selection
    of Goethe not previously read or discussed, students
    will translate five pages accurately.

Exercises in Conditioned Stated Objectives:
    Examine the objectives below and draw a single line
under the condition segment.

1. Given a baseball and a target, set at a distance
    of fifty feet, the learners will hit the target.
2. Students will demonstrate the concept of positive
    and negative numbers using a number line at their
    desk.
3. Given an unlabeled anatomical chart of the human
    body, the class will label the parts of the
    digestive system.
4. From five bibliographical sources on Piaget's
    stages of cognitive development, the class will
    write a composition paper on the three stages of
    cognition.
5. On an electric IBM typewriter, students will acquire
    a typing speed of seventy-five words per minute.

ANSWERS:

1. Given a baseball and a target set a distance of
    fifty feet...
2. ...using a number line at their desk.
3. Given an unlabeled anatomical chart of the human body...

4. <u>From five bibliographical sources</u>...
5. <u>On an electric IBM typewriter</u>...

Write three conditional objectives in your area of
expertise:

EXERCISE:

1.

2.

3.

COMPETENCY STATED OBJECTIVES

   Most behavior can be measured, evaluated and
described. The statement of behavioral objectives in
terms of specific measurable outcomes facilitates the

process of evaluation. It not only enables the teacher to evaluate instructional goals, but gives the student a diagnostic tool for self-evaluation. It gives both teacher and students tangible criteria by which to measure curricular and student progress. Competency objectives may be written as follows (the competency level to be obtained by students is underlined):

1. Given a list of spelling words from a geography lesson, all pupils will spell at least <u>85% of the words correctly</u>.
2. Given twenty problems using Ohm's Law and a VTVM to measure voltage drop, all students will correctly calculate the amount of current passing through different size, color-coded resistors, <u>with 90% accuracy</u>.
3. At the end of the week, pupils will correctly solve problems dealing with division of fractions at a <u>75% level of proficiency</u>.

Exercises In Competency Level Statements In Behavioral Objectives:

Underline Competency Level with a <u>single line</u>.

1. Students will demonstrate interest in the poetry of Carl Sandburg by volitionally reading at least two poetic works by Sandburg.
2. Reading Mike Royko's <u>Boss</u>, all students will write a ten page term paper identifying at least ten current political figures and personalities involved in politics today.
3. To make the varsity squad, prospective candidates must make 7 out of 10 one-handed free throws.
4. Beginning electronic students, studying the schematic of a television receiver, must be able to identify all symbols representing resistors,

transformers, condensors, speakers, chokes,
induction coils and transistors.
5. Tryouts for the debate team must discuss the theme
   dictatorship vs. democracy and win at least one-
   half their debates to make the team.

ANSWERS:
1. ...<u>by reading at least ten poetic works by Sandburg</u>.
2. ...<u>at least ten current political figures and personalities involved in politics today</u>.
3. ...<u>make seven out of ten free throws</u>.
4. ...<u>all symbols representing resistors, transformers,
   condensors, speakers, chokes, induction coils
   and transistors</u>.
5. ...<u>at least one-half of their debates to make the team</u>.

Write three competency based objectives in your area of
specialty:

EXERCISE:

1.

2.

MULATION OF LEARNING ACTIVITIES

 The preceding material has illustrated the methods
which general and specific objectives are formulated
 stated. The process of curriculum development
ins with the formulation of general objectives which
e the overall purpose and direction and proceeds to
 development of specific instructional objectives
 the classroom. To implement the specific objectives
y must be translated into learning experiences or
ivities. On the following page is a schema for
riculum development:

41

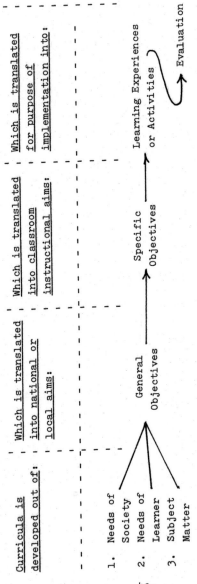

Curricula is
developed out of:

Which is translated
into national or
local aims:

Which is translated
into classroom
instructional aims:

Which is translated
for purpose of
implementation into:

1. Needs of
   Society
2. Needs of
   Learner
3. Subject
   Matter

General
Objectives

Specific
Objectives

Learning Experiences
or Activities

Evaluation

Activities or learning experiences are the means by
which the objectives are met and carried out. They are
the experiences students have in the process of meeting
the objectives of the instructional program. The basic
difference between specific instructional objectives and
activities is that activities are stated in present tense,
whereas the objectives are stated in future tense, goals
to be attained. The activity is generally more concrete
and specific than the objective, although it may not
always be the case. On the other hand, objectives and
activities are very similar in their formation, each
contains both a behavior and a content. For example,
behavior is underlined with a single line, content with
a double line):

Objective: To be able to recognize geographic symbols
               on a topographical map.

Activity: Identify three mountain ranges in the
               Western part of the United States on a
               topographical map.

Objective: To understand the molecular structures.

Activity: View a filmstrip on "Chemical Particles."

Activity: Prepare charts on three molecular structures.

Exercise In Writing   Activities:
Below are five activities. Underline the behavior
with a single line, the content with a double line:

Locate and measure the area of the Rocky Mountains
in the State of Colorado.

2. Prepare charts on three molecular structures.
3. Role play editor and copywriter of a newspaper.
4. Draw a cartoon for a comic strip.
5. Locate forest areas on a Great Lakes map which supply paper for our city newspapers.

ANSWERS:

1. <u>Locate and measure</u> <u>the area of the Rocky Mountains in the State of Colorado</u>.

2. <u>Prepare</u> <u>charts on three molecular structures</u>.

3. <u>Role play</u> <u>editor and copywriter of a newspaper</u>.

4. <u>Draw</u> <u>a cartoon for a comic strip</u>.

5. <u>Locate</u> <u>forest areas on a Great Lakes map which supply paper for our city newspapers</u>.

Write three activities in any content area, using the foregoing criteria:

EXERCISE:

1.

2.

3.

DEVELOPING ACTIVITIES FROM OBJECTIVES
      As indicated, activities implement the objectives.
The objective is that which the learner is supposed to
achieve. The activity is the means by which the learner
carries out the objective. The instructional process
begins with the overall or general objective, out of
which the specific or instructional objective is
extracted and developed. It is from the specific
objective that the activities are developed. Following
is an example of this sequence.

General Objective:
      To become familiar with Eugene O'Neill's life to
      understand the autobiographical nature of his plays.

Specific Objectives:
1.   To know the significance of O'Neill's philosophical
      views as reflected in <u>Long Day's Journey into Night</u>.
2.   To be able to select autobiographical elements in
      <u>Long Day's Journey into Night</u>.

Activities:
1. Choose two members of O'Neill's family whom you feel
   influenced him most. Write an essay, supporting
   your opinion or readings, discussions and lectures
   on O'Neill's life.
2. Dramatize a scene between Eugene O'Neill and one of
   his family members as shown in <u>Long Day's Journey
   into Night</u>.

A comparison of the above sequence of objectives to
the formulation of activities shows the continuity as
well as the integration of content in the general and
specific objectives and the activities. Each element--
from general to the more specific, to the activitity--
flows out of the other. Any number of specific objectives
could be developed from the general objective. Similarly
a number of activities could be developed from the
specific objectives.

<u>Exercise In Developing Activities From Objectives</u>:
Select and write a general objective from your subject
area.

General Objective:

Now that you have written your general objective,
does it meet the criteria of a well stated objective? If
so, write two specific objectives in the same content
area, which naturally evolve out of and are an integral
part of your general objective:

Specific Objective:
1.

2.

Are the specific objectives specific in content?
Could they be used in a daily lesson plan? If not,
rewrite them until they could be used in a daily lesson
plan. Do they contain both a specific and observable
behavior as well as a specific area of content?

Are the objectives stated in terms of the learner?
If so, proceed to write five (5) activities that reflect
the specific objectives:

Activities:
1.

2.

47

3.

4.

5.

    Do your activities accurately reflect the intent of
the objectives? If not, rewrite them. And write
additional activities that would adequately meet the
goals of the objectives.

The reader has been through a programmed method of
mulating objectives and activities. The rationale
the formulation of objectives at two levels--general
specific--is based on a systems approach which
ferentiates complex concepts, attitudes and skills
single, definable instructional objectives.* It
es structure, continuity and accountability to the
riculum. The continuity from objectives to activities
ilitates the process of evaluation because of the
ination of ambiguity. It provides a functional
ework for any instructional program.

---

*For an expanded and detailed program of objectives
and activity writing, the reader is referred to:
Ogletree, Earl J., and Hawkins, Maxine: <u>Writing
Instructional Objectives and Activities for the
Modern Curriculum</u>, New York, Mss Info, 1973, pp. 7-72.

APPENDIX

*Categorized List of
Behavioral Terms

*The following list was developed by Calvin K. Claus,
Psychology Department, National College of Education,
Evanston, Ill. Printed by permission from a paper
presented at the annual meeting of the National Council
on Measurement in Education (Chicago: Feb. 1968).

Additional list of action verbs for writing
behavioral objectives according to categories.

CREATIVE BEHAVIORS

k	Modify	Regroup	Paraphrase	Generalize
ter	Predict	Reorder	Question	Reconstruct
ange	Rename	Rephrase	Rearrange	Reorganize
sign	Retell	Restate	Recombine	Restructure
ry	Revise	Rewrite	Simplify	Synthesize

COMPLEX, LOGICAL, JUDGEMENTAL BEHAVIORS

sess	Analyze	Compare	Criticize	Structure
duce	Appraise	Conclude	Designate	Substitute
'end	Combine	Contrast	Determine	
'er	Induce	Discover	Formulate	
n	Suggest	Evaluate	Generate	

GENERAL DISCRIMINATIVE BEHAVIORS

t	Detect	Choose	Describe	Differentiate
ch	Order	Collect	Indicate	Discriminate
t	Place	Define	Isolate	Distinguish
k	Point	Select	Separate	Identify

SOCIAL BEHAVIORS

Admit	Allow	Accept	Contribute	Communicate
Agree	Argue	Answer	Disagree	Compliment
Aid	Dance	Execuse	Discuss	Cooperate
Help	Greet	Invite	Forgive	Participate
Join	Laugh	Permit	Interact	Volunteer
Meet	React	Visit	Praise	
Talk	Reply	Thank	Smile	

ARTS BEHAVIORS

Cut	Heat	Blend	Frame	Assemble
Dab	Hold	Brush	Hammer	Construct
Dot	Melt	Build	Handle	Illustrate
Draw	Nail	Carve	Paint	Polish
Mix	Pour	Color	Paste	Sculpt
Pat	Roll	Drill	Press	Sketch
Rub	Sand	Fold	Shake	Smooth
Saw	Stir	Form	Stick	Stamp

DRAMA BEHAVIORS

Act	Clasp	Express	Initate	Pantomime
Exit	Cross	Direct	Perform	
Move	Emit	Display	Proceed	
Pass	Enter	Leave	Respond	
Show	Tally	Verify	Tabulate	

LABORATORY SCIENCE BEHAVIORS

Align	Attach	Balance	Calibrate	Demonstrate
Apply	Insert	Conduct	Decrease	Operate
Feed	Limit	Connect	Lengthen	Manipulate
Grow	Plant	Convert	Prepare	Straighten

Keep	Remove	Dissect	Replace
Set	Reset	Increase	Specify
Time	Weigh	Report	Transfer

GENERAL APPEARANCE, HEALTH AND SAFETY BEHAVIORS

Comb	Clean	Clear	Button	Eliminate
Eat	Lace	Close	Fasten	Unbutton
Fill	Stop	Cover	Stack	Uncover
Go	Wait	Dress	Taste	
Tie	Wash	Drink	Untie	
Zip	Wear	Empty	Unzip	

MATHEMATICAL BEHAVIORS

Add	Bisect	Conduct	Calculate	Circumscribe
Check	Insert	Connect	Decrease	Demonstrate
Feed	Limit	Convert	Increase	Manipulate
Grow	Plant	Dissect	Lengthen	Straighten
Keep	Remove	Operate	Replace	
Set	Reset	Prepare	Specify	
Time	Weigh	Report	Transfer	

LANGUAGE BEHAVIORS

Call	Accent	Hyphenate	Abbreviate	Alphabetize
Edit	Print	Indent	Articulate	Capitalize
Read	Speak	Outline	Punctuate	Syllabicate
Say	Spell	Pronounce	Summarize	
Sign	State	Recite	Translate	
Tell	Write	Whisper	Verbalize	

STUDY BEHAVIORS

Cite	Chart	Circle	Arrange	Categorize
Copy	Label	Follow	Classify	Reproduce
Find	Name	Gather	Compile	Underline
Look	Note	Locate	Diagram	
Map	Quote	Record	Itemize	
Mark	Sort	Search	Organize	

MUSIC BEHAVIORS

Bow	Play	Blow	Compose	Harmonize
Hum	Pluck	Clap	Finger	Practice
Tap	Sing	Mute	Strum	Whistle

PHYSICAL BEHAVIORS

Arch	Face	Carry	Catch	Pitch
Bat	Grab	Push	Chase	Skate
Bend	Grip	Skip	Climb	Somersault
Hit	Jump	Step	Float	Stand
Hop	Kick	Swim	Grasp	Stretch
Ski	Lift	Toss	Knock	Swing
Run	Pull	Walk	March	Throw

APPENDIX B

COMMON VERBS USED IN WRITING EDUCATIONAL OBJECTIVES

abbreviate	balance	circle	contrast
act	bat	circumscribe	contribute
accent	begin	cite	convert
accept	bend	clap	cooperate
add	bisect	clasp	copy
admit	blend	classify	correct
agree	blow	clean	count
aid	bow	clear	cover
aim	bring	climb	crease
align	brush	close	criticize
allow	build	collect	cross
alphabetize	button	color	crush
alter	buy	comb	cumulate
analyze	calculate	communicate	cut
answer	calibrate	compare	dab
apply	call	compile	dance
appraise	capitalize	complete	decrease
arch	carry	compose	deduce
argue	carve	compute	defend
arrange	catch	conclude	define
articulate	categorize	come	demonstrate
ask	change	combine	derive
assemble	chart	compliment	describe
attach	chase	conduct	designate
attempt	check	connect	design
attend	choose	construct	detect

determine	extract	handle	label
differentiate	face	hang	lace
direct	fasten	harmonize	laugh
disagree	feed	heat	lay
discover	feel	help	lead
discriminate	fill	hit	leave
discuss	find	hold	lend
display	finger	hook	lengthen
dissect	finish	hop	lift
distinguish	fit	hum	limit
distribute	fix	hunt	light
divide	flip	hyphenate	list
do	float	identify	locate
dot	fold	illustrate	make
draw	follow	imitate	manipulate
dress	forgive	include	map
drill	form	indent	march
drink	formulate	indicate	mark
drop	frame	induce	match
eat	gather	infer	measure
edit	generalize	inform	meet
edliminate	generate	insert	melt
emit	get	integrate	mend
empty	give	interact	miss
end	go	interpolate	mix
enter	grab	invite	modify
erase	graph	isolate	mold
estimate	grasp	itemize	move
excuse	greet	join	multiply
exit	grind	jump	mute
expand	grip	keep	nail
express	grow	kick	name
extend	hammer	kneel	note
extrapolate	hand	knock	number

	prepare	sharpen	stir
˙er	present	shoot	stop
˙t	press	shorten	store
˙n	print	shovel	straighten
˙rate	proceed	show	stretch
˙er	produce	shut	strike
;anize	reset	sign	structure
˙k	respond	signify	strum
nt	restate	simplify	substitute
.tomime	restructure	sigh	subtract
˙aphrase	retell	sit	suggest
˙ticipate	return	skate	sum
s	revise	sketch	summarize
t	rewrite	ski	supply
	ride	skip	support
˙l	rip	slip	swim
˙form	roll	slide	switch
mit	rub	smile	syllabicate
k	run	smooth	synthesize
	sand	solve	systematize
˙ch	save	somersault	tabulate
˙ce	saw	sort	take
˙n	say	speak	talk
˙nt	scratch	specify	tally
˙y	sculpture	spell	tap
˙t	search	spread	taste
˙ck	select	square	tear
˙nt	send	stack	tell
ish	separate	stake	thank
ition	serve	stamp	throw
r	set	stand	tie
˙ctice	sew	start	time
˙ise	shake	step	toss
˙dict	share	stick	touch

trace	uncover	visit	weigh
transfer	underline	volunteer	whistle
translate	untie	vote	whisper
trim	unzip	wait	wipe
try	use	walk	work
turn	varnish	wash	wrap
twist	vary	watch	write
type	verbalize	weave	zip
unbutton	verify	wear	

COGNITIVE DOMAIN

ATING BEHAVIORAL OBJECTIVES FOR CLASSROOM INSTRUCTION

Examples Of General Instructional Objectives
And Behavioral Terms For The Cognitive
Domain Of The Taxonomy

LUSTRATIVE GENERAL STRUCTIONAL OBJECTIVES	ILLUSTRATIVE BEHAVIORAL TERMS FOR STATING SPECIFIC LEARNING OUTCOMES
know common terms	Define, describe
know specific facts	Identify, label
know methods and procedures	List, match, name
know basic concepts	Outline, reproduce
know principles	Select, state
understand facts and principles	Convert, defend
interpret verbal material	Distinguish, estimate
interpret charts and graphs	Explain, extend
translate verbal material	Generalize, give
use mathematical formulas	Example, infer
estimate future consequences	Paraphrase, predict
evaluate the relevancy of data	Relate, select
distinguish between facts and inferences	Illustrate, infer, outline, point-out
analyze the organizational structure of (art, music, writing)	Separate, subdivide

To write a well organized theme	Categorize, combine
To imply in data	Rewrite, summarize
To apply concepts and principles to new situations	Change, compute, demonstrate, discover
To apply laws and theories to practical situations	Operate, predict manipulate, modify
To solve mathematical problems	Prepare, produce
To construct charts and graphs	Relate, show, solve
To demonstrate correct usage of a method or procedure	Use
To recognize unstated assumptions	Break down, diagram
To recognize logical fallacies in reasoning	Identify, distinguish, differentiate
To give a well organized speech	Compile, compose
To write a creative short story (or poem or music)	Create, devise, design explain, generate
To integrate learning from different areas into a plan for solving a problem	Plan, rearrange, reconstruct, relate, reorganize, revise
To propose a plan for an experiment	Modify, organize
To formulate a new scheme for classifying objects (or events, or ideas)	Rewrite, summarize, tell, write
To judge the logical consistency of written material	Appraise, compare, conclude, contrast
To judge the adequacy with which conclusions are supported by data	Criticize, describe, discriminate, explain

To judge the value of a work (art, music, writing) by use of internal criteria and external standards of excellence

Justify, interpret, relate, summarize, support

AFFECTIVE DOMAIN

CHARACTERIZATION BY A VALUE OF VALUE COMPLEX

At this level of the affective domain, the individual has a value system that has controlled his behavior for a sufficiently long time for him to have developed a characteristic life style. Thus the behavior is pervasive, consistent and predictable. Learning outcomes at this level cover a broad range of activities, but the major emphasis is on the fact that the behavior is typical or characteristic of the student. Instructional objectives that are concerned with the students general patterns of adjustment (personal, social, emotional) would be appropriate here.

USING THE TAXONOMY OF EDUCATIONAL OBJECTIVES

Examples Of General Instructional Objectives And Behavioral Terms For The Affective Domain Of The Taxonomy

ILLUSTRATIVE GENERAL INSTRUCTIONAL OBJECTIVES	ILLUSTRATIVE BEHAVIORAL TERMS FOR STATING SPECIFIC LEARNING OUTCOMES
To listen attentively	Ask, choose, describe
To participate in class discussion	Discuss, greet
To complete laboratory work	Help, label

To volunteer for special tasks	Perform, practice
To show interest in subject	Present, read, recite
To enjoy helping others	Report, select, tell, write
To show awareness of the importance of learning	Follow, give, hold, identify, locate
To accept differences of race and culture	Name, point to, select, sit, erect
To attend closely to the classroom activities	Reply, use
To complete assigned homework	Answer, assist
To obey school rules	Comply, conform
To demonstrate belief in the democratic process	Complete, describe, differentiate, explain
To appreciate good literature (art or music)	Initiate, invite, follow, form
To appreciate the role of science (or other subjects) in everyday life	Join, justify propose, read, report, select, share, study
To recognize the need for balance between freedom and responsibility in a democracy	Adhere, alter, arrange, combine, compare, complete
To show concern for the welfare of others	Work
To recognize the role of systematic planning in solving problems	Generalize, identify, defend, explain
To display safety consciousness	Act, discriminate

To accept responsibility for
his own behavior

Integrate, modify,
order, organize

To understand and accept his
own strengths and limitations

Prepare, relate,
synthesize

To demonstrate self-reliance in
working independently

Display, influence,
listen, modify

To practice cooperation in group
activities

Perform, practice,
propose, qualify

To use objective approach in
problem solving

Question, revise,
serve, solve, use

To demonstrate industry, punctu-
ality and self-discipline

Verify

APPENDIX C

PSYCHOMOTOR DOMAIN

LIST OF ACTION VERBS FOR WRITING OBJECTIVES IN THE PSYCHOMOTOR DOMAIN

QUENCY

write smoothly and legible	assemble	hammer
draw accurate reproduction	build	heat
of picture (or map, biology	calibrate	hook
specimen, etc.)	change	identify
set up laboratory equipment	clean	locate
quickly and correctly	compose	make
RGY	connect	manipulate
operate a sewing machine	construct	mend
skillfully	correct	mix
operate a saw safely and	create	nail
skillfully	design	paint
perform skillfully on the	dismantle	sand
violin	drill	saw
TION	fasten	sharpen
perform a dance step correctly	fix	set
demonstrate correct form in	follow	sew
swimming	grind	sketch
demonstrate skill in driving	grip	start
an automobile		stir
repair an electric motor		use
quickly and effectively		weigh
create new ways of performing		wrap

Bibliography

Airasian, Peter W.: Use of hierachies in curriculum analysis and instructional planning. _California Journal Educational Research_, 54:34-41, 1971.

Airasian, Peter W.: Behavioral objectives and the teaching of English. _Engl J_, 60:495-499, 1971.

Ammerman, Harry L., and Melching, William H.: _The Derivation, Analysis and Classification of Instructional Objectives_. Washington, D.C.: George Washington University Human Resources Research Office, 1966.

Armstrong, Robert J. et al.: _Developing and Writing Educational Objectives_. Tuscon, Educational Innovations Press, Inc., 1968.

Symposium: Behavioral objectives and human values. _Educ Tech_, vol. 2, pp. 35-51, June, 1971.

Bloom, Benjamin S. (Ed) et al.: _Taxonomy of Education Objectives: The Classification of Educational Goals_, _Handbook I: Cognitive Domain_. New York, McKay, 1956.

Grunlund, Norman E.: _Stating Behavioral Objectives for Classroom Instruction_. New York, Macmillan, 1970.

Krathwohl, D. R., Bloom, B. S., and Masia, B. B.: _Taxonomy of Educational Objectives Handbook 2: Affective Domain_. New York, McKay, 1964.

Mager, Robert F.: _Preparing Instructional Objectives_. San Francisco, Fearon, 1962.

Ogletree, Earl J., and Hawkins, Masine: _Writing Instructional Objectives and Activities for the Modern Curriculum_. Mss Info, 1973.

CHAPTER III

DEVELOPING THE RESOURCE UNIT

Introduction

A unit of work is a method of individualizing the curriculum in which subject matter, materials and teaching procedures are organized around the learning interest of students and relevant topics, problems and issues. Unit planning varies from the general and exploratory overview of the <u>resource unit</u> to the more in depth <u>teaching or experience unit</u> to the very specific level of the <u>daily lesson plan</u>. There are different levels of units of work: 1) There is the preparation or preteaching unit better known as the <u>Resource Unit</u>.

There is, in addition, the teaching, experience or instructional unit which is used in the class with the children. 3) Lastly, there is the lesson plan, which in a sense, is a miniature unit used on a daily or weekly basis. All three forms or levels of units are related.

<u>The Resource Unit</u> is a method of organizing the content, objectives, materials and evaluative techniques for a teacher or a group of teachers in preparation to teach subject matter(s). It is a reservoir of ideas, materials, content and resources for the teacher from which to develop the teaching or experience unit which will be taught in the classroom. It is out of the experience unit that a series of daily lesson plans are developed and implemented. Therefore, there is a

three step process: The <u>resource unit</u>, the <u>teaching or experience unit</u> and the <u>lesson plan</u>.

This chapter will deal with the elements of and the steps needed to develop a resource unit. Chapter IV will explain and demonstrate the construction of the teaching or experience unit, and Chapter V will discuss the development of the lesson plan.

Definition of a Resource Unit

The resource unit is aptly referred to by some as the <u>source</u>. It is indeed a rich source of a great variety of learning activities, of multimedia instructional materials, of community resources from which the teacher can select for implementing and supplementing the textbook that still prevails in most schools. The unit approach not only richly implements the traditional textbook with a variety of other kinds of learning experiences but it also provides a convenient source of supplementary books to extend those experiences into more worthwhile and meaningful areas of learning.[1]

Mannello defines the resource unit as:

a statement of possibilities...a comprehensive guide from which the teacher may select to organize his instruction, a rich reservoir of alternative ideas some of which will be chosen by the teacher in preference to others.[2]

Aldrich, on the other hand, characterizes the resource unit in terms of its implementation.

A. It guides the teacher in a problem area or topic. It supplements the experience and background and provides new information on the topic for the teacher.

---

[1]Marcella H. Nerbovig. <u>Unit Planning: A Model for Curriculum Development</u>. Worthington, Ohio: Charles A. Jones Publ. Co., 1970, p. 12.

[2]George Mannello. "Resource Unit Versus Instructional System," <u>The Education Forum</u>, Vol. 35, November, 1970, p. 85.

B. The resource unit is a pool of activities, materials, resource and evaluative devices. It provides for different ability interest levels and needs of the students.

C. It is a guide to the development of a teaching unit. It provides directions or goals, variety and guidance. It clarifies objectives and suggests and describes competency based objectives, methods and instruments of evaluation.[3]

Jarolimek describes the resource unit as a collection of suggested teaching materials and activities organized around very broad topics such as "Transportation," "Nigeria" or "Communication."[4]

The construction of a resource unit is an exhaustive preparation by individual teachers or group of teachers on the background research of significant problem areas or selected topics. This research involves these individuals, whether singly or in groups, in the basic steps of learning, exploration and investigation of content and materials.

Preparing the Resource Unit

In many cases, it is not necessary for teachers either to develop their own resource units or to revise available units. Some school districts have prepared resource units for each grade level or for a block of grade levels, such as for the primary grades and middle grades. The resource units are sometimes bound into courses of study or curriculum guides or are simply kept in a file. Curriculum materials centers of most

---

[3]Julian C. Aldrich. How to Construct and Use a Resource Unit. New York: The Joint Council on Economic Education, (Mimeograph) 1941, p. 44.

[4]J. Jarolimek, Social Studies in Elementary Education. New York: MacMillan, 1967.

universities and teacher colleges keep a collection of commercial or published units as well as teacher-made or unpublished resource units. Examples of resource units can be found in "Selected Resource Units, Curriculum Series #11," National Council for the Social Studies, NEA, 1961. More recent sources of resource units can be found in the Education Index. (See the appendix for additional sources.)

The "ready-made" resource unit or school curriculum guide can save the teacher considerable time. In most cases some revision is necessary. Revising the "ready-made" resource unit is simply a matter of up-dating subject matter, content, materials and resources and revising the objectives and activities to meet grade level and pupil needs.

In some school districts where "platooning" or "departmentalization" of subject areas--such as mathematics, English, physical science, etc.--is practiced, it is possible for the teachers in these departments to develop teaching units or "work units" without first developing resource units. (See Chapter IV.) Often content area supervisors and curriculum specialist provide advice, resources, and materials that can be helpful to the teacher in the preparation of the unit.

The resource unit, if it is being prepared by a group of teachers, and possibly administrators, is generally designed to serve several grade levels and age spans, covering a broad subject area on such topics as "Germany" or "Latin America" or "The American Colonial Period," etc. Saylor and Alexander state that the teaching unit is prepared on specific content and is focused towards a specific grade level and ability of learning while "...the resource unit, if used in its entirety and without adaptation to a particular classroom, may have all of the weaknesses of a single textbook."[5]

Jarolimek suggests the following outline for a resource unit:[6]

1. Significance of Topic
2. Brief Outline of Topic
3. Possible Outcomes
4. Inventory of Possible Activities
5. Evaluation Suggestions
6. Listing of Materials for Reference Purposes

Strickland outlines some suggestions for selecting both a resource and teaching unit.[7] Steps three and four are more applicable to the resource unit, steps one and two to the teaching unit for the reasons given above:

1. The unit of work can be chosen cooperatively by teacher and children out of the interest and on-going activities of the group and in line with their self-appointed goals for the year.

   Pros: Best fits needs and interests of children; offers most chances to practice democratic procedure; unified year curriculum; teacher-pupils curriculum makers.

   Cons: Danger of repetition of other grades; omission of important areas; selection of unimportant areas.

2. The unit of work can be chosen cooperatively by teacher and children within the framework of flexible curriculum requirements so that it fits the needs and interests of children.

---

[5]Saylor, J. Galen and William M. Alexander, Curriculum Planning for Modern Schools. New York: Holt, Rinehart and Winston, Inc., 1966.

[6]Jarolimek, op. cit.

[7]Ruth G. Strickland, How to Build a Unit of Work. Washington, D.C.: U.S. Office of Education, 1962, p. 2. Pamphlet out of print.)

71

Pros: Pattern of continuity from grade to grade;
insures selection of important areas;
utilize cooperative planning by several
teachers; apt to be based on community-
pupil needs; teacher given broad outline
of goals, work; teacher-children plan units
and details.

Cons: Danger of areas of little interest to pupils;
less opportunity for value judgments; less
chance for democratic action.

3. The unit can be selected from source volumes which
list units of work or from collections of units and
logs or units which are sold.

Pros: Saves time of teacher planning; utilizes
knowledge of others on resources; probably
well prepared by experts.

Cons: Apt not to fit needs or interest of own
class; requires careful editing and adapting.

4. The unit of work can be developed from and around
required textbook material so that it meets the
textbook course-of-study requirement and still
incorporates as much as possible of child interest
and opportunities for initiative, enrichment, and
differentiated work.

Pros: Easiest to prepare; affords security of textbook for new teachers; generally units for
text given in teacher's guide.

Cons: May not be compatible to the achievement and
ability level and interest of the class.

Consideration of the interests and viewpoints of
the pupils can lead to the development of a more
exciting and relevant unit. This is why it is important to make the resource unit flexible and comprehensive.

Strickland emphasizes this point:

When an area of interest has been selected that
merits study over a period of time, the teacher
is ready to work out an overview of possibilities
and sum up teaching objectives of the resource
unit. The more thoroughly she has thought through

the learning possibilities of the area and her
own objectives the better prepared she is to
recognize and pick up leads from the children
and to guide their thinking as they make their
plans and set up their work. The teacher must
plan so that the children may plan. The children's planning will fall within the framework
of the teacher's planning, for the most part,
though there be times when their thinking
brings out points which had not entered into
the teacher's plan...The teacher's resource unit
should be comprehensive and contain many more
possibilities than appear in the actual teaching
unit for the children.[8]

structing the Resource Unit

The format of the resource unit can vary in terms of
ject-matter content and organization. Generally,
ever, the basic format contains the following
nents:

1. GENERAL OR OVERVIEW OBJECTIVES: Reasons and
   rationale for covering the unit work.
2. SUBJECT-MATTER CONTENT from one or more
   related areas.
3. LEARNING ACTIVITIES that will involve pupils
   intellectually, emotionally and physically.
4. INVENTORY OF SKILLS: Cognitive, affective
   and psychomotor that will help students
   modify their behaviors and enable them to
   cope with new problems, learnings and
   situations.
5. EVALUATION TECHNIQUES for continuous assessment
   procedures to help achieve the objectives of
   the unit.
6. RESOURCE MATERIALS: Teacher and pupil bibliography, audio visual aids and media, and
   community resources.

---

[8]Ibid.

Certain elements of the resource unit are emphasized and developed more than others. Since the unit is intended to include a broad area of subject-matter content and span several grade levels, the subject-matter content section should be expanded considerably as should the section on resource materials to include a multiplicity of immediate resources and projected resource materials.

Let us now examine the details of a resource unit. The following format is similar to the outlined form of the elements of the resource unit, except that each step or element is annotated to guide the student. Following the detailed resource unit format are sample resource units and further suggestions for the preparation of the unit.

Detailed Format of a Resource Unit

I. <u>A Title</u>: This might be a brief descriptive statement on the topic, or a question, about the content of the unit. The value of the unit can be enhanced by the use of an imaginative title. (See the appendix for unit titles.)

II. <u>Overview</u>: This is similar to a short preface. It is a concise descriptive summary of the content. Its purpose is to give direction to the unit and to orient teachers and administrators to what the unit is about. Others may wish to use it.

III. <u>General Objectives</u>: These statements should cover the scope of the unit adequately. They could be categorized into various domains of the cognitive, affective and psychomotor. The objectives are the "Why" for the unit

of work being important to study. (See Chapter II
for review on writing objectives.)

. Content or Subject Matter: The content can
be in outline form but must include the
actual facts, information, concepts, generalizations, issues, problems or questions to be
learned or answered. The content, in whatever
form it is to be presented, must be adequately
stated in the unit to assure the teacher both
the efficiency and the economical use of such
extensive preplanning. This part is the "What"
of the unit.

. Learning Activities: This part consists of
lists of suggested teaching activities through
which the content and skills can be taught
more effectively than if the straight textbook
approach were being used. Either of the
following approaches (A, B, C or D) may be used
to construct learning activities. This is the
"How" of the unit.

A. The activities may be categorized in terms
   of: Initiatory, developmental and
   culmination.

B. Or they can be categorized according to
   the ability, interest, and/or need levels
   of the class or individuals within it.

C. Activities listed under each of the three
   domains of learning--cognitive, affective
   and psychomotor--helps the teacher to be
   more aware of their inclusion in the
   actual plans for teaching--the teaching
   unit or lesson plan.

D. Use no categorization of activities. In
   this format, the various kinds of activities,

75

as many as possible, are simply listed
and are sorted out later when the teacher
selects from them for the teaching unit.
This is the most popular method of
categorization.

Classifying Learning Activities Into Initiatory, Developmental, Culminating Categories

1. **Initiatory** activities may consist of some of the following suggestions:
   a. Arrange room environment to include bulletin boards, display tables or exhibit cases of books, real objects, magazines, etc.
   b. View films, filmstrips, tapes, cassettes, or other visual aids.
   c. Take field trips to community resources.
   d. Invite resource people to the classroom.
   e. Do exploratory reading.
   f. Pretest pupils to discover informational background of the pupils.
   g. Teacher-pupil planning.
2. **Developmental** activities may be comprised of some of the following suggestions:
   a. Do research activities.
   b. Make presentation-type activities: oral reports, planning panel discussions, debates, dramatizations.
   c. Develop creative expression activities.
   d. Develop reinforcement-type activities: drill, practice and recitation sessions.
   e. Devise appreciation activities.
   f. Develop observation and listening activities.
   g. Invent group cooperative activities.
   h. Create experimental-type activities.

        i. Organize evaluative-activities that can be
            used on a daily or weekly basis.
3. <u>Culminating</u> activities may include some of the
    following suggestions:
        a. Exhibit pupils' work relating to the unit.
        b. Demonstrate skills and content learned in such
            activities as dramatics, panel discussions,
            original T.V. shows, radio skits, etc.
        c. Provide cognitive-type activities such as
            summary, review, transfer of learning, and
            sharing with others.
        d. Paper-pencil tests.

Culminating activities might be terminal or
continuing activities. The successful conclusion of one
unit can be the introduction to the next one, depending
on the particular intention of both the teacher and
the students. Thus, a final examination of the content
studied indicates a termination of that particular unit
of study, whereas panel discussions or debate-type
activities might introduce other aspects of the problem
or issue and can offer continuity to other units on
another level.

    VI. <u>Evaluation Techniques</u>: When employing
         evaluation techniques, stress should be placed
         on trying to find methods of evaluation that
         bring out not only what the pupils learn
         about a topic but also what they do with that
         learning. The process of evaluation should
         be continuous and cumulative. Samples of
         evaluation techniques may include some of the
         following:
         A. Devise sample test (teacher-made).
         B. Interview students.
         C. Employ pupil self-analysis inventories.

D. Use rating scales.

E. Use observation techniques.

F. Evaluate transfer of learning skills.

VII. <u>Bibliography of Materials and Resources</u>: This section of the resource unit should include all the books and journals, instructional materials, audiovisual media, community resources (both persons and places), and sources for obtaining additional information and appropriate materials. If this section of the resource unit is thoroughly investigated, and the feasibility of appropriate and adequate materials established, the success of the unit is enhanced. Many units fail to get off the ground because of the unavailability of materials for the type of teaching demanded by the unit approach. The following breakdown of the various categories of instructional materials will help the teacher in his initial explorations:

A. Teacher's bibliography of texts for background reading and reference

1. Reference Books

a. Encyclopedia

b. Atlas

c. Yearbook and almanac

d. Textbook--college level as well as student level

2. Non-Fiction--history, science, or whatever the subject of the unit

3. Fiction--The subject of the unit treated in fiction form, e.g.: Civil War: <u>Gone With the Wind</u>

B. Student's bibliography
  1. Student reference books
     All references listed above if suitable
     for students, too.
  2. Textbooks
     a. Grade-level textbooks in both the
        subject matter and related areas.
     b. Multi-grade level textbooks, both
        above and below to assure appro-
        priate reading levels for the class.
  3. Trade books
     Include all books pertaining to the
     subject, but not included under the
     textbook category.
C. Other readings
  1. Magazines and journals
  2. Newspapers
  3. Music
D. Audio-Visual Aids
  1. Films, filmstrips, slides
  2. Flat pictures and other graphics
  3. Tapes, cassettes, and records
E. Community Resources
  1. Places to visit
     a. Museums
     b. Special interest places in the
        local community
     c. Industry
     d. Businesses, etc.
     e. Governmental agencies
  2. Resource persons
     a. Experts in specific fields
     b. Travelers

79

    c. Hobbyists

    d. Foreign guests

  F. Manipulative--games, puzzles, art,
    equipment, instructional aides,
    programmed materials.

  The above format has been developed in some detail.
It is, of course, not necessary that a resource unit
should contain all these suggestions and sub-elements.
The length and detail of a resource unit depends on
the subject-matter content and the grade levels to be
covered. Generally units designed for the elementary
and intermediate grades would be of greater length than
units for junior high and senior high school grade
levels. A unit on literature, history or language arts
would probably be more extensive than a unit on mathematics and science. A lower grade level unit would
probably be longer than an upper-grade unit. Following
are two sample resource units--"Animals We Should Know"
for the 5th grade and "Business Organization and
Management" for the 10th grade level.

RESOURCE UNIT

ANIMALS WE SHOULD KNOW

OVERVIEW

The purpose of this unit is to introduce students
the various types of animals. It is also hoped
t the students will develop an awareness of the
ctions, uses, and relationships of these animals
our society. This unit is designed for the 5th grade
el.

OBJECTIVES

1. To be able to identify the various kinds of
   animals
2. To understand the importance of animals to man
3. To know some facts about the origin of animals
4. To develop a comprehensive view of the
   life of the various species of animals
5. To acquire some knowledge of the relationships
   between certain classes of animals and man as
   related to physiology and certain anatomical
   structures
6. To be able to understand the classification of
   the animal kingdom
7. To comprehend the necessity of animal conservation

OUTLINE OF CONTENT

I. How animals are classified
   A. Scientific classification
      1. Binomial nomenclature
         a. Scientific name
         b. Common name

81

B. Groups of classification
    1. Kingdom - shows how kinds of animals
        are related
    2. Phylum - 1 or more of same body
        characteristics
    3. Class - further division of phylum
    4. Order - sub-division of class
    5. Family - sub-division of order
    6. Genus - sub-division of family
    7. Species - sub-division of genus

II. Animals of the past
    A. The earliest animals
        1. Paleozic period
        2. Mesozoic period
        3. Cenozoic period
    B. Kinds of animals
        1. Vertebrates - those that have backbones
        2. Invertebrates - those without backbones
    C. First land animals
        1. Amphibians
        2. Reptiles
    D. Age of Dinosaurs
        1. Began 200 milion years ago
        2. Most spectacular land animals in this
            period
        3. Both plant and flesh eaters
    E. Why ancient animals disappeared
        1. Earth changed
        2. Unable to adapt to the earth's changes
        3. Evolutionary changes in other animals
    F. The age of Mammals
        1. Began 65 million years ago
        2. Prehistoric man developed $3\frac{1}{2}$ million
            years ago
        3. Many changes in earth's surface and climate

G. Living Fossils
    1. Resemble their ancestors
    2. Enable scientists to study their
       prehistoric ancestors and times
II. Kinds of Animals
    A. Tame and wild animals
        1. Kinds of animals
            a. Grouped according to the way they
               act with people
            b. Mostly pets and farm animals
            c. Majority of animals are still wild
        2. Functions of
            a. Tamed for food
            b. Used to help man hunt for food
            c. Used to carry burdens
            d. Hunted or grown for fur, skin, or
               wool to be used by man
    B. Land and Water animals
        1. Kinds of
            a. Strictly land animals (butterflies,
               apes, and eagles)
            b. Water animals (clams, sponges,
               and whales)
            c. Land or water animals (frogs,
               dragonflies, and toads)
        2. Functions or uses of
            a. Food for man
            b. Food for other animals
    C. Warm and Cold blooded animals
        1. Warm blooded - body temperature remains
           the same all the time
        2. Cold blooded - body temperature varies
           with the external temperature
            a. Includes all other animals

IV. The Importance of Animals
    A. Animals that help man
        1. How they help man (functions)
            a. Balance of nature
            b. Supply with food
            c. Provide food for most plants
            d. Used to increase man's knowledge about many diseases
            e. Supply many important drugs, such as insulin, used to fight disease
        2. Kinds of tamed animals
            a. Dogs, bees, ducks, geese, chickens, horses, pigs and cats
            b. Sheep, cattle, turkeys, reindeer, goats, donkeys
            c. Silkworms, guinea pigs, alpaca
    B. Animals that harm man
        1. How they harm man
            a. Eating him
            b. Poison
            c. Parasites (carrying deadly diseases)
        2. Kinds of harmful animals
            a. Snakes
            b. Lions and tigers
            c. Crocodiles and sharks
            d. Mosquitoes and tsetse flies
            e. Lice, blood flukes, and tapeworms
    C. Animals that man changes
        1. Ways changed
            a. By killing them
            b. Removing their living places
            c. Developed types that did not exist
            d. Breeding them for domestication

        2. Kinds of
            a. Wild oxen
            b. Mammoths and cave bears
            c. Buffalos
            d. Antelopes, elephants, zebras,
                and rhinoceros
    D. How man protects animals
        1. Where
            a. Wildlife preserves
            b. National parks
        2. How
            a. Laws and regulations
            b. Restrictions on hunting
V. Where animals live
    A. Mountain Animals
        1. Kinds of
            a. Rocky Mountain goats (North America)
            b. Chinchillas (South America)
            c. Vicunas (South America)
            d. Giant Pandas (Asia)
            e. Ounce (Asia)
        2. Environment (why there)
            a. Similar types of animals are there
            b. Move about easily
    B. Grassland Animals
        1. Kinds of
            a. African lions
            b. African elephants
            c. Kangaroos
            d. Giraffes
            e. Hippopotamuses
        2. Environment
            a. Openness easily adaptable to their
                swiftness

      b. Openness adaptable to largeness of
         the animals

C. Woodland Animals
    1. Kinds found in North America
      a. Brown bears
      b. White-tailed deer
      c. Moose
      d. Beavers
    2. Environment
      a. Small bodies allow ease of movement
         in brush
      b. Accessibility to both land and stream
      c. Food easily accessible

D. Desert Animals
    1. Kinds of
      a. Dromedaries (Africa and Asia)
      b. Scorpions (North America)
      c. Bobcats (Southwestern United States)
      d. Coyotes (Southwestern United States)
    2. Environment
      a. Can endure arid and hot climates
      b. Can live without water for several days

E. Polar Regions - Arctic and Antartic Circle
    1. Kinds of
      a. Polar bears (Arctic)
      b. Penguins (Antarctic)
      c. Walruses (Arctic)
      d. Caribou (Arctic)
    2. Environment
      a. Accessibility of fish
      b. Cold climate

F. Oceans
    1. Kinds of
      a. Whales
      b. Anemones

        c. Sharks

        d. Octopuses

VI. Ways of Life

  A. Animal Defenses

     1. Hiding (camouflage)

     2. Protective coloration

     3. Protective resemblance

     4. Playing dead

  B. Animal Weapons

     1. Built in armor

     2. Flight

     3. Lighting

     4. Chemical weapons (poisons)

  C. Animals and their Young

     1. Types of care

        a. No care at all

           1. Mollusks, starfishes

           2. Sea turtles, sea urchins

        b. Special care (feed their young,
           keep them warm, teach them to hunt
           for food)

           1. Sea horses

           2. Ants, bees, many mammals

        c. To fear man

           1. Deer

           2. Wolves

  D. Animal Homes

     1. Permanent homes

        a. Chipmunks

        b. Beavers

        c. Lions

        d. Ants

     2. Boundaries

        a. Usually set up by animals themselves

                     b. May extend from 3 feet to 15 miles
                         in any direction from home
             3. Types of homes
                     a. Nests
                     b. Dens
                     c. Burrows
                     d. Colonies
                     e. Hives
     E. Animals that live together
             1. Kinds of
                     a. Animals that do not fear each other
                     b. Animals that do not hunt other
                         animals for food
             2. Where animals live in
                     a. Communities
                     b. Herds
                     c. Flocks
                     d. Colonies
     F. Animals that travel long distances
             1. Reason for travel
                     a. Weather
                     b. Food
                     c. To reproduce
             2. Types of animals that migrate
                     a. Birds
                     b. Insects
                     c. Ocean animals
     G. Animals and climate
             1. Adaptation
             2. Hibernation
             3. Reasons for change
VII. Animal Bodies
     A. How animals move about
     B. How animals eat

C. How animals reproduce

D. How animals breathe

LEARNING ACTIVITIES

Teacher   I = Individual   G = Group

Visit Zoos   G

Compare human system with other vertebrates.   G

Divide students into groups and have each group
give presentation on one particular phylum of
animal.   G

Have students visit museum and write paper on one
type of pre-historic animal.   I

Have students construct bulletin boards on animals
in danger of extinction.   G

Have open discussion on what students feel they
can do to help conservation.   G

Have students find out what types of conservation
programs, if any, their particular city or state has.   I

Arrange a field trip to a wildlife preserve.   T

Assign students to discover what animals are native
to North America.   G

Show filmstrip.   T

Select a student to invite a speaker from a local
conservation or wildlife society.   I

Have students evaluate what they feel they have learned
up to this point.   G

View set of filmstrips on mammals.   G

Study and review vocabulary list.   G

Review for a quiz.   G

<u>Vocabulary</u>

prehistoric	genus	warm-blooded
kingdom	spawn	gestation period
environment	order	asexual reproduction
families	tundra	cold-blooded
reptiles	phylum	protective resemblance
conservation	cilia	migration
camouflage	fossil	sexual reproduction
adaptation	classes	regeneration
hibernation	species	fertilization
amphibians	trachea	tentacles

How Animals Are Classified

<u>Kingdom</u> Animalia	Includes all animals
<u>Phylum</u> Chordata	Includes all animals with backbones
<u>Class</u> Mammalia	Includes: 1. Animals with backbones 2. Animals that nurse (feed milk) to their young
<u>Order</u> Rodentia	Includes: 1. Animals with backbones 2. Animals that nurse their young 3. Animals with long, sharp front teeth

mily	
Sciurdage	Includes:
	1. Animals with backbones
	2. Animals that nurse their young

nus	
Tamiasciurus	Includes:
	1. Backbones
	2. Nurse their young
	3. Long, sharp front teeth
	4. Bushy tails
	5. Climb trees

ecies	
Tamiasciurus Hudsonicus	Includes:
	1. Backbones
	2. Nurse their young
	3. Long, sharp front teeth
	4. Bushy tails
	5. Climb trees
	6. Have brown fur on backs and white fur on their underparts

EVALUATION

pil Evaluation

1. Have pupils evaluate by means of oral reports and class discussion what they have learned in the unit
2. Have each pupil construct a notebook or scrapbook on a certain phylum, class and family of animals; the pupil-made notebook could include stories, photographs, pictures, newspaper clippings and poems

3. Have groups of pupils assigned to develop and construct a bulletin board each week, dealing with certain aspects of animal life

Teacher Evaluation

1. Do the pupils understand the different classifications of animals?
2. Do the pupils appreciate the role of animals in the world and the dependent relationship of man to animal?
3. Have the pupils developed their perceptual and problem solving skills?
4. Have the pupils gained skill in organization and classification of material?
5. Have the pupils grown in self-expression?
6. Do the pupils work cooperatively in group activities and class discussions?

BIBLIOGRAPHY OF MATERIALS AND RESOURCES

Student References

Chinery, Michael. Animals in the Zoo. New York: Taplinger, 1974. (Gr 4-6)

Dobler, Lavinia. Animals at Work. New York: School Bk. Serv., 1974. (Gr 5-6)

Fenton, Carrol L., and Kitchen, Hermine B. Animals That Help Us. rev. ed. New York: John Day, 1973. (Gr 4-6)

Fisher, Arleen. Animal Houses. Glendale, CA: Bowmar, 1973. (Gr K-6) Filmstrip and record also available.

Laycock, George. Wild Animals, Safe Places. New York: Four Winds, 1973. (Gr 5-7)

Ommanney, F. D. Animal Life in the Antarctic. New York: McGraw, 1971. (Gr 3 and up)

Teacher References

Bailey, Bernardine. <u>Wonders of the World of Bears</u>.
    New York: Dodd, 1975.

Cohen, Daniel. <u>Animal Territories</u>. New York: Hastings,
    1975.

Cole, William. <u>A Book of Animal Poems</u>. New York:
    Viking, 1973.

Hopf, Alice L. <u>Wild Cousins of the Dog</u>. New York:
    Putnam, 1973.

Milne, Lorus J., and Milne, Margery. "Animals," in
    <u>World Book Encyclopedia</u>. Chicago: Field
    Enterprise, 1975.

Sheldrick, Daphne. <u>Animal Kingdom</u>. Indianapolis, IN:
    Bobbs Merrill, 1974.

Shuttleworth, Dorothy E. <u>Animals That Frighten People</u>:
    <u>Fact Versus Myths</u>. New York: Dutton, 1973.

Audio Visual Aids

Films

<u>Animal Predators and Balance of Nature</u>. color, JRN,
    10 min., 1964.

<u>Animal Tracks and Signs</u>. color, EB, 11 min., 1961.

<u>Animals and How They Communicate</u>. color, COR, 14 min.,
    1966.

<u>Learning About Bears</u>. color, EB, 11 min., 1970.

<u>New Born Calf</u>. color, EBF, 11 min., 1970.

Filmstrips with Records or Cassettes

<u>Beishung: The Giant Panda</u>. color, #402-2, SVE, 60
    frames, 16 min., 1974.

<u>Kiboko the African Hippo</u>. color, #126-4, SVE, 55 frames,
    12 min., 1974.

<u>Koolah: The Koala</u>. color, #402-6, SVE, 60 frames,
    16 min., 1974.

<u>Marsu the Red Kangaroo</u>. color, #126-5, SVE, 56 frames,
    13 min., 1974.

<u>Tapes</u>

<u>Animal Classification: Reptiles</u>. Wollensak Teaching
    Tape, #C-7106, St. Paul, 3M Co., 1968.

<u>Animal Classification: Vertebrates</u>. Wollensak Teaching
    Tape, #C-7101, St. Paul, 3M Co., 1968.

RESOURCE UNIT
BUSINESS ORGANIZATION AND MANAGEMENT

OVERVIEW

The purpose of this unit is to familiarize 10th grade
students with Business Organization and Management.
The students will discover the importance of management
as a major function in our society. Management can
best be understood in relation to the role which
business plays in our society. Several significant
aspects of management will be introduced to the students.

OBJECTIVES

1. To develop an understanding of the evolutionary
    development that led to the modern concept of
    business organization
2. To discover the legal forms of ownership of
    business structures used as devices to
    facilitate the carrying out of business
    objectives
3. To recognize business organization and the need
    for careful planning
4. To appreciate the duties performed by personnel
    management and administration and their
    importance to successful business operations
5. To understand that a successful business must
    be conducted on the basis of sound financial
    principles
6. To learn the many factors involved in the
    logistic and purchasing procedures for a
    modern business enterprise
7. To be able to identify the various factors and
    characteristics of production

95

8. To know the marketing procedures of business
9. To develop an understanding for the need of a clearly defined system of control, services, and management in modern business
10. To show the importance of complex relationships existing among business, government, labor and the public.

OUTLINE OF CONTENT

I. Background in business organization
   A. Business difficulties in early civilization
   B. Development of cooperation among business groups
   C. Industrial Revolution
   D. Modern business in the United States
II. Legal forms of ownership
   A. Introduction to legal forms of ownership
   B. Individual proprietorship
   C. Partnerships
   D. Common advantages of proprietorship and partnership
   E. Corporations
   F. Cooperatives
III. Internal structure of business organizations
   A. Characteristics of a business organization
   B. Role of management
IV. Personnel management
   A. Role of personnel management and administration
   B. Determination of labor requirements and location of sources of labor
   C. The right person for the right job
   D. Provision for personnel changes
   E. Wage structure
   F. Determination of organizational stability

V. Finances
   A. Financial requirements of a business
   B. Sources and uses of funds
   C. Problems of financial management
I. Logistics and purchasing
   A. Logistics
   B. Purchasing
I. Production
   A. Definition of production
   B. Production processes
   C. Production control
   D. Production methods improvement
   E. Characteristics of production
   F. Factors of production
I. Marketing
   A. Nature of marketing
   B. Classification of goods
   C. Market information
   D. Distribution of information
   E. Promotion
   F. Prices and pricing
I. Auxiliary services
   A. Record-keeping
   B. Budget
   C. The office
I. Business, government, labor and the public
   A. Government controls and private enterprise
   B. Legislation affecting business
   C. Business ethics

LEARNING ACTIVITIES

. Lead a discussion of, "Why England was the
logical country for the origin of the Industrial
Revolution?"

2. Explain that businesses may have many forms, according to social, economic, and legal criteria, and discuss with students the fact that not all businesses can choose the form they wish and assume it.

3. Introduce management from a positive point of view.
   a. Place the students in a management position as small store owners.
   b. Challenge the students to solve representative management problems of a small store owner.

4. Present an overview of the problems, duties, and responsibilities facing personnel management administration.

5. Point out that it is much easier to gauge the financial needs of an existing business rather than a completely new one. Require that students list ways in which they might evaluate the capital of a business.

6. Ask the students to list types of businesses in which closeness to the market, not to the raw materials, is of prime importance.

7. Point out that while many laborers may lose jobs because of automation, many new ones will be created in the industry planning, building, installing, and serving automated systems.

8. Describe marketing as a function which takes into account all the people and the media involved in getting a product from the producer to the consumer. Name and briefly describe the people involved in the movement of the product.

9. Show the need for the keeping of records in various phases of business activities by

stressing the uses of record-keeping.
10. Begin a discussion of government control by
    suggesting it is necessary for the maintenance
    of private enterprises and fair competition
    and is designed to benefit ultimately the
    consumer.

cabulary

Industrial Revolution	insurance
social security	scheduling
business	automation
individual proprietorship	quality control
partnership	division of labor
corporation	specialization
managerial employee	skilled labor
committee	real capital
current asset	liability
job description	equity
labor market	securities

EVALUATION

oil Evaluation

1. Have students present a critique of business
   management problems of a store owner, small
   businessman, and corporation.
2. Have panel discussions on the influence and
   role of private enterprise.
3. Have students write a paper on the need for
   accurate record-keeping for the businessman
   for private enterprise.

Teacher Evaluation
1. Observe students throughout the unit for:
    a. Level of involvement and interest
    b. Knowledge of content and mastery of technical words related to the unit
    c. Attitude toward the subject
    d. Cooperation with others
2. Successful attainment of objectives:
    a. Do the students understand the marketing process?
    b. Are they able to define the role and appreciate the duties of management and administration?
    c. Have the students gained skill in business record keeping?
    d. Do they recognize the factors and stages of production and finance?

Teacher evaluation can be accomplished by an objective test which is devised from the test or constructed by the teacher.

BIBLIOGRAPHY OF MATERIALS AND RESOURCES

Student References

Grieco, Victor A. Management of Small Business. new ed. Columbus, Ohio: Merrill, 1975.

McFarland, Dalton. Management: Principles and Practices. 4th ed. New York: Mcmillan, 1974.

Mantell, Leroy H., and Sing, Francis P. Economics for Business Decisions. New York: McGraw, 1972.

Salzman, Stanley A. and Miller, Charles D. Business Mathematics. Glenview, ILL: Scott F, 1974.

Sharpe, William F. Introduction to Managerial Economics. New York: Columbia U Pr., 1973.

Teacher References

Flipp, Edwin B. and Musinger, Gary M. _Management_. 3rd ed. Boston, MA.: Allyn, 1975.

Hellriegel, Don and Slocum, John W. Jr. _Management in the World Today: A Book of Readings_. Reading, MA.: A-W, 1974.

Rosenberg, Robert R., et al. _Business Mathematics_. 8th ed. New York: McGraw, 1975.

Schmiedicke, Robert E. and Nagy, Charles F. _Principles of Cost Accounting_. 5th ed. Cincinnati: South Western, 1973.

Taylor, Bernard and Keith (Eds.) _Business Policy: Teaching and Research_. New York: Mcmillan, 1973.

Audio Visual Aids

Films

Basic Elements of Production. black and white, EBF, 14 min., 1954.

Challenge of Leadership. color, BNA, 14 min., 1961.

My Financial Career. color, NFBC, 7 min., 1962.

Poor Pay More. black and white, NET, 60 min., 1967.

Production Control Pt. 2. color, MGHT, 10 min., 1951.

Promise. color, IL BELL, 31 min., 1967.

World Trade for Better Living. black and white, EBF, 17 min., 1951.

There are additional resource units on other subject areas for different grade levels at the end of this chapter.

Practical Suggestion for Unit Writing:

As a conclusion to this chapter on the writing of a resource unit, an additional few practical suggestions of procedures are offered for those about to take this task to hand. The first task is to decide on the particular topic, question, or problem statement with which the unit will deal. This is best done by referring to the specific courses of study and curriculum guides available in the school district. After perusing the general areas of study recommended by the school district through the course of study, the teacher should also consult other curriculum guides outside his own area school district. This will help him not only get a better perspective of the subjects that are taught in his school but also those that are generally taught on his grade level elsewhere. Consulting outside guides also helps the teacher get new ideas about how to teach with different activities suggested by teachers outside his own system. This experience alone offers an opportunity to interact with other ideas and other teachers.

The topic or area of exploration for the unit having been decided the next step should be the statement of objectives. The objectives in a resource unit are most often written as general objectives. Ideas for writing these might be suggested by the courses of study and the curriculum guides from which the teacher is working.

The next logical step would seem to be to follow the outline suggested earlier in this chapter. However, the authors suggest a departure from the outline at

this point and suggest that the next step be the last
step of the outline: This is also called the <u>Bibliog-
raphy of Materials and Resources</u>. The student is
advised to explore all the materials both for background
and reference information as well as for instructional
materials and resources as his next step. This will
indicate to him right at the outset whether his topic
is worth the effort of such extensive research as he is
undertaking. If ample materials are available, these
are listed in their appropriate categories using
correct bibliographic entries. The **teacher** then can
proceed to the other parts of his outline with the
assurance that his efforts are worthwhile and that the
teaching units to be derived later from his resource
unit are feasible.

The reader goes through each section of the outline
listing all the facts and information, concepts and
generalizations he can find. Under the lists of
suggested activities it should include not only the
familiar types but should also include activities found
in other courses of study, those suggested by other
teachers and also ideas developed by the students themselves. This is an excellent opportunity to exercise
the imaginations of each student and to incorporate
new and fresh ideas into the curriculum through the
medium of unit teaching.

After the teacher has completed the various parts
of the unit outline, he will collate it into the suggested
format with the last part being the bibliography and
materials. The following is a summary of the suggested
procedure for working through the writing of the unit:

Guide for Compiling a Resource Unit

A. Select title
B. Write statements of general objectives
C. Explore the background of materials and resources
D. Write statement of content
E. List all possible kinds of learning activities
F. Devise inventory of evaluation techniques

The person who has expended the effort needed to construct a good resource unit will find later on in his teaching from it that it has been well worth the time. The new learning experiences encountered by the teacher in this endeavor will surely be passed on to the students, making their learning experiences more enthusiastic and more meaningful in the process than they would otherwise have been.

The construction of a resource unit pays off in other ways too. In truth, a resource unit, however complete it may appear to be when the teacher completes it, is never completed. The teacher who has constructed a good unit of work will find that it can become a process of constant renewing by the addition of new facts and information, the addition of new and different activities of newer materials of instruction and the discarding of those contents, activities, and materials that no longer are appropriate or valid. With such a resource at hand, no teacher should ever have to be afraid of outdated teaching practices.

(For additional information for sources and on the construction of resource units, see the Appendix.)

RESOURCE UNIT
THE STUDY OF MAN

OVERVIEW

The purpose of this unit is to increase the student's
erstanding of man's rise from the bow and arrow stage
the long ago Stone Age to the modern way of civi-
ed living. This unit on understanding the history
modern man through the study of fossils, rock
nations, legends, and other written records, was
igned for the sixth or seventh grade level.

OBJECTIVES

1. To know about the Prehistoric Period as the
   time of man's greatest invention which ended
   with the achievement of writing and written
   records
2. To understand the history behind modern man
   through investigation of the cultural stages
   of man two million years ago
3. To understand that the Greeks of 2,000 years
   ago built upon the accomplishments of the
   past and were the first to develop a democratic way of life
4. To understand that the cultural traits of man
   are the results of his physical inheritance
5. To realize that the physical traits of man
   are the result of his physical inheritance
6. To understand that the cultural traits of
   man are the result of his learning
7. To understand that man's physical inheritance
   and his culture change over the ages

8. To show an understanding of the relation of the present to the past by analyzing present conditions and problems in at least one culture
9. To manifest a knowledge of the use of research tools in the following ways:
   a. Efficient use of the encyclopedia to collect data
   b. Effective examination of the index and contents from at least three books other than the classroom text for completion of a classroom assignment
   c. Correct use of the library card catalog to locate authors, books, tapes, film-strips or other audio-visual reference for assigned topics
10. To demonstrate an appreciation for the achievements of at least one culture by means of creative expression, e.g. making a mural on the theme or constructing a bulletin board
11. To locate in an encyclopedia, or other references, the elements of culture left by Prehistoric races of man
12. To locate in an encyclopedia or other references, the classification of the races of modern man
13. To recognize that the things one spends time on shows one's value

OUTLINE OF CONTENT

I. Prehistoric Era
   A. Animals through the ages
      1. Determining existence of prehistoric animals

106

      2. Discussing disappearance of pre-
         historic animals
B. Earth
    1. Is a ball of solid land (lithosphere)
    2. Covered in part by water (hydrosphere)
    3. Surrounded by an envelope of gases
       (atmosphere)
C. Investigations of the lithosphere
    1. Rocks formed through heating and
       cooling of material in a molten state
    2. Rocks worn down by natural forces such
       as wind and water
    3. Fossil remains showing what life was
       like long ago
       a. Coal formation
       b. Amber formation
D. Classification of rocks
    1. Igneous
       a. Obsidian (Oregon)
       b. Basalt (Michigan)
       c. Pumice (Utah)
       d. Phyolite (Colorado)
    2. Metamorphic
       a. Quartzite (Wisconsin)
       b. Pink marble (Georgia)
       c. Green slate (Vermont)
       d. Dolomitic marble (Massachusetts)
    3. Sedimentary
       a. Bituminous coal (Pennsylvania)
       b. Limestone (Florida)
       c. Shale (Colorado)
       d. Sandstone (New York)
I. Anthropology
A. Physical anthropology

1. Human development
2. Fossil men
3. Classification of races
   a. Negroid race
   b. Australoid race
   c. Mongoloid race
   d. Caucasoid race
      1) The Nordics
      2) The Alpines
      3) The Mediterraneans
      4) The Hindus
B. Elements of cultural or social anthropology
   1. Paleolithic Age (1½ million - 8,000 B.C.)
      a. Used stones without being shaped
         or sharpened
      b. Handles fastened to spearheads
         with rawhide
      c. Used fire for heating and cooking
      d. Buried their dead
      e. Drew pictures on cave walls
      f. Used tendons of animals for thread
      g. Sewed with bone needles or with
         sharp thorns or pieces of wood
   2. Mesolithic Age (8,000 - 7,000 B.C. or
      longer in some other places)
      a. Bridged the gap between the Old
         and New Stone ages
      b. Disappearance of open plains
      c. Appearance of forests
      d. Hunting difficult
      e. Improved weapons by using tiny
         flints called microliths
      f. Polished and sharpened stones shaped
         to fit various needs
      g. Smoked fish to preserve it

3. Neolithic Age (7,000 - 3,000 B.C.)
    a. Cultivated wheat, barley, and other plants
    b. Domesticated animals such as dogs, horses, sheep, pigs and goats
    c. Formed clans, tribes and villages
    d. Baked clay and shaped into pottery
    e. Weaved flax and hemp into cloth
    f. Believed in gods of rain and sun

III. Early civilizations of man and their contributions
    A. Civilization in the Nile River (Egypt)
        1. Invented picture writing called hyroglyphics
        2. Made first convenient writing material called papyrus
        3. Worked out a calendar of twelve months of thirty days each
        4. Invented shadow clocks to measure time during the day
        5. Used numeral system based on 10 excluded zero as a symbol and use of the principle of place value
        6. Constructed irrigation system of ditches and dams
        7. Believed in many gods and life after death
        8. Developed a method of embalming or preserving bodies after death
        9. Built pyramid for pharoahs and their families
        10. Introduced stone architecture for homes, temples and pyramids
        11. First to develop the stone column

12. Developed world's first national government
13. Set up basic procedures of geometry and surgery
B. Civilization around the Tigris and Euphrates rivers in Mesopotamia (Iraq)
    1. The Sumerians
        a. Made earliest wheel yet discovered
        b. Invented the arch
        c. Developed cuneiform, a wedge-shaped writing
        d. Developed an economy based on farming
        e. Used a stylus (wooden stick) when writing on clay tablets which were later baked to preserve the message
        f. Counted by sixties
        g. Established a primitive democracy for their city-states
        h. Constructed houses and temples in cities of sun-dried brick
    2. The Babylonians
        a. Decorated bricks with color and with enamel
        b. Constructed tall buildings with outside inclines or ramps connecting the various floors
        c. Invented new ways of measuring by pounds and ounces
        d. Counted by twelves (dozen and foot)
        e. Divided the year into months, weeks and days
        f. Became world's first bankers

g. Created written laws, Code of
   Hammurabi
h. Believed in astrology
3. The Assyrians
   a. First to use horses and war
      chariots made of iron
   b. Used towers on wheels with
      battering rams to make a breach
      in the walls of a city
   c. Remembered for spreading fear and
      destruction
   d. Invaded and leveled the great city
      of Babylon to the ground
   e. Built new capital called Nineveh
      on the Tigris River
   f. Built a system of roads
4. The Chaldeans
   a. Defeated Assyrians and destroyed
      Nineveh
   b. Rebuilt city of Babylon
   c. Built the Hanging Garden of Babylon
      (Nebuchadnezzar)
. Civilizations beyond the Two Rivers
   1. Lydians in Asia Minor
      a. Became a great commercial center
      b. First country to cast coins
   2. Phoenicians in coastal areas of Syria,
      Lebanon and Israel
      a. First to send out explorers
      b. Spread civilization as they were
         seagoing traders
      c. Founded colonies throughout the
         Mediterranean Sea area

111

               d. Learned methods of manufacturing
                   from the Egyptians
               e. Left alphabet to the western world
                   which consisted of 22 consonant
                   signs
IV. Insights into Greek Civilization
     A. Beginning of Greek civilization before
         650 B.C.
         1. Added vowel signs to Phoenician alphabet
         2. Borrowed Lydian practice of using
             coins in business transactions
         3. Were buyers not sellers
         4. Improved use of sails for merchant
             shipping from the Egyptian invention
         5. Established trading posts which grew
             into colonies
     B. Greek civilization after 650 B.C.
         1. Were sellers not buyers
         2. Established independent city-states
         3. Established a system of sea laws later
             adopted by the Romans
         4. Produced first great dramatists,
             historians, orators, philosophers
             and poets
         5. First to study botany, geometry,
             medicine, physics and zoology on a
             scientific basis
         6. Gave us present day democracy

              LEARNING ACTIVITIES
1. Visit local museum to view accomplishments of
    man from prehistoric times to present day
    modern man
2. Make a time line of events covered

                    112

Find evidence for cultural borrowing in cook-
books, clothing, language, machines and so
forth

Have children locate geographical places
mentioned on maps

Keep a record of the services received and
given to show our dependence and need for
cooperation to live and accomplish all that
we do

Construct a bulletin board entitled, "Who
Will Depend on Me"

Compare norms of behavior of the past with
that of the present of a citizen, merchant,
woman and man

Scan newspapers or magazines for reference to,
or illustration of (a) barbarism (b) immortality
and (c) archaeology

Compare powers of our president with those of
the pharoahs

Make a salt and flour map of the Tigris and
Euphrates Rivers

Interview the oldest person in the neighborhood
to learn about how things were when he was
younger

Note the significant changes evident in one
person's lifetime

Draw a tree labeled "Roots and Fruits." Let
the roots represent the past, and the fruits
the present accomplishments

Start a rock collection and discuss the uses
of rocks

Make a fossil out of plaster of paris

Model out of sand, soil or clay a stream or gully

Find evidence of Greek architecture still in
existence

18. Draw wall murals on facts learned
19. Compare an American city with a Greek city-state
20. Compare art of ancient civilization of the Near East with the art of today
21. Establish a new city on another planet or in another place on earth. (a) Which characteristics of a modern city would you plan to have? (b) Which would you plan to avoid?
22. Build a model city or the city-states of Greece
23. Note in how many ways people who live near you adapt their patterns of living to the natural environment
24. Analyze the varying life style of a youth of ancient Athens and a youth of ancient Sparta

Vocabulary

igneous	physical anthropologist	Assyrians
fossil	cultural anthropologist	cunneiform
granite	paleontologists	metamorphic
talc	anthracite coal	caucasoid
topaz	bituminous coal	hieroglyphics
pumice	paleolithic	Sumerians
metallic	mesolithic	democracy
Sparta	Rosetta Stone	geologist
papyrus	phoenicians	Mesopotamia
quartz	nonmetallic	Chaldeans

EVALUATION

Pupil Evaluation

1. Have the pupils give oral reports on different sections of the unit
2. Have them discuss what they learned from or like most about the unit

3. Allow them to construct bulletin boards on different themes of the unit each week
4. Have them write stories or make up a skit or play about anthropologists in the future reconstructing our own present culture
5. Let them develop and construct the sequence of historical events as they unfold in the unit

acher Evaluation

1. Observe the pupils in the various activities of the unit:
   a. Did they enjoy the unit?
   b. How much did they learn before and after the unit?
   c. Did they cooperate in group activities?
2. Evaluate written and oral reports and projects on various aspects of the unit:
   a. Have they improved their research and investigative skills?
   b. Do they have good working knowledge of the vocabulary of the unit?
   c. Have the pupils improved in both written and oral expression?
   d. Are they able to initiate a project or piece of research and follow it through to completion?
3. Observe and evaluate pupils' attitudes.
   a. Do they really appreciate and recognize the contributions and struggles of past civilizations?
   b. Are the pupils able to relate to and appreciate people of other cultures?
4. Give oral and written tests to determine if the pupils have mastered the significant points of interest in the unit.

BIBLIOGRAPHY OF MATERIALS AND RESOURCES

Student References

Baldwin, Gordon C. <u>Inventors and Inventions of the Ancient World</u>. New York: Four Winds. School Book Service, 1973. (Gr 6-9)

Chard, Chester S. <u>Man in Prehistory</u>. New York: McGraw, 1973. (Gr 6-9)

Foster, Genevieve. <u>Birthdays of Freedom</u>. New York: Scribner, 1973. (Gr 6-7)

Goode, Ruth. <u>People of the Ice Age</u>. New York: Crowell-Collier Press, 1973. (Gr 5-7)

Leacroft, Helen, and Leacroft, Richard. <u>The Buildings of Ancient Man</u>. Reading, MA.: Young Scott Bks, 1973. (Gr 5-7)

Wallbank, Walter T. et al. <u>Civilization Past and Present</u>. 4th ed. Glenview, Illinois: Scott F., 1975. (Gr 6-9)

Teacher References

Larue, Gerald A. <u>Ancient Myth and Modern Man</u>. Englewood Cliffs, NJ: P-H, 1975.

Morgan, Lewis. <u>Ancient Society</u>. New York: Gordon Pr, 1974.

Sabloff, Jeremy A. and Lamberg-Karlovsky, C.C. Albuquerque, NM: U of NM Pr, 1975.

Seton, Lloyd et al. <u>Ancient Architecture: Egypt, Mesopotamia, Crete</u>. New York: Abrams, 1974.

Short, Luke. <u>Man from Two Rivers</u>. New York: Bantam, 1974.

<u>World Book Encyclopedia</u>. Field Ent. Chicago, 1975.

Audio Visual Aids

Films

<u>Ancient Egypt</u>. color, COR, 11 min., 1952.

<u>Ancient Mesopotamia</u>. color, COR, 11 min., 1953.

<u>Anthropology, A Study of People</u>. color, BFA, 16 min., 1970.

116

Life in Ancient Greece, Role of the Citizen. black and
     white, COR, 13 min., 1959.

Life in the Nile Valley. color, COR, 11 min., 1962.

What's So Important About a Wheel. color, FAC, 14 min.,
     1970.

Filmstrips

Earth and It's Neighbors in Space: Our Earth. color,
     #8412, Chicago, EBF, 48 frames, 1956.

Earth and It's Wonders: Story of Ice and Glaciers. color,
     #7485, Chicago, EBF, 52 frames, 1952.

Earth and It's Wonders: Story of Rivers. color, #7481,
     Chicago, EBF, 54 frames, 1952.

Earth and It's Wonders: Story of Volcanoes. color,
     #7486, Chicago, EBF, 54 frames, 1953.

Earth Science Series: Metamorphic Rocks. color, #FS-6,
     New York, Ward's, 56 frames, 1961.

Earth Science Series: Sedimentary Rocks. color, #FS-5,
     New York, Ward's, 62 frames, 1961.

Golden Age: The Ascendancy of Athens (480 B.C. - 448 B.C.).
     color, #5690, SVE, 52 frames, 18 min., 1969.

Rise of the City States (750 B.C. - 480 B.C.). color,
     #5689, SVE, 54 frames, 18 min., 1969.

Tapes

Democracy: Ancient Greece. Wollensak Teaching Tape,
     #C-5771, St. Paul, 3M Co., 1968.

RESOURCE UNIT
TESL -- TEACHING ENGLISH AS A SECOND LANGUAGE

OVERVIEW

The development of wide-spread TESL (Teaching English as a Second Language) programs has made it necessary for teachers to develop different ways of teaching subjects in English to her non-English speaking pupils. Language arts to pupils who are learning English as a second language becomes a drill in vocabulary, pronunciation and basic American English conversation.

This unit is designed to cover approximately a six-week period of time in an intermediate classroom during the early part of the school year. The first few weeks of school are spent in getting into the habit of speaking, hearing, and writing English. Basic vocabulary on classroom objects, clothing, family, etc. as well as structure patterns is learned and intensively practiced.

OBJECTIVES

1. To learn a useful vocabulary related to sports that are familiar to native Spanish speakers and native English speakers
2. To learn how to conduct a class meeting
3. To exchange and enjoy various games and sports of the Americans
4. To grasp the structure of simple sentences using the personal pronouns, vocabulary and verbs in the unit

118

5. To learn the names of the parts of the body in English
6. To learn popular singing games
7. To develop the ability to pantomime
8. To understand the simple past and future tenses of the verbs in this unit
9. To spell the contractions involving some personal pronouns and the verb will
10. To learn the use of the telephone in conducting a polite and clear conversation
11. To exchange food recipes typical of different cultures in America
12. To become acquainted with the neighborhood grocer in a small ethnic store and with the local supermarket
13. To effectively order groceries at the store or by telephone
14. To correctly pronounce all new words
15. To correctly spell all new words

OUTLINE OF CONTENT

I. Pan-American games and sports
   A. Story for motivation*
      1. Collection of equipment
      2. Illustration and dramatization of equipment needed
      3. Vocabulary for games and sports
   B. Conducting a student council meeting
      1. Officers elected in charge of forming teams
      2. Go over rules and regulations of game chosen
      3. Each group goes through a drill to emphasize the vocabulary and language structure of the unit

C. Pantomiming a song
   1. Sing to the tune of "Mulberry Bush" about playing sports
   2. Pan-American sports can be pantomimed by native Spanish pupils
   3. Learn the names of the parts of the body
   4. The "Hokey Pokey" dance-game using parts of the body vocabulary
   5. Dictation on story from part A
   6. Differentiate fruits from vegetables from vocabulary list
D. Simple future and past tenses of verbs in the unit

II. The Supermarket
A. Telephone conversation
   1. Read a conversation**
   2. In pairs, pupils go over conversation from dittoed sheets
   3. Spelling vocabulary (initial b & sh sounds)
   4. Plan a Pan-American meal with the class
B. Grocery Store
   1. Vocabulary for groceries
   2. Telephone a grocery order
      a. Read to class***
      b. Have pairs practice conversation
      c. Trip to neighborhood ethnic food store
C. Games
   1. "What does she have?" (Have students guess what food you are thinking of as you ask them questions.)
   2. Discuss the seven basic food groups and play various games

a. Group I includes meat, poultry, fish, eggs, dried beans and peas and nuts.
b. Group II includes leafy, green and yellow vegetables.
c. Group III includes citrus fruits, raw cabbage, salad greens and tomatoes.
d. Group IV includes potatoes and other vegetables and non-citrus fruits.
e. Group V includes bread, breakfast cereals and flour.
f. Group VI includes butter and fortified margarine.
g. Group VII includes milk and milk products.
3. Play grocery store in classroom using empty containers
4. Drill on pronunciations and spellings of new vocabulary
5. Drill on word usage in a sentence

LEARNING ACTIVITIES

Have pupils bring in personal belongings related to games or sports to introduce to the class
Pupils bring in pictures to put in vocabulary notebooks of different sports and equipment taken from newspapers, magazines, catalogs, etc.
Go to the gym as a class to examine all equipment used by the physical education department
Read the story "We Want to Play"
Make vocabulary lists of different sports and games and equipment used for each

121

6. Hold a class officer's election
7. Form teams to play and/or explain games and sports
8. Invite P.E. teacher to give further assistance to groups on specific games or sports
9. Make a bulletin board including ethnic sports stars
10. Include various sports books in the class library for leisure reading
11. On a given day each week, children will compete in games or sports they have chosen through their teams as a reward for good work.
12. Learn the singing game related to sports to the tune of "Mulberry Bush."
13. Learn the "Hokey Pokey" dance-game to practice parts of the body vocabulary.
14. Engage in a pre-prepared telephone conversation.
15. Plan a meal for the class so they can sample various Latin dishes. Have Spanish pupils bring samples from home, if possible.
16. Set up a grocery store in the class so that children can go shopping.
17. Drill on various vocabulary, sentence structure and grammar used in the unit.

Vocabulary

Spelling			Comprehension	
bat	shield	dominoes	soccer	bounce
vat	halls	checkers	marbles	sugar
ball	heel	baseball	uniform	pepper
vase	she'll	basketball	helmet	pork
vast	they'll	tortilla	mask	onion
vault	we'll	football	whistle	rice
base	fast	cock fights	glove	bacon

il	very	bull fights	catch	cheese
sket	falls	checkerboard	throw	dribble
il	heat	corn meal	pitch	lettuce
at	calls	green pepper	pass	tomatoes
eet	he'll	chicken	mitt	salt
d	he'd	vanilla	tacos	sugar

*We Want To Play

Juan is President of the Student Council in room
_____. He is starting our first meeting.
want to make teams. We want to play games. "What
you see on the table?" asks Juan.

"I see a baseball," says Joseph.

"I see a box of dominoes," says Mary.

"We see a soccer ball, too," says Luisa.

"We see a bag of marbles and a box of checkers,"
aron and Paul say together.

"What do you want to play?" asks Juan.

"I want to play soccer," says Jose.

"And I want to play marbles with Paul," says Jerry.

"We want to have a bullfight," says Richardo and
ingo.

"What do you need?" asks Juan.

"I need a soccer ball and a uniform," says Jose.

"We need the bag of marbles and a chalk to draw a
rcle," says Paul.

"I need a mask of a bull," says Domingo.

"And I need the mask of a matador and a cape," says
ardo.

Juan asks the vice president, "Do the teams have
rything they need?"

"Yes," he answers. "They have the equipment to
y soccer and marbles. And they have the equipment
have a bullfight.

123

**Planning a Pan-American Fiesta

Jorge: Hello.

Eva: Hello, Jorge! This is Eva. How're you?

Jorge: I'm fine, Eva. And how're you?

Eva: Fine. I want to invite you to a Pan-American
        fiesta at my house.

Jorge: Wonderful, Eva. When is it?

Eva: It's next Saturday evening. Can you come?

Jorge: Sure, I'd love to! Do you want me to bring
        anything?

Eva: Yes. I want you to bring some typical (Puerto
        Rican) food.

Jorge: O.K. I will make (pasteles). Everybody likes
        (pasteles).

Eva: Thanks, Jorge. Please come at six o'clock.

Jorge: O.K., Eva.

Eva: See you Saturday, Jorge. Bye.

Jorge: Good-bye, Eva.

Substitutions for the words in parentheses may
be used if desired to better fit the class situation.

***Telephone Order for Groceries

Senor Gonzales: Hello. Gonzales Food Store.

Jorge: Hello, Sr. Gonzales. This is Jorge.

Sr. Gonzales: Hello, Jorge. How are you?

Jorge: I'm fine, thanks. How are you?

Sr. Gonzales: I'm fine, too. What can we do for you?

Jorge: I want to make (pasteles) for a Pan-
                 American Fiesta.

Sr. Gonzales: Good. What do you need?

Jorge: I need (plantain leaves).

Sr. Gonzales: (to Sra. Gonzales) Jorge needs (plantain
                 leaves). (to Jorge) O.K. we have them.
                 What else?

124

Jorge:	I need ground pork.
Sr. Gonzales:	(to Sra. Gonzales) He needs ground pork. (to Jorge) Yes, we have that. What else?
Jorge:	I need potatoes and olives.
Sr. Gonzales:	He needs potatoes and olives. All right. Is there anything else?
Jorge:	That's all I need, Sr. Gonzales. Thank you.
Sr. Gonzales:	You're welcome, Jorge. And thank you!
Jorge:	You're welcome, Good-bye.
Sr. Gonzales:	Good-bye.

EVALUATION

Pupil Evaluation

1. Have pupils participate in one of the following plays, "We Want to Play," "Planning a Pan-American Fiesta," or "Telephone Order for Groceries"
2. Have them practice using the telephone correctly using conversational English
3. Have them participate in the selling and purchasing of grocery items in a "mock" classroom grocery
4. Have them take weekly spelling quizzes
5. Have them participate in choral speaking in English
6. Have them display their English notebooks

Teacher Evaluation

1. Did the pupils enjoy the unit?
2. How much comprehension did they gain in the use of English?

3. Did the pupils increase their vocabulary and
    spelling skills of the words included in the
    unit?

4. Are the pupils more versatile in conversational
    English?

5. Do the pupils enjoy and appreciate their
    second language?

BIBLIOGRAPHY OF MATERIALS AND RESOURCES

Student References

Anderson, Valerie and Bereiter, Carl. <u>Catching On</u>.
    LaSalle, Illinois: Open Court Pub. Co., 1973.

Archibald, John. <u>Baseball</u>. Chicago: Follett, 1972.

Cebulash, Mel. <u>Baseball Players Do Amazing Things</u>.
    Westminister, Maryland: Random, 1973.

Hall, Eugene J. <u>English Self Taught Levels 1-6</u>. New York:
    Regents Pub. Co., 1974.

Herber, Harold L. <u>Go Reading in the Content Areas</u>.
    New York: Scholastic Book Services, 1973.

Savaiano, Eugene and Winget, Lynn W. <u>Bilingual Dictionary
    of Spanish Idiomatic Phrases and Sentences</u>. Woodbury,
    New York: Barron, 1975.

Teacher References

Castillo, Carlos and Bond, Otto F. <u>Spanish Dictionary</u>.
    revised ed. Chicago: U. of Chicago Pr., 1972.

<u>Curriculum Guide-Language Arts for Non-English Speaking
    Children</u>. Chicago: Board of Education, 1974.

Fries, Charles C. <u>Teaching and Learning English as a
    Foreign Language</u>. Ann Arbor: U. of Mich. Pr., 1973.

Poster Cards

<u>Antonym: Poster Cards</u>. (11¼" X 14"), #7529, 30 cards,
    Springfield, Massachusetts: Milton Bradley Co., 1968.

Homograph: Poster Cards. (11¼" X 14"), #7552, 30 cards,
     Springfield, Massachusetts: Milton Bradley Co., 1971.

Homonym: Poster Cards. (11¼" X 14"), #7510, 30 cards,
     Springfield, Massachusetts: Milton Bradley Co., 1971.

Synonym: Poster Cards. (11¼" X 14"), #7513, 30 cards
     Springfield, Massachusetts: Milton Bradley Co., 1966.

Vowel Combinations: Wall Reference Charts. (8½" X 11"),
     #1442, 16 cards, New York: McGraw Hill, 1971.

Activity Cards

Schaffer, Frank. Creative Writing Activity Cards for Fun.
     (5½" X 8½"), 48 cards, Palos Verdes Peninsula,
     California: Frank Schaffer, 1974.

Furlong, Kaye. Dictionary Activity Cards for Fun. (5½" X
     8½"), 40 cards, Palos Verdes Peninsula, California:
     Frank Schaffer, 1974.

Schaffer, Frank. Read and Reason Activity Cards: Middle
     and Upper Grades. (5½" X 8½"), 42 cards, Palos Verdes
     Peninsula, California: Frank Schaffer, 1974.

RESOURCE UNIT
EUCLIDEAN GEOMETRY

OVERVIEW
The purpose of this unit is to develop in the
student a background in Euclidean geometry as a prerequisite for a liberal education. The geometry
presented in this unit is a mixture of intuition, logical
reasoning, and careful examples of the various mathematical methods and models. This entire unit encompasses
more than a two semester sophomore course can cover in
detail, but many of the sections are useful as a
review for other mathematics and science courses.

OBJECTIVES
1. The student will learn various geometric
   relationships.
2. The student will develop the skills of
   geometric proof.
3. The student will strengthen his mathematical
   vocabulary.
4. The student will understand physical and
   space geometry.
5. The student will acquire an understanding of
   the metric system and uses.
6. The student will appreciate the need for
   precision of language in mathematics.

OUTLINE OF CONTENT
I. Abstraction and logic in geometry
   A. Definitions
   B. Axioms and postulates
   C. Theorems

128

Sets
A. Basic concepts and symbols for sets
B. Operations with sets
C. One-to-one correspondence
Real numbers
A. Diagrams
B. Inequalities
C. Absolute value
Distance
A. Distance axioms
B. Betweenness
C. Segments
D. Rays
E. Midpoints
Lines, planes, separation
A. Definitions and examples
B. Separation axioms
C. Convexity and separation
Angles
A. Definition and examples
B. Measurements of angles
C. Right angles and perpendicular lines
D. Congruence of angles
E. Construction of congruent angles
Triangles
A. Definition and examples
B. Congruence of triangles
C. Requirements for congruence of triangles
D. Applications for congruence of triangles
E. Exterior and interior angles and their
   measures
F. Isosceles triangles
G. Construction of congruent triangles

VIII. Right triangles
    A. Definition and examples
    B. Congruence for right triangles
    C. Pythagorean theorem
    D. Introduction to trigonometric ratios

IX. Parallel lines
    A. Transversals
    B. Conditions for parallel lines
    C. Angles whose sides are
    D. Relationship to
    E. Applications and examples of
    F. Construction of parallel lines

X. Quadrilaterals
    A. Classification
    B. Properties of a parallelogram
    C. Properties of a trapezoid
    D. Rhombus, rectangle, square

XI. Applications of parallel lines
    A. Segments joining midpoints of two sides
       of a triangle
    B. Symmetry
    C. Simple solids

XII. Geometric inequalities
    A. Symbols and applications
    B. Triangle inequality

XIII. Areas of polygonal regions
    A. Polygons
    B. Area relations
    C. Proofs of area formulas
    D. Applications to triangles
    E. General applications

XIV. Similarity
    A. Intuitive similarity
    B. Proportional measures

C.   Meaning for triangles

D.   Applications

E.   Area of similar triangular regions

F.   Examples of similarity in space

XV.   Circles

A.   Definition and examples

B.   Construction

C.   Areas, circumference and other measures

D.   Applications of circle measurements

E.   Spheres and volume and surface area
     formulas

F.   Lines of circles

G.   Central and inscribed angles

H.   Areas of circles

I.   Congruence for circles and congruent arcs

J.   Concurrent circles

K.   Polygons and circles

VI.   Volume and solids

A.   Prisms

B.   Pyramids

C.   Cavalieri's principle

D.   Cylinders and cones

E.   Volume of cylinders, cones, prisms and
     pyramids

II.   Vectors and trigonometry

A.   Vector algebra

B.   Magnitude of a vector

C.   Values of sine, cosine, tangent

D.   Trigonometric formulas

LEARNING ACTIVITIES

1.   Have students do short homework readings and
     assigned problems.

2.   Have students work in groups to discuss proofs
     that were assigned.

131

3. Have students put assigned problems on board.
4. Have students illustrate pictorially the textbook problems.
5. Have students write reports on problems and people in the history and development of geometry.
6. Have students construct triangles with sides of 3 inches and 5 inches with included angles of 35° and compare the results. Do this also to demonstrate ASA, AAS, AAA, SSA and SSS.
7. Have students note congruence in patterns, art and furniture.
8. Have students note inequalities around them in sizes and ages of students and heights of buildings.
9. View films.
10. Have students see mathematics room at the Museum of Science and Industry.

Equipment

chalkboard	parallel rules	yardstick
flannelboard	T-square	compass
graph board	chalkboard	triangle
solid models	protractor	flexible curve

EVALUATION

Pupil Evaluation

1. Have pupils demonstrate their work at workout proofs.
2. Have them demonstrate on the blackboard their ability to explain the solution to geometric problems to the class.
3. Have the pupils write reports on history and development of geometry to be given orally.

4. Have them keep class and homework assignment
   notebooks for the evaluation purposes at the
   end of the unit.

Teacher Evaluation

1. Administer weekly examinations to reinforce
   and evaluate the material learned by the
   pupils.
2. Evaluate notebooks during and at the completion
   of the unit.
3. Observe and evaluate group and total class
   discussions on the solution and proofs of
   geometric problems.
4. Observe the precise use of mathematical
   vocabulary by each student.

BIBLIOGRAPHY OF MATERIALS AND RESOURCES

Student References

Ballard, William R. Geometry. Philadelphia: Saunders,
1970.

Blumenthal, Leonard Mascot and Menger, Karl. San Francisco:
Freeman C, 1970.

Dodge, Clayton W. Euclidean Geometry and Transformation.
Reading, Massachusetts: Addison-Wesley, 1972.

Fishback, William Thompson. Projective and Euclidean
Geometry. 2nd ed. New York: Wiley, 1969.

Levy, Lawrence S. Geometry: Modern Mathematics via the
Euclidean Plane. Boston: Prindle, 1970.

Teacher References

Lanczos, Cornelius. Space Through the Ages; The Evolution
of Geometrical Ideas From Pythagoras to Hilbert and
Einstein.

Mihalek, R. J. Projective Geometry and Algebraic Structures.
New York: Acad. Pr., 1972.

Weiss, Sol. Geometry: <u>Content and Strategy for Teachers</u>. Belmont, California: Bogden & Quigley, 1972.

Yale, Paul B. <u>Geometry and Symmetry</u>. San Francisco: Holden-Day, 1968.

<u>Audio Visual Aids</u>

Films

<u>Area and Volume Measurement</u>. Color, Sterling, 10 min., 1970.

<u>Congruent Figures</u>. black and white, Knowledge Builders, 12 min., 1945.

<u>Discovering Solids: Surface Areas of Solids - Part I and II</u>. color, Delta, 18 min., 1959.

<u>Discovering Solids: Volumes of Pyramids, Cones and Spheres</u>. color, Central Scientific Co., 15 min., 1960.

<u>Understanding Solids in Geometry</u>. black and white, Owens and Rodriguez, 19 min., 1955.

CHAPTER IV

DEVELOPING THE TEACHING UNIT

ntroduction:

The teaching unit is known by various title, e.g.,
ubject matter, correlated, broadfields, fused, and
ntegrated units, project, activity and experience units.
he difference between these units is the organization
f content, the teaching methods, activities and
hether the emphasis of the unit is on subject-matter
ontent or the interest and needs of the learner.

Table I illustrates this point by showing the
rganizational scope of various teaching units. The
ubject matter and correlated units stress subject-
atter content over the needs and learning experiences
f the learner, as explained in Chapter I. On the
ther hand, there is increasing emphasis placed on
earning experiences as one moves toward the experience
nit.

The varying degrees of emphasis placed on subject-
atter content and student learning experiences has led
o confusion in the definition of unit types. It is
uite obvious that even the most organized subject-
atter unit must provide learning experience activities
or the student. On the other hand, even the non-planned
xperience unit must contain subject-matter content
rganized in a meaningful fashion.

TABLE I

ORGANIZATION SCOPE OF TEACHING UNITS

Types of Units

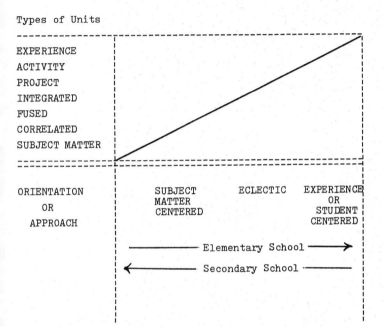

EXPERIENCE
ACTIVITY
PROJECT
INTEGRATED
FUSED
CORRELATED
SUBJECT MATTER

ORIENTATION
OR
APPROACH

SUBJECT
MATTER
CENTERED

ECLECTIC

EXPERIENCE
OR
STUDENT
CENTERED

Elementary School →

← Secondary School

Therefore, for the purposes of clarity and consis-
cy, the two divergent unit types are reconciled and
bined to form the teaching unit. An effective unit
t be based on rational planning and cogent principles
learning essential for meaningful learning experiences.
emphasis should not be upon acquisition of subject-
ter content but upon the processes of learning and
behavioral changes in the learner.

The teaching unit is the modern approach to
riculum implementation at the primary, elementary
secondary grade levels. At the primary and elemen-
y school levels, the emphasis is on learning exper-
es supported by multi-varied activities. The
roach is more affective and psychomotor oriented.
the secondary school level, however, the unit tends
e more subject-matter oriented, the approach more
llectual, and the variety of activities limited.
maturity and interest of the secondary school student
t the variety and types of activities that can be
. In either case, the essential ingredient of the
hing unit is student participation at all levels.

Student participation is not only the basis of the
but the unit is so designed as to capitalize on
e experiences. The projects, activities, demon-
tions, etc. are the means to understanding and
riencing the topics under study. It is the meaning-
ss of the experiences and the degree of involvement
he students that determine the level of retention
the quality of learning. For example, persons
rally retain

10% OF WHAT THEY <u>READ</u>
20% OF WHAT THEY <u>HEAR</u>
30% OF WHAT THEY <u>SEE</u>

137

50% OF WHAT THEY <u>SEE AND HEAR</u>
70% OF WHAT THEY <u>SAY</u>
90% OF WHAT THEY <u>DO</u>

It is for this reason that for an experience or teaching unit to be effective it should:

1. have a useful and significant purpose,
2. replicate actual life situations as closely as possible,
3. utilize materials as they occur in everyday life,
4. provide a considerable amount and variety of learning activities,
5. provide a variety of direct sense and motor experiences,
6. provide for some free, informal interaction of students,
7. provide ample opportunity for students to create, plan, and implement direct activities,[1]
8. develop meaningful methods of evaluation of the goals and outcomes of the unit for both students and teacher

Characteristics of the Teaching Unit:

The teaching unit, a form of individualized curriculum planning for a particular class and grade level, has a number of advantages over other methods of curriculum planning. It allows for teacher-pupil planning. In this sense, it is a democratic approach to teaching. It is also convenient in handling extensive ranges of interrelated fields of contemporary information and knowledge. The teaching unit has been defined in a variety of ways. Pounds and Garretson state:

---

[1]Maria Mehl, Hubert H. Mills, and Carl R. Douglass, <u>Teaching in the Elementary School</u>. New York: Ronald Press Co., 1958, p. 179.

Unit teaching offers more opportunity for
the optimum transfer of learning to real-
life situations. The flexibility of unit
teaching enables it to be adapted to student
problems...to utilize more effectively good
psychological principles of teaching.[2]

Mehl, Mills and Douglas add that "...the most
significant factors are the characteristics of the
children, particularly their abilities, educational
status, interest, and social maturity."[3]

Hanna, Potter and Hagaman in their book Unit
Teaching in the Elementary School, define the unit of
work or teaching unit:

...as a purposeful learning experience focused
upon some socially significant understanding
that will modify the behavior of the learner
and enable him to adjust to a life situation
more effectively.[4]

Gwynn and Chase characterized the teaching unit as
having four characteristics:

1. It has a central theme, around which class work
   and activities revolve,

2. implies the use of more than one method of
   teaching,

3. makes use of different kinds of learning
   activities on the part of the student through
   provision for the well-balanced large-group
   activity, small group activity, and individual
   activity...

---

[2]Ralph L. Pounds and Robert L. Garretson. Modern
Curriculum. New York: Macmillan, 1967, p. 415.

[3]Mehl, Mills and Douglass, op. cit., p. 179.

[4]Lavone Hanna, Gladys Potter and Neva Hagaman, Unit
Teaching in the Elementary School. New York: Holt,
Rinehart and Winston, 1963, p. 117.

4. requires careful advance planning by the teacher[5]

Alberty defined the teaching unit in a similar way. It has: 1) a broad comprehensive problem, or project of common concern to the group, 2) a series of related activities selected and organized to provide common learnings for the entire group and individual students based on specific needs, abilities or interest, and 3) a program of continuous cooperative evaluation of outcomes.[6]

Risk made a distinction between non-planned (experience or student-centered units) and preplanned (subject-centered) units. "The teaching unit," according to Risk, "emphasizes the importance of student learning experiences centered upon some problem, purpose or goal. Teacher planning is anticipated, but student sharing in planning is not included."[7]

The teaching unit formats and sample units presented in this chapter are in accordance with Risk's definition. The units are preplanned by the teachers in terms of general curriculum guidelines, concepts, values and skills that should be provided for effective learning outcomes, and the formulation of objectives for the unit. However, there is enough flexibility in the planning of the unit to permit student input for their development, interest and needs. Preplanning allows the teacher to anticipate curricular and student needs. Teacher - student planning gives the teacher insight into the

---

[5]J. Minor Gwynn and John B. Chase, _Curriculum Principles and Social Trends_. New York: Macmillan Co., 1969, pp. 188-89.

[6]Harold Alberty, _Reorganizing the High School Curriculum_ rev. ed., New York: Macmillan Co., 1957, p. 295.

[7]Thomas M. Risk, _Principles and Practices of Teaching in Secondary Schools_. New York: American Book Co., 1958, p. 164.

140

interests, concerns and abilities of the student. The
process is a period of confirmation and enlightenment
for both the students and the teacher. This can lead
only to more effective learning.

<u>Preparing the Teaching Unit</u>:
Preparation of the teaching unit requires more
detailed work than the resource unit. It demands
greater insightful information about the students,
specific knowledge of the curriculum of the school and
the school district, and an overview of the practical
availability of school and community resources. The
actual construction of a functional teaching unit
requires a detailed sequence of subject-matter content,
the formulation of classroom instructional objectives
and the organization of relevant and specific learning
activities.

The content of the teaching unit, like the resource
unit, is determined by the curriculum goals of the
school and the particular grade level. Generally, it is
the teacher who determines the magnitude and scope of
the topics, projects, and learning activities. In most
cases, the teacher is able to exercise some choice over
the selection of specific units for the classroom.

However, the teacher is generally obliged to follow
curricula guidelines or a course of study as far as
determining what subject-matter content is to be taught
at a certain grade level.

Some school systems have developed rather extensive
and specific guidelines in the form of curriculum guides
divided into units of work. They may have units on file
available to the staff. Other school districts use a
course of study, general guideline, supplemented by a
textbook series. While in other school districts, there
may be no prescribed curriculum and it is left to the

141

teacher to develop her own units of work -- both the
resource and the teaching units. If the teacher has
been fortunate enough to have developed a resource unit,
the amount of work necessary to construct a teaching unit
will be minimized.

Therefore, subject-matter content to be taught may
be dictated by the framework of the curriculum set
down in the course of study or curriculum guide (see
appendix for samples and explanation of courses of study
and curriculum guides). Or the teacher, as indicated,
may have few guidelines available to her. Therefore,
the subject for the teaching unit may be developed out
of previous learning experiences of the pupils or out
of unplanned experiences. The unplanned experiences
may arise out of national or local news items, a visitor,
a holiday, an event such as the "skylab" or the Watergate
hearings, election processes, sports events, or other
local, national or international issues. Or the teaching
unit may be developed from the resource unit, previously
prepared from the curriculum guidelines. Unlike the
resource unit, the teaching unit has to be modified to
fit the specific class(es) for which it is intended.

Initial Preparatory Steps:

In addition to the curriculum demands of the school,
the teacher must consider several subsequent factors in
the preparation of the teaching unit.

Sowards and Scobey recommended the following
preparatory steps:

1. To be aware of the units of work already
   experienced by the students.
2. To know something of the background and nature
   of the students.
3. To be certain of the significance of the
   proposed units of work.

4. To know the local community, its socio-
    economic and cultural bases.
5. To consider his own competence, knowledge,
    skill and experience in relation to the
    proposed units of work.
6. To know the ability, maturity, and level of
    interest of students.
7. To know the material resources, such as
    reading materials, audio-visual aids,
    construction materials, community materials,
    and other resources to develop a unit
    efficiently and comprehensively.[8]

Preparation of the teaching unit gives the teacher
a unique opportunity to become acquainted with the
students. Student participation in the teaching unit
is an essential ingredient for its successful implementation. It not only emphasizes learning by wholes and
continuity of learning but also the integration of the
learning experiences of the students. It must incorporate adequate provisions for individual interests and
intellectual differences in the classroom as well as
for specific curriculum content needs. This is accomplished by the involvement of the pupils in the planning
and development of the unit. Strickland suggests the
following steps for teacher-student planning.

Steps in Teacher-Student Planning

Teacher Planning
    A. Survey the needs and interests which justify
        this unit and make it significant. General

---

[8]Wesley G. Soward and Mary-Margaret Scobey. The
Changing Curriculum and the Elementary School. California:
Wadsworth Pub., 1968, p. 359.

needs, life problems, community needs,
students' needs, and interests.
- B. List important objectives or goals which
might be achieved through this study.
- C. Make an overview of subject matter, good
experiences, integration of different
subjects with this area.
- D. List books and other materials for student use.
- E. Plan possible ways of introducing and
arousing interest.

Teacher-Student Planning
- A. Preplan work period. Then plan with students
by:
    1. Discussion - learn attitudes, interest,
knowledge of topic
    2. Get work under way by:
        a. Listing questions to be answered
        b. Making work charts showing what to do
        c. Planning trips
        d. Constructing projects
        e. Finding and using sources of infor-
mation (books, pamphlets, and people)
        f. Listing materials needed
        g. Discussing responsibilities of
committees and individuals
    3. Gather information and use in reports and
discussions.
    4. Organize information to answer questions.
    5. Summarize total learning by parent programs,
assemblies, plays, murals, classbooks.
- B. Plan evaluation techniques for entire unit
including:
    1. Growth and changes which have taken place
in students in terms of achievement and the
acquisition of skills.

144

2. Areas needing further study for
    understanding
3. Daily log or record of teacher comments
    briefly indicating useful, useless, and
    additional activities
4. Possible student logs to keep goals
    in mind.[9]

To obtain full class participation, which is
ther dominated by a small group of articulate
ients nor by the teacher, the following suggestions
given:

s and Don'ts of Teacher-Student Planning

1. The teacher should ask questions and make
    comments which will bring about a reflective
    and deliberative mood.
2. Pupils need to know where they are headed and
    why they are doing what they are doing.
3. The teacher must know how to offset the
    frequent tendency of a few pupils to
    monopolize the discussions or planning
    sessions.
4. The teacher must strive for wide participation--
    even from those children who prefer not to
    participate.
5. The teacher should give recognition to
    contributions.
6. Pupils should have some opportunity to handle
    the leadership role in planning, particularly
    as they grow older.
7. The teacher will need to serve as the influence
    that keeps planning moving towards a course

---

[9]Ruth Strickland. How to Build a Unit of Work.
etin, No. 5, Washington, D.C.: U.S. Office of
ation, 1961 (pamphlet out of print), p. 2.

145

of action or solution to the problem posed.

8. Manipulation by the teacher to force acceptance of his preconceived plan is essentially dishonest. It is better for the teacher to announce outright or vote a plan outright than resort to dishonesty through subtle manipulation.

9. When asking for an opinion, the teacher is obliged to honor the opinion by respecting it when it is given.

10. Provisions should be made for carefully recording of plans as they are made to help insure their more adequate completion.

These suggestions are not only applicable in the preparation of the unit, but are excellent teaching principles for every stage of the learning process.

We have examined the basic preparatory steps for the development of the teaching unit. Now let us consider the steps involved in its construction. As indicated, the teaching unit must have purpose, significance, continuity and integration of learning, a variety of relevant and worthwhile learning activities and concrete methods of evaluation. It must be tailored to the needs and interests of the students as well as conform to the curriculum requirements of the school.

The remainder of this chapter will deal with the presentation and discussion of four different formats with sample units under each one to guide the reader.

Constructing the Teaching Unit

What are the steps in the construction of the teaching unit? There are a number of specific ways that the unit can be organized. Basically, in terms of an

146

verview, the following format was developed by
hicago State University student teaching personnel.[10]

eneral Format for a Teaching Unit:

1. _Initiating Stage_ In this stage, teacher and
   students consider the general nature of the
   unit and determine its purpose and broad
   objectives. It is important that the unit
   be placed in perspective with previous
   learnings and that the students understand
   what it is and why it should be undertaken.
   (Here is where teacher-student planning is
   also included.)

2. _Developing Stage_ This stage begins with the
   formulation of specific objectives, typically
   expressed in terms of desired pupil behaviors,
   and proceeds to a determination of activities
   which will lead to the achievement of goals.
   This is followed by an extended period of
   work in the selected learning experiences
   which will include, among other things, the
   developing of needed skills. The teacher's
   role is to guide and direct the progress of
   the learning so that it is meaningful and
   productive.

3. _Culminating Stage_ During this stage, the
   learnings which have taken place are organized
   and directed for final effect. Reports,
   culminating activities, and evaluations are
   undertaken to insure classwide understandings.
   Further provision is made for sharing learnings

---

[10]Used with the kind permission of the student
aching personnel, Chicago State University, 1974.

with others in the school, the home and
in the community.

Perhaps the most effective way to describe the
teaching unit is to show a detailed format. The
following specific unit <u>Format One</u> was developed from
the foregoing general format:

TEACHING UNIT
FORMAT ONE [11]

Name _____

School _____

Date _____

Unit Title _____ Unit No. _____

Subject Area _____

Grade Level _____

Periods per week _____ Minutes per period___

   I.   INITIATING STATE

       A.   <u>Teacher Preparation</u>

           1.   Consider the general selection of
               the unit

           2.   Determine specific unit of study

       B.   <u>Approach</u> (to enlist pupils' participation)

           1.   Motivation planned to stimulate pupil
               interest

           2.   Activities devised to:

               a.   Develop pupil understanding of
                    the nature of the unit

               b.   Develop reasons for undertaking
                    the unit

---

[11]Used with permission of Student Teaching Department,
Chicago State University, 1974.

II. DEVELOPING (WORK) STAGE
   A. Determination of Objectives (pupil-teacher oriented)
      1. Relate to the major functions of living
      2. Relate to subject-matter achievement goals
      3. Relate to pupil-personality objectives
   B. List and Arrange Resource Activities
      Comprehensive list of all pertinent and related activities, each activity listed with code letter as appropriate (I-Individual, S-Sub-group, T-Total group)
   C. Integrate Classwork with Other Learning Areas (select those which meet the needs of the class)
      1. Language Arts
      2. Social Studies
      3. Fine and Practical Arts
      4. Healthful Living
      5. Science (arithmetic, science)
      6. Homeroom (on-going activities)
      7. Home and Community
      8. Unit Vocabulary Development (extend and enrich vocabulary during unit progress through word list derived from unit learnings)
III. CULMINATION STATE (EVALUATION)
   A. Unifying Activities
   B. Evaluation Procedures
      1. Teacher
      2. Teacher-Pupil

IV. INSTRUCTIONAL MATERIALS
    A. Bibliography
        (List books really available for use in
        developing unit. Supply page numbers and
        chapter heading to designate specific
        references rather than whole books. Place
        asterisk before those reading-books and
        periodicals - for teacher only.)
    B. Films and Filmstrips
        (Preview and reserve visual materials in
        an A-V Center. List title, publisher, time,
        publication, a Board of Education or
        other catalog number.)

    This Teaching Unit Plan, _Format One_, is illustrated
in the following pages with three sample units: **Pages 155-202.**
    1. A fifth grade unit:
        "Becoming Acquainted with the Southern States."
    2. An eighth grade unit:
        "Oral Communication."
    3. An eleventh grade unit:
        "Computer Programming."
    Format One unit plan has an initiating stage,
whereas Format Two does not. Format One is generally
used when a resource unit has not been developed before-
hand. The initiating stage indicates the preparatory
steps through which the teacher proceeds to develop the
teaching unit. A comparative examination of the two
unit plan formats shows that Format One does not have a
separate outline subject-matter of content, whereas
Format Two does. Format One is generally used in
conjunction with a textbook, a curriculum guide or a
course of study. (The outline of subject-matter is
further explained later in the chapter.) Format Two is

generally preceded by the development of a resource
unit. However, the use of a resource unit is dependent
upon the availability of curriculum resource materials
and the experience of the teacher.

Following are sample units illustrating developmental procedures for both Formats One and Two:

TEACHING UNIT
FORMAT TWO[12]

I. INTRODUCTORY STATEMENT
   A. State the age and grade level for which the
      unit is planned.
   B. Duration of time needed for the unit.
   C. Show briefly how this unit fits into the
      overall plan.

II. OBJECTIVES STATED IN THE COGNITIVE, AFFECTIVE
    AND PSYCHOMOTOR DOMAINS
    A. Write general objectives
    B. Write specific objectives in each of the
       three domains

III. CONTENT OUTLINE
    A. Outline the major subject-matter content, or
    B. Outline the problems to be solved, and
    C. Vocabulary

IV. ACTIVITIES IN WHICH STUDENTS WILL ENGAGE
    A. Initiatory Activities
       1. Outline a series of activities which
          will get the students off to a
          successful beginning. Indicate the
          sequence of these activities on the

---

[12]This outline was taken from Herbert L. Klausmeir,
eaching in the Secondary School. New York: Harper Row,
958, pp. 151-152. Revised by authors (used with
ermission of publisher).

basis of your ideas as to how to
initiate a good teaching-learning
situation.
2. Indicate the time that will probably
be required for initiation of the unit.
B. Developmental Activities*
1. Outline the activities in which the
students will engage to develop understandings, skills, and attitudes.
Indicate a sequence in terms of the
order in which you think they may be
learned.
C. Integration with Other Subject Matter Areas
1. Mathematics
2. Science
3. Social Science
4. Language Arts
5. Fine Arts
6. Practical Arts
7. Physical Education
8. Community
D. Culminating Activities
1. Outline a summarizing activity or a
group of activities to which each
student can participate, to which the
whole group will direct its efforts
during the major portion of the learning
period, which will best satisfy each
student's need for approval from classmates and others, and which will promote
good attitudes toward classmates,
teacher, and school.

---

*Developmental and initiatory activities are some-
times combined.

>   2. Indicate the estimated length of time
>   necessary for this phase, allowing for
>   appropriate student participation.
>   V. EVALUATION PROCEDURES
>   A. Outline the procedures you will employ to
>   determine where students are when the unit
>   starts.
>   B. Outline the methods you will use in
>   assisting students to measure their own
>   progress.
>   C. Outline the procedures you will use to
>   measure growth in understandings, skills
>   and attitudes during the entire unit.
> VI. MATERIALS AND RESOURCES
>   A. Locate appropriate reading materials
>   1. Student texts
>   2. Teacher texts
>   3. Magazines
>   B. Select audio-visual materials, demonstra-
>   tions, and experimentation materials which
>   are needed to make the activities worthwhile.
>   C. Locate and outline facilities in the school
>   (outside the classroom) and in the commu-
>   nity which will be used.
>   D. Devise procedures for bringing people from
>   the community to the classroom and for
>   taking the students into the community.
>   E. Outline procedures you will use when students
>   make contact with persons outside the class-
>   room to secure materials you will need to
>   facilitate activities.

Following are sample teaching units of <u>Format Two</u>.
student should compare the format to the sample units,

when constructing his own teaching unit. The sample
units include: Pages 203-257.

1. A third grade unit:
    "Plants and How They Grow."
2. An intermediate grade level unit:
    "Simple Machines Make Our Work Easier."
3. A fifth grade unit:
    "How Newspapers Serve Us."

TEACHING UNIT

Format One

UNIT TITLE: Becoming Acquainted with the
                     Southern States
SUBJECT AREA: Social Studies
GRADE LEVEL: 5th
PERIODS PER WEEK: Six   MINUTES PER PERIOD: Forty

INITIATING STAGE

A. Teacher Preparation
    1. Considering the general selection of the
        unit:
        a. (1) Determine the specific content
                 material to be covered.
            (2) Determine methods of using the
                 pupils in committee activities.
            (3) Determine the value of the
                 teaching aids.
            (4) Determine the possibility of using
                 a variety of activities which call
                 for additional permissiveness.
        b. Review the emotional, intellectual,
            social, and physical characteristics of
            the pupils at the 5th grade level.
        c. Peruse the Course of Study in Social
            Studies for the Chicago Public Schools
            to verify curriculum level and expected
            learnings for the 5th grade level.
    2. Determining the specific unit of study:

155

   a. Study the grades achieved by the pupils
     on the activities in previously
     presented units. (To determine whether
     any of these activities should be
     excluded because of lack of interest or
     whether they should be used again to
     strengthen certain weaknesses.)
   b. List possible weaknesses displayed by
     the pupils during the presentation of
     previous units and devising activities
     to strengthen in these areas.
   c. Gather and distribute special materials
     for use by the weaker pupils to increase
     their comprehension of the subject
     matter under consideration.
   d. Inspect instructional materials available
     for my use:
     (1) Copies of supplementary texts
     (2) Audio-Visual materials
     (3) Library references
     (4) Pictures and pamphlets for pupil use

B. Approach
  1. Motivation planned to stimulate pupil
   interest:
   a. Display pictures and discuss the terrain,
     people, climate, and industries of the
     Southern States.
   b. Discuss the Southern States in terms of
     the great historical events which have
     occurred in this region and a general
     overview of the settlement of this region.
   c. Discuss the importance of the Southern
     States in terms of the economic and
     cultural heritage of this region.

d. Have pupils who have visited the Southern States give oral accounts of what impressed them most about this region.

2. Activities devised to:
   a. Develop pupil understanding of this unit.
      (1) Present and discuss the geological aspects of the Southern States which will be studied during the presentation of this unit.
      (2) Present the pupils with a list of beneficial and detrimental geological factors which account for the social and economic development of the Southern States.
      (3) Remind the pupils of the procedures used in determining the geological aspects of the Northeastern States, and discussing ways of doing the same for the Southern States.
   b. Develop reasons for undertaking the unit.
      (1) Discuss that the unit of study will help them to understand the variations in the way the people of the Southern States live.
      (2) Discuss purposes of the unit which will enable them to understand why the economy and society of the Southern States developed the way they did.
      (3) Discuss the unit of study which contains interesting information on how man is improving his living

conditions by overcoming geological
characteristics in his community.

II. DEVELOPING STAGE

    A. <u>Determining Objectives</u>

        1. Relating to major functions of living

            a. To use the tools of communication
effectively through participation in
activities involving reading, writing,
and speaking.

            b. To develop economic competence by under-
standing economic values of everyday
living and the principles involved in
conserving the nation's resources.

        2. Relating to subject matter achievement goals

            a. To gain knowledge of the physical
aspects of the Southern States through
understanding the geological formations
and climatic controls of the region.

            b. To gain knowledge of the industries,
major cities, and occupations found
within the Southern States through a
comprehensive understanding of the
content material and discussions
presented during the unit.

        3. Relating to pupil personality objectives

            a. To develop a sense of responsibility
through seeing the relationship of the
self to increasingly larger community
groups.

            b. To develop social effectiveness through
an understanding and appreciation of
individual and cultural differences
and similarities.

    B. <u>Listing of Resource Activities</u>
       (T-Total, I-Individual, S-Sub-group, *T-Teacher)

*T&T - Observe the pictures of the Southern
         States on the bulletin board display
         and discuss them in terms of their social,
         economic, and geological significances.
*T&T - View the regional wall map showing the
         topography of the Southern States.
*T   - Discuss the organization of all work
         done during the unit into a notebook on
         the Southern States.
T   - Locate the states in the Southern region
         by checking textbook maps with listings
         of the Southern States in the appendix.
*T&T - Read and discuss the content material on
         the Southern States. (To be repeated.)
T   - Read stories and collect pictures
         about the mountain people of the Southern
         States.
T&I - Select words for a class vocabulary list
         and an individual vocabulary list.
*T   - Analyze the geographic factors which
         contributed to the crop specialization
         of the Southern States.
T   - Work the exercises on the Southern States
         which are found in the workbook. (To
         be repeated.)
T   - Discuss the historical reasons why the
         Southern States have lagged behind the
         rest of the nation in economic progress.
     - Make area maps of the Southern States
         showing the capitals, mountains, lakes,
         rivers, and outstanding points of interest.
T&T - Compare a vegetation map with a rainfall
         map of the Southern States and discuss
         the fertility of this region on the basis
         of its climate and rainfall.

I   - Become acquainted with the resource
materials pertaining to the Southern
States found in the library and the
classroom.

T   - Note the latitude through which the
Southern States extends and compute the
distance from the equator to make pre-
dictions about the climate.

T   - Make charts listing the major occupations,
important industries, climatic features,
major cities, products grown and manu-
factured, and natural resources found
in the Southern States.

*T   - Discuss how early methods of plantation
farming depleted the fertility of the
soil in this region, and introduce the
pupils to methods of soil and forest
conservation which are helping to overcome the waste of natural sources.

T   - Have pupils pretend they are tourists
and have them list the points of interest
in the Southern States.

T   - Have pupils answer "Which Belongs Where"
questions. (This consists of selecting
the correct answer from a list of words
and placing it in the correct sentence
which is found in a series of sentences
above the list.)

*T   - Explain why the varied climate, adequate
rainfall, and natural resources of the
Southern States have encouraged the
diversification of farm crops.

T   - Construct a products map of the Southern
States. (Consists of having the pupils

paste small cut out pictures of the
products on a large outline map.)
- Discuss how modern transportation has
helped to provide us with out-of-season
foods.
&T - Locate the T.V.A. dams and power sites
on a large outline map. Explain their
value to the surrounding areas. Compare
life in rural areas prior to electrifi-
cation with the present ways of living.
- Construct a model of a T.V.A. dam and
power plant. Prepare a short oral
report to explain how electrical power
is transferred from the plant to rural
areas.
T - View and discuss the following films:
Tennessee River: Consideration and
Power. 15 min.
U. S. Geography: The Gulf Coast. (The
South's Land of Opportunity) 15 min.
- Discuss reasons why the steel industry
in the South developed even though steel
industry in the from the North.
- Determine from a number of sources why
the aluminum industry has been developing
plants in the Southern States.
T - Organize the pupils into committees to
make oral reports on the people, their
occupations, industries, tourist attrac-
tions, major cities, major ports, and
topography of the Southern States.
- Discuss and evaluate materials pertaining
to the Southern States brought in by the
children.

161

*T   - Discuss the future role the Southern
       States will play in the Nation's economy.
C. Integrating Classwork With Other Areas
    1. Language Arts
        a. Read the content material in the text.
        b. Utilize the library resources.
        c. Listen during class discussions.
        d. Write the answers to questions.
    2. Science
        a. Discuss the climatic controls operating
            in the Southern States.
        b. Become acquainted with the forces that
            helped shape the topography of the
            Southern States.
        c. Discuss the natural resources of the
            Southern States.
        d. Discuss the conservation programs of
            the Southern States.
    3. Practical Art
        a. Make charts listing the major occupations,
            important industries, major cities,
            products grown and manufactured, and
            natural resources found in the Southern
            States.
        b. Make area maps of the Southern States,
            the capitals, mountains, lakes, rivers,
            and outstanding points of interest.
    4. Home and Community
        a. Discuss the value of soil conservation.
        b. Discuss the assets of industry to a
            community.
        c. Promote human relationships through
            group projects.
        d. Discuss the importance of products needed
            for the home and community.

162

5. Unit Vocabulary Development
   a. Enrich vocabulary through planned activities.
   b. Enrich vocabulary through the addition of words found in the content material.
   c. Find value in words other than meanings
   d. Vocabulary list:

peninsula	bayous	derrick
tributaries	resin	refineries
flood plain	rosin	phosphate
levees	cultivator	bauxite
channel	cotton gin	erosion
delta	legume	

I. CULMINATING STAGE
   A. Unifying Activities
      1. Review study for the purpose of enriching understanding.
      2. Complete notes, maps, charts, and vocabulary list, and turning this work in, in the form of a notebook.
      3. Evaluate and discuss notebooks.
      4. Use knowledge gained during presentations of this unit to write about a typical day in the Southern States.
   B. Evaluation Procedures
      1. Teacher
         a. Determining the effect of the teaching unit
            (1) Note the degree of increased interest in the Southern States.
            (2) Note the attention given during discussions.
            (3) Note the quality of work produced by the children.

163

                    (4) Note the degree of the children's
                         participation in the classroom
                         discussions.
               b. Determining to what extent the objectives
                   have been accomplished
                    (1) Prepare for and give a written test.
                    (2) Evaluate the written test.
                    (3) Evaluate written and oral assignments
                         which stress the objectives.
          2. <u>Teacher - Pupil</u>
               a. Discuss the test to clarify misunder-
                   standings.
               b. Appraise workmanship on the class note-
                   books.
               c. Appraise completed area maps.
               d. Appraise completed charts.
               e. Appraise completed workbook assignments.
IV. INSTRUCTIONAL MATERIALS
     A. <u>Bibliography</u>
          1. <u>*Teacher-Pupil Texts</u>
               a. Alderman, Clifford L. <u>Colonists for
                   Sale: The Story of Indentured Servants
                   in America</u>. Riverside, New Jersey:
                   Macmillan, 1975. (Gr 4-6)
               b. Brown, Ira L. <u>Georgia Colony</u>. Riverside,
                   New Jersey: Macmillan, 1970. (Gr 4-6)
               c. Haynes, Betsy. <u>Slave Girl</u>. New York:
                   School Book Service, 1974. (Gr 4-6)
               d. Jones, James. <u>Appalachian Ghost Stories
                   and Other Tales</u>. Parsons, West Virginia:
                   McClain, 1975. (Gr 5 and up)
               e. *Jones, E.L. <u>Agriculture and the Indus-
                   trial Revolution</u>. New York: Halsted
                   Press, 1974.

f. *Kenworthy, Leonard S. _Social Studies_
    for the Seventies. Lexington, Massa-
    chusetts: Xerox College, 1973.

g. Lacy, Dan. _Colony of North Carolina_.
    New York: Watts, 1975. (Gr 4-6)

h. Lyman, Nanci A. _Colony of Southern_
    Carolina. New York: Watts, 1975. (Gr 4-6)

i. *McDonald, Nancy and McDonald, Jack.
    This Is America's Story. New York:
    Monarch, 1975.

j. *Ragan, William B. and McAulay, John D.
    Social Studies for Today's Children.
    2nd ed. Englewood Cliffs, New Jersey:
    Prentice-Hall, Inc., 1973.

k. Suttles, Patricia H. (Ed.). _Elementary_
    Teachers Guide to Free Curriculum Materials.
    revised 32nd ed. Randolph, Wisconsin:
    Ed Prog, 1975.

B. Audio-Visual Materials
    1. Films 16 mm
        a. _George Washington_. black and white,
            ENCYCLOPEDIA BRITANNICA EDUCATIONAL FILMS,
            19 min., 1951.

        b. _North America: The Continent_. color,
            CORONET, 16 min., 1966.

        c. _Southeastern States_. second edition.
            color, ENCYCLOPEDIA BRITANNICA EDUCATIONAL
            FILMS, 11 min., 1956.

        d. _Tennessee River: Conservation and Power_.
            color, ART EVANS PRODUCTIONS, INC.,
            15 min., 1970.

        e. _U. S. Geography: The Gulf Coast_. (The
            South's Land of Opportunity). color,
            McGRAW-HILL BOOK COMPANY, 15 min., 1963.

f. U. S. Geography: The Southeast (Challenge and Change). color, McGRAW-HILL BOOK COMPANY, 14 min., 1965.

C. Graphic Materials
   1. Full orbital globe (12") with cradle base
   2. World map (40" x 54") physically colored showing true population center size
   3. United States Maps (40" x 54") the physical-political type
      a. One map with mercator projection
      b. One map with conic projection
   4. North American map showing thirteen original colonies and routes of the explorers
   5. Chalkboard outline maps of the United States and North America (46" x 62")
   6. Individual desk outline maps for students (8" x 10½") corresponding to the classroom wall maps
   7. U. S. Relief Map (22" x 35") showing how altitude and landforms relate to cities and land use
   8. Tagboards (12" x 18") and (18" x 24") for constructions of
      a. Circle or pie graphs
      b. Bar graphs
      c. Line graphs
      d. Pictorial graphs
      e. Time and sequence charts
      f. Flow charts

D. School Equipment Resources
   1. 16 mm sound projectors
   2. 8 mm projectors
   3. Film loop (8 mm)
   4. Audio-tape recorders

166

5. Opaque projectors
6. Overhead projectors
7. TV cassette
8. Videotape
9. Slide projector (2" x 2")
10. Tachistoscopic projector
11. Filmstrip and record player

TEACHING UNIT

Format One

UNIT TITLE: Oral Communication
SUBJECT AREA: Language Arts
GRADE LEVEL: Eighth
PERIODS PER WEEK: Five   MINUTES PER PERIOD: Forty

I. INITIATING STAGE
    A. Teacher Preparation
        1. Considering the general selection of the
            unit.
            a. Consulted the Language Arts Curriculum
                Guide.
            b. Checked students' past achievement
                scores to determine the ability span
                in order to pace the work accordingly.
            c. Examined various textbooks dealing
                with the subject.
            d. Referred to what was previously covered
                in the subject in seventh grade.
            e. Surveyed the community.
            f. Considered the needs, interests,
                abilities, and backgrounds of the
                students.
            g. Consulted other resource books for
                teachers.
            h. Discussed verbal communication with the
                students to acknowledge their specific
                needs.
        2. Determining the specific unit of study

                            168

a. Obtained information about specific students from other faculty members.
b. Consulted students files and cumulative records for test scores and other pertinent information.
c. Consulted the seventh grade test scores in language achievement.
d. Listened carefully to the students speaking at various times, during lunch, class discussion, in the halls, socializing.
e. Noted faults in language common to the entire class.
f. Kept notes of serious speaking faults of particular students.
g. Distributed questionnaires to discover students' attitudes, interests, and behaviors
h. Interviewed some of the parents.
i. Surveyed the school to determine what supplementary materials were available.
j. Consulted books written by subject specialists in the field of speaking and communication.
k. Perused resource units dealing with the subject.
l. Reviewed my philosophy of education, psychology of learning, function of the subject.
m. Noted aspects of the contemporary lives of the students outside the school.

Approach (to enlist students' participation)
1. Motivation planned to stimulate student interest

a. Discuss construction of bulletin board depicting various professional people in different life situations which require different types of communication etiquette.

b. Distribute two mimeographed speeches after listening to a tape recording of each; criticize the grammatical structure of the content of each. One should exemplify good speaking; the other poor speaking.

c. Display newspaper articles about language.

d. Display magazines which appeal to the students - <u>Seventeen</u>, <u>Popular Mechanics</u>, <u>Sports Illustrated</u>. Use for selection of topics for reports.

e. Brief discussion about the value of a common understanding of social issues.

f. Tape voices of students speaking; make general comments about acceptable speaking.

g. View the film <u>English Language: Patterns of Usage</u>. Discuss this question: Is there a pure language?

h. Display the wall chart - <u>The Meeting Will Please Come to Order</u>.

i. Display teletrainer unit.

2. Activities devised to:

a. Develop student understanding of the nature of the unit
   (1) Taking part in conversation
   (2) Discussing
   (3) Giving reports

(4) Taping student speeches
(5) Making explanations and giving directions
(6) Making announcements
(7) Showing courtesies demanded in social situations of various types
(8) Viewing film and filmstrips
(9) Listening to speeches on the radio
(10) Reading speeches from the newspaper or magazines
(11) Inviting and listening to guest speakers
(12) Listening to recordings of other students' speeches
(13) Skits depicting communication courtesies
(14) Listening to recordings of historic speeches

Develop reasons for undertaking unit
(1) Using the telephone effectively
(2) Making introductions easily
(3) Greeting callers and guests
(4) Discussing weaknesses in oral presentations
(5) Partaking in panel discussions
(6) Sharing information, feelings, opinions
(7) Making speeches in social gatherings
(8) Explaining or persuading
(9) Presenting ideas with courtesy and an awareness of the feelings and response of the listeners
(10) Contributing constructively in committee deliberation as a member or a chairman

171

       (11)   Giving oral reports on books read

       (12)   Using parliamentary procedures

       (13)   Partaking in daily conversations

       (14)   Listening to formal talks

II.   DEVELOPING STAGES

    A. <u>Determining Objectives</u>

        The student:

1. Uses grammatically correct English which permits him to participate competently and without fear in the society of which he is a part.

2. Uses common conversational courtesies and etiquette while speaking.

3. Assumes an active role in meaningful, inquisitive discussion.

4. Increases and develops his communicative skills and abilities while improving his attitudes and developing his understandings through sharing ideas, feelings, and information.

5. Experiences the pleasure of speaking before a group.

6. Is able to solve problems through analyzing and evaluating the techniques and content of a spoken work as well as the motives of the creator.

7. Develops self-confidence, personal development, maturity, and the ability to present ideas and convince others.

8. Expresses his thoughts and emotions better and thereby achieves the self-expression important to mental health and maximum contribution to others.

9. Becomes increasingly thoughtful of persons
   with whom or to whom he is talking or to
   whom he is listening, and gives evidence
   of the improved attitude.

The student:
1. Has a thorough knowledge of his subject and
   what he wants to say. (This develops self-
   confidence.)
2. Understands the interests of others.
3. Makes his conversation interesting through
   the use of adequate vocabulary.
4. Knows how to use the dictionary to find the
   proper pronunciations.
5. Knows how to organize material.
6. Knows how to select the things that have
   great need to be said, stressing them in the
   order of their importance.
7. Makes conversation convincing by developing
   poise, proper posture, appropriate gestures,
   and facial expressions.
8. Knows how to give clear and explicit
   directions.
9. Uses language which is clear, dynamic,
   forceful, imaginative, and creative.
10. Develops the art of talking to the whole
    audience not to just a part of it. Looks
    at and speaks directly to the audience.

The student:
1. Knows when to interrupt and when not to
   interrupt.
2. Knows how to interrupt adults and how to
   interrupt each other.

3. Knows when to converse quietly - before,
    after, and during intermissions of lectures,
    musical performances, plays, and programs;
    before and after formal services such as
    weddings, funerals, initiations. He knows
    the common conversational courtesies in
    the sick room and/or other places or
    occasions when conversation may be annoying
    such as in class when someone else is
    speaking.
4. Knows how to show appropriate conversational
    courtesies in the following situations:
    when he is a guest or entertaining a guest,
    while at the table (choose only pleasant
    topics), when being introduced to another,
    and when receiving generous favors.
5. Knows how to talk over the telephone.
6. Knows how to introduce people.

B. Listing and Arranging Resource Activities
    (T-Total, I-Individual, S-Sub-group)
    T - Plan conversational periods with the students
        discussing topics of conversation interesting
        to them.
    S - List a number of conversational possibilities
        in a notebook under the headings:

        Participants   Situation
        Mother and grocer   ordering by phone
        John and Margo   accepting an invitation

        Prepare, with a partner, the two opening
        speeches of the conversations suggested on
        the list. Explain the situation to the
        audience before giving the speeches.
    T - Discuss the characteristics of an effective
        speaker; then list the standards of a good

speaker with contributions made by the
students.

T - Discuss the importance of the library as a
resource for materials that will make
interesting programs or talks. Spend a
library period making an inventory of
resource materials for talks.

S - Choose one of the following topics. Organize
ideas on the subject and prepare for dis-
cussion of:
"Girls Should Become Astronauts"
"A Dress Code Should Exist at School"
"World Food Shortage "

S - Prepare for the discussion by reading or by
other investigation in an effort:
to bring out some facts not previously
known
to give accurate information to the
listener
to present some new ideas on the subject
to test the completeness of any statements.

S - The students compile a class book of words
used for each discussion about usage.

S - Use the word game Prefixes and Suffixes -
the leader says a prefix or suffix as he
points to a specific student. Then he
begins counting from one to ten. As the
leader counts, the other student names as
many words containing the stated prefix or
suffix as possible.

S - Present a socio-drama with one class member
impersonating the conversational bore and
the other members reacting to the speaker
and the situation.

I - Each student makes his own list of items
S - where his usage needs improvement. He then
      joins a small buzz group to discover whether
      the members have similar problems. The
      group then discusses these similar problems
      and solutions to them listing the solutions
      on the board.
G - Discuss the place of appropriate conversa-
      tion in such circumstances as the following:
      1) appearing for a job interview
      2) attending a "get-acquainted" meeting
      3) meeting the parents of friends
      Tell what might be said in a first conver-
      sation with a doctor, a famous coach, and/or
      a sculptor.
I - An individual student could construct a
      chart indicating the characteristics of an
      able conversationalist. An Able Conversa-
      tionalist...
           emphasizes a point by story or gesture
           encourages others to participate
           has a wide variety of interests
           knows when to stop talking
           listens as well as he speaks
G - Students work out some guidelines to serve
      individuals occupying the three possible
      positions:
           leader — Gives everyone a fair chance
                       to contribute.
           audience — Listens to the end of a state-
                       ment without interrupting.
           speaker — Speaks clearly and distinctly
                       so that all participants may
                       hear.

- Students act as receptionists during Open
  House introducing visiting parents to school
  faculty.
- Giving directions, the student may practice
  common conversational courtesies. He
  should keep in mind the age of the person
  he is directing. Varying the situation
  offers the student this opportunity. Have
  the student give directions to a child who
  is lost; an elderly person who does not
  know the town or city.

Record these dramatizations on tape. The
students listen to their own introductions
and jot down points of constructive
criticism which will enable them to improve
in their area of weakness.

Interview the principal, the nurse, physician,
grocery market manager.

Use actual definite classroom situations
to instruct students how and when it is
permissible to interrupt adults, and when it
becomes a breach of etiquette.

The student reads sections of books by
Emily Post, Amy Vanderbilt, and other
writers of good manners; he reports his
findings to the class.

Chart the characteristics of a courteous
conversationalist.

Discuss difficulties students may have
experienced because of inaccurate directions
or lack of care in following instructions.
Stress the need for courteous answers to
questions instead of a curt "No" or "I don't
know." Include in this discussion the idea
of offending someone through curt replies.

177

G - Topics for discussion:

    1. The characteristics of a bore (self-centeredness, long-windedness, boast-fulness.)

    2. The importance of talking about other persons' interests as well as your own.

    3. The dangers and impropriety of gossip.

I - The student gives directions or explains how to make something.

I - The student contributes to unit discussion

S - plans. A topic presented by one of the students is discussed in small groups, and opinions are collected from each group for consideration by the class. The instructor can sit in with different groups and lead summary discussions.

G - Students participate with each other in creating an evaluation form to be used in expressing an opinion of a discussion leader's performance.

I - A student makes the evaluation check list available for ready reference by reproducing it on a classroom chart.

S - The students submit a topic to be the subject of a panel discussion. Consider one that is slightly controversial and suited to the interests of the class. Choose such a topic as, "Should There Be A Dress Code at School?" Suggest one aspect of the subject for each of four panel members chosen by the group. Find facts to support a series of statements on one phase of the proposed topic. Decide upon a time limit for each panelist. Select a moderator to conduct the discussion.

- Listen to a radio or television broadcast
  of a panel discussion program. Pay
  particular attention to the moderator and
  prepare a report for classmates by answering
  such questions as:

  Did his remarks consume too much time?
  By what means did he keep the discussion
  moving?
  When did he summarize?
- Serve as a member of the audience during a
  class panel discussion. Write, at the
  close of the discussion, a summary to show
  briefly and clearly what has been accomplished.
  Follow these guidelines:

  Describe the situation or topic
  discussed.
  Record the important contributions and
  suggestions that were offered.
- The students choose a committee of three
  members to interview a neighborhood merchant
  who makes a practice of employing students.
  Instruct the committee to approach this
  employer to find out which things impress
  him favorably in an interview and which
  things are likely to result in an unfavorable
  reaction. Use the committee's report to
  the class as the basis for a class discussion
  of the topic "Do's and Don't's for Job
  Interviews."
- Write and act out an interview in which a
  high school student applies for a job in a
  bank or factory. Perform the task in these
  four sections:

  Prepare for the Interview   Conduct the Interview
  Arrange for the Interview   Close the Interview

I - Choose a subject and prepare an interview
      of solicitation in which the housewife is
      approached about:

         purchasing a new magazine
         signing a petition for noise abatement

I - The student brings to class some kind of
      tool or instrument and explains how it
      works.

G - Review and observe the standards for
      explanations, announcements and directions
      which have been learned in the interme-
      diate grades.

I - Prepare an announcement about an event
      which is important to members of the
      class. Present it orally and omit one
      essential detail. Ask class members to
      detect the missing particular.

S - Analyze announcements given:

         in an assembly, a class, a club, or
         church
         on the radio or television.

I - Use a map of Chicago and give directions
      for traveling by public transportation
      from the school to one of the following
      places:

         Adler Planetarium   McCormick Place
         Art Institute   Museum of Science
         Brookfield Zoo   and Industry

G - Students discuss the skills applied in
      preparing an oral report. Consider the
      need for mastery of the following skills:

         locating   reading for detail
         skimming   taking notes
         interviewing   outlining

The instructor should present a series of
lessons that will show students how to
locate materials, select only the pertinent
information, organize it in an interesting
manner, and present the ideas concretely.

G - Develop some standards for speaking
behavior. Include:

Look directly at the audience.
Speak so as to be heard by everyone.
Stand easily erect.
Use appropriate gestures and facial
expressions.

I - Use the standards to evaluate the delivery
of classmates who give reports.

S - Compose a list of subjects, such as current
events, what's happening in the community,
which have possibilities for interesting
reports. Work together in small groups to
designate enough phases of a single subject
for each member to investigate for a report,
such as, "Vietnam." Choose these phases:

government	reaction to the U.S.
people	economy
land	religions

I - Select significant details from notes or
assigned topics and make outlines to serve
as the framework for individual reports.
Take turns with classmates in placing a
personal outline on the board and in
speaking from it. Ask the group to anticipate the steps of the report as it progresses.

S - Participate in a group book report. Divide
the report into four or five segments with
each member assuming one of the following
responsibilities:

                Title, author, setting   Student 1
                Description of characters   Student 2
                Story-line without conclusion Student 3
                Opinion of book   Student 4
      S - Provide the students with role-playing
          situations which include timely events
          such as President Ford and Secretary of
          Agriculture Earl Butz being interviewed.
C. Integrating Classwork With Other Learning Areas
    1. Social Studies
        a. Students discuss contemporary problems
            and offer individual possible solutions.
        b. Students investigate democratic practices
            in the school; hold a panel discussion
            to present ways in fostering these
            practices.
    2. Science
        a. Students will read and analyze scientific
            papers and present basic ideas and
            concepts to the class.
    3. Fine Arts
        a. The students research and present reports
            about musicians, music of a state or
            nation, festivals, and periods of
            history.
        b. Students sketch the portrait of one of
            the characters in their book reports and
            then give a personality sketch of the
            character orally.
    4. Unit Vocabulary Development
                usage   reporting
                interview   outline
                panel discussion   communication
                formal talks   standard
                etiquette   criticize
                conversation

                        182

II. CULMINATING STAGE
  A. <u>Unifying Activities</u>
     1. Students guided by the instructor plan
        the programs for graduation.
     2. Students plan an assembly program having
        oral communication as its theme.
  B. <u>Evaluation Procedures</u>
     1. <u>Teacher</u>
        a. Keeps a daily log of the apparent
           understandings of the students.
        b. Carefully observes student participation
           and enthusiasm while learning activities
           are in progress.
        c. Notes the attention given to particular
           learning activities; which activities
           developed the interests of the students.
        d. Observes the students' social and
           emotional behavior.
        e. Observes methods of procedures used by
           students.
        f. Were the reports well-organized? Did
           they indicate that the reporter was
           making good use of the study skills, such
           as finding and using reference books,
           selective data, taking notes, collating
           them, outlining?
        g. Did the students grow in ability to
           absorb new ideas from reading and
           listening, to form thoughtful opinions,
           to organize their thoughts, to define
           problems, to make decisions, and to plan
           solutions?
        h. Develops a check list of questions to
           be considered in respect to each student:

183

Is he being motivated by a desire to
improve in speech?
Does he participate voluntarily in
expressional activities and cooperate
as a listener in an audience situation?
Does he understand that a mastery of
mechanics will help him to express
himself more effectively?
Is he progressing in ability to organize
his thoughts and ideas logically?
Can he find required date, take notes,
outline, and summarize?
Can he stand before an audience with
ease and confidence and express himself
clearly and forcefully?
Does he accept criticism gracefully and
try to correct his weaknesses?

i. Was the instruction geared to provide
optimal language experience based upon
the students' home conditions, experiences, interests and hobbies, levels of
maturity and capacities, to learn,
current and emerging needs and maladjust-
ments (social, emotional, or intellectual)?

j. Formulate tests to describe status in
specific areas assumed important for a
particular group and individuals based
upon the behavior and content of the
objectives.

k. The instructor observes his students in
terms of specific purposes to collect
specific information concerning behavior
of pupils in various types of situations:
Work habits
Socializing

Relationships with other students
Relationships with other adults
Use of time

The instructor keeps anecdotal records
of the results of listening to the
students' discussions, conversations,
and comments to identify speech and
discussion needs; to collect leads which
enable the instructor to better understand the interests, attitudes, anxieties,
and concerns of his students.
Collect students' work and keep on file
to continuously analyze the status of
learning, find evidences of improvement
in specific areas, discover needs,
misconceptions, strengths and weaknesses,
discover interests, identify values.
Have individual students raised their
standards for their individual work?
Determine the individual's place in a
group and a group's acceptance or
rejection of the individual and the
individual's place in a group.
Interviews of students - Interviews
provide evidence of major understanding,
maturity of insight, growth.
Tape recordings of the panel discussions
will provide an immediate source of data
from which value judgements can be made.
Various types of tests made up by the
instructor can be used to test content
of certain objectives:
(1) Oral examinations
(2) Essay examinations

185

      (3) Objective examinations

      (4) Performance tests and scales -
           Giving a speech or recording a
           sample of written expression under
           controlled conditions.

2. <u>Teacher-Pupil</u>

    a. Questions the students may apply to
        themselves individually:

        (1) Am I acquiring a fund of facts and
             ideas so that I have something
             worth communicating?

        (2) Am I trying to enrich my vocabulary
             so that I can find the best words
             with which to express my ideas?

        (3) Do I express myself in clear-cut
             sentences?

        (4) Do I assume a good, easy posture
             before an audience, and speak with
             confidence?

        (5) Am I gradually getting rid of errors
             in word usage, pronunciation, and
             enunciation?

        (6) Is my voice pleasing, and do I
             speak loudly and clearly enough for
             all to hear?

        (7) Do I correctly use capitalization,
             punctuation, and spelling in
             writing?

        (8) Have I learned to reread, criticize,
             edit, and revise my own written
             work?

        (9) Am I thoughtful and courteous in
             conversation and discussion?

      (10) Do I listen courteously and atten-
             tively to others?

- The students compile their own evaluation check lists.
- The students may evaluate themselves
  through use of voice improvement cards:
(1) My voice is pitched
     (a) high
     (b) medium
     (c) low
(2) I speak
     (a) too loudly
     (b) too softly
     (c) Just right for my audience
          to hear
(3) I speak with
     (a) Variety
     (b) Monotony
     (c) Too much variety
(4) I speak
     (a) Too rapidly
     (b) Too slowly
     (c) At a satisfactory rate
(5) I speak with
     (a) Good rhythm
     (b) Poor rhythm
     (c) Repetition
(6) I articulate
     (a) Carefully
     (b) Too carefully
     (c) Carelessly
(7) My voice is pleasant
     (a) Nasal
     (b) Hoarse
     (c) Harsh
     (d) Breathy

187

d. Evaluation of discussion
   (1) Was the problem stated clearly?
   (2) Were varied opinions expressed and considered?
   (3) Did the discussants keep their remarks focused on the problem?
   (4) Was there unnecessary repetition?
   (5) Were the elements of the speech appropriate?
   (6) Were the participants courteous and interested?
   (7) Did most members of the group participate?
   (8) Were the goals of the discussion attained?
   (9) To what extent was a measure of agreement reached?
e. Evaluation of an interview
   (1) Did the interviewer gain the information desired?
   (2) Did the individuals concerned part amicably with a measure of mutual satisfaction?
f. Evaluation of an oral report
   (1) Are the students increasingly able to discriminate between the significant information to be included in the report?
   (2) Do the students have a feeling for accuracy in presenting details of a situation?
   (3) Have the students developed the habit of observing sequence in reports?

188

　　　　(4)　Are they able to address an
　　　　　　audience with reasonable ease and
　　　　　　confidence?
　　　　(5)　Is there evidence of ability to
　　　　　　incorporate the use of visual aids
　　　　　　in oral reporting?
　g.　Questionnaires
　　　　(1)　Questionnaires contributed by the
　　　　　　students should enable them to
　　　　　　appraise progress of the class and
　　　　　　individual students based upon the
　　　　　　standards set up by themselves under
　　　　　　the guidance of the instructor.
　　　　(2)　Questionnaires should be contrived
　　　　　　by the students to appraise their
　　　　　　behavior and study-work habits.
　h.　Review points illustrated in the charts
　　　made by individual students.　The
　　　students then ask themselves questions
　　　which evaluate points to be observed.
　　　Example:　Chart Points to Observe When
　　　Speaking
　　　　(1)　Enunciation
　　　　(2)　Pronunciation
　　　　(3)　Voice
　　　　(4)　Manner
　　　　(5)　Sentence structure
　　　　(6)　English
　　　　(7)　Looking at the listeners
　　　Students then apply questions to the
　　　above appraising themselves.

　　　　　INSERT - EVALUATIVE TECHNIQUES
　　The following list of evaluative techniques show
some of the many means of evaluation that can be used:

Activity records
Adjustment inventories
Anecdotal records
Autobiographies
Case studies
Check lists
Collections and scrapbooks
Cumulative records
Dramatic play
Diaries

Essays, themes, and poems
Flow charts
Group discussions
Health and medical histories
Interviews

Intelligence tests
Inventories - of interests, attitudes, etc.
Logs of periods or events
Neighborhood studies
Observation: directed, time-sampling, and informal

Oral reports
Parent conferences
Peer-group studies
Personality inventories
Photographs

Questionnaires
Rating scales
Readiness tests
Recordings and films
Sociograms and other projective techniques

IV. INSTRUCTIONAL MATERIALS
  A. Bibliography
    1. *Teacher-Pupil Texts
      a. *Applbaum, Ronald et al. Speech Communication. Riverside, NJ: Macmillan, 1974.
      b. *Burton, Dwight et al. Teaching English Today. New York, NY: Houghton Mifflin, 1975.
      c. Diamond, Harriet and Dutwin, Phyllis. Grammar in Plain English. new ed. Woodbury, NY: Barron, 1975 (Gr 7 and up)
      d. Hance, Kenneth G. Principles of Speaking. 3rd ed. Belmont, CA: Wadsworth Pub., 1975. (Gr 7-12)
      e. *Kean, Personke. Teaching and the Language Arts. New York: Intext, 1975.
      f. *Linkugel, William A. and Buehler, Christian E. Speech Communication for the Contemporary Student. Scranton, PA: Har-Row, 1975.
      g. Nadeau, Ray E. Speech-Communication: A Modern Approach. Reading, MA: Addison-Wesley, 1973. (Gr 7-12)
      h. Pulaski, Mary A. Step by Step Guide to Basic English. New York: Arco, 1974. (Gr 7-10)
  B. Audio-Visual Materials
    1. Films 16 mm
      a. English Language: Patterns of Usage. color, CORONET, 11 min., 1970.
      b. Speech: Conversation. black and white, YOUNG AMERICAN FILMS, 11 min., 1953.

c. <u>Speech: The Function of Gestures</u>.
   black and white, YOUNG AMERICAN FILMS,
   10 min., 1950.
d. <u>Verbs: Recognizing and Using Them</u>.
   black and white, CORONET, 11 min., 1960.

TEACHING UNIT
Format One

T TITLE: Computer Programming
JECT AREA: Data Processing
DE LEVEL   11th grade
IODS PER WEEK: Five   MINUTES PER PERIOD: Forty

INITIATING STAGE
A. Teacher Preparation
    1. Considering the general selection of the
        unit:
        a. Unit Material
            (1) Determine the general areas of
                 computer programming to be
                 covered
            (2) Determine specific languages to
                 be covered
            (3) Determine percentage of class time
                 to be used by the students in
                 testing and debugging their programs
            (4) Determine the value of available
                 teaching aids, such as films,
                 charts, and transparencies for the
                 over-head projector
        b. Review the emotional, social, physical,
            and intellectual characteristics of the
            11th grade student.
        c. Compare unit with curriculum guide of
            the Chicago Public Schools to verify
            that required material will be covered.

193

2. Determining specific unit of study
   a. Study grades earned by students in previously presented units and weigh these grades according to the dependence of the material in this unit on that of previously presented units.
   b. Determine how areas of pupil weakness in previous unit can be incorporated into this unit to overcome those weaknesses.
   c. Review and select films, charts, supplementary texts, and transparencies for the over-head projector for class use.
   d. Review and select pamphlets, manuals and other special material available for students according to need.

B. Approach
   1. Motivation planned to stimulate student interest
      a. Discuss ways in which the computer affects our everyday life.
      b. For comparison, demonstrate the running of a job on the computer in different programming languages.
      c. Have each student bring a want ad for a computer programmer from a newspaper to show the financial rewards of computer programming.
      d. Show samples of different programming languages and discuss with the students similarities and differences.
   2. Activities devised to:
      a. Develop pupil understanding of the nature of the unit.

194

           (1)   Discuss the nature of language
                    assemblers comparing and contrasting

                    them with foreign language inter-
                    preters.

           (2)   Discuss the assembler languages
                    in relation to machine language.

           (3)   Discuss similarities and differences
                    between computer languages and the
                    English language.

           (4)   Have students give criteria for
                    deciding which language is used when.

     b.   Develop reasons for undertaking unit

           (1)   Choose several students at random
                    to read their want ads for pro-
                    grammers.

           (2)   Discuss the demand for computer
                    programmers.

           (3)   Discuss the history of assembler
                    languages and why they came into
                    being.

           (4)   Discuss present needs and advantages
                    of assembler languages.

. DEVELOPING STAGE

A. <u>Determining Objectives</u>

    1. Relating to major functions of living

       a. To develop competence in communication
           with peers and adults through writing,
           speaking, and listening.

       b. To develop respect and consideration for
           others in working with the total class
           and in groups.

       c. To learn to think in a logical manner.

    2. Relating to subject matter achievement
       goals

      a.   To gain a better knowledge of the
            workings of a computer and programming
            language

      b.   To gain a knowledge of the various pro-
            gramming languages and their appropriate
            times of use

      c.   To gain skill in working with the
            computer and various languages to
            solve problems

3. Relating to pupil personality objectives

      a.   To develop a sense of responsibility in
            working with equipment entrusted to the
            student

      b.   To develop a sense of competence and
            self respect in being able to improve
            his position in life through a good job

      c.   To develop competence in forming
            adequate decisions based on information
            supplied to him.

B. <u>Listing of Resource Activities</u>

(T-Total, I-Individual, S-Sub-group)

T - Discuss ways in which the computer affects
    everyday life of everyone.

I - Have each student bring in a want ad for a
    computer programmer.

T - Read and discuss the following pamphlets:
        <u>What Do You Want</u> Sperry Rand Corporation
        <u>You and The Computer</u>   General Electric Co.

T - Show examples of programming languages and
    have the students discuss similarities and
    differences.

T - Discuss the history of assembler languages
    and why they came into being.

T - Discuss the need for and advantages of
    assembler languages.

T - Discuss the nature of compilers and compare
    them to foreign language interpreters.
T - Discuss similarities and differences in
    writing a flow chart and an outline.
T - Have students discuss which language should
    be used when.
T - Discuss the role of mnemonics in writing a
    symbolic language.
T - Discuss types of instructions used in pro-
    gramming and how they are represented in
    various languages.
T - Discuss how programs can restrict parts of
    files and how this affects the individual's
    right to privacy.
T - View and discuss the following films:
    Computers and You
    Data Processing: Introductory Principles
I - Have each student write a short program in
    each language to produce desired output from
    given input. (To be repeated.)
S - Have groups of students all work on the same
    problem--each group using a different
    language.
T - Discuss aspects of previous problem and how
    they were affected by the languages.
I - Have each student write programs to solve
    a series of given problems. (To be repeated.)
S - Have groups of students write programs to
    process a given set of files. Each student
    will write one program.
I - Have each student give an oral report on an
    article from the library in the field of
    data processing. (To be repeated.)
T - Discuss the future of assembler languages
    and computer programming.

I - Collect and organize the various languages
to form a "Programming Dictionary."

C. Integrating Classwork With Other Areas
   1. Language Arts
      a. Read the text and supplementary materials.
      b. Utilize the library in reporting an
         outside assignment.
      c. Listen and speak during class discussions.
      d. Write reports, programs, and answers to
         questions.
   2. Science
      a. Discuss ways in which science and math
         have been affected by the computer.
      b. Discuss which language is most adequate
         in handling scientific problems and why.
      c. Discuss which language is most adequate
         in handling arithmetic problems and why.
   3. Practical Art
      a. Construct flow charts.
      b. Construct diagrams showing the assembly
         of symbolic language.
      c. Discuss the role of computer programs
         in having the computer draw pictures,
         diagrams, maps, and "sing" songs.
   4. Home and Community
      a. Discuss the effects of the computer on
         the home and community.
      b. Promote human relationships through
         group projects.
   5. Unit Vocabulary Development
      a. Enrich vocabulary through new words
         found in materials.
      b. Enrich vocabulary through learning new
         meanings to familiar words.

c. Vocabulary list:

algol	maching language
assembler	macro
assembler language	mnemonic
autocoder	monitors
bootstrap	NPL
cobol	One-for-one instructions
compilation	operands
compiler	poerations
console	PL/I
constant	problem-oriented
control	procedure-oriented
debugging	program execution
flow chart	report generator
fortran	routine
hardward	simulators
indexing	software
instruction	sort system
instruction repertoire	SPS
load	stored-program computer
load-and-go system	symbolic language
logic	tabular language
loop	utility programs

II. CULMINATING STAGE

    A. <u>Unifying Activities</u>

        1. Review the relationship between the computer
machine language, compiler, and flow chart.

        2. Have the students form groups and write
programs for a hypothetical company.

        3. Evaluate and discuss the programs written
by the groups.

        4. Organize and finish the dictionary of
computer instructions.

B. Evaluation Procedures
   1. Teacher
      a. Determining the effects of the teaching unit
         (1) Evaluate "programming dictionaries."
         (2) Evaluate programs written by the students.
         (3) Note the quality of the work done.
         (4) Note the degree of student participation in discussions and activities.
      b. Determining to what extents the objectives have been met by:
         (1) Prepare and give a written test.
         (2) Evaluate the test results.
         (3) Evaluate the output produced from written programs.
         (4) Evaluate written and oral assignments which stress the objectives
   2. Teacher-Pupil
      a. Discuss the test results to clarify misunderstandings.
      b. Evaluate the dictionary and programs written for class.
      c. Evaluate all completed assignments.
IV. INSTRUCTIONAL MATERIALS
   A. Bibliography
      1. *Teacher-Pupil Texts
         a. Bacon, M.D. and Bull, G.M. Data Transmission. New York: Am Elsevier, 1975. (Gr 11 and up)
         b. Clifton, H.D. and Lucey, T. Accounting and Computer Systems. New York: Petrocelli Books, 1973. (Gr 11 and up)

c. *Dixon, W.J. and Nicholson, W.L.
    Exploring Data Analysis: The Computer
    Revolution in Statistics. Berkeley, CA:
    U of Cal. Pr., 1974.
d. *Exposito, Anthony. Machine Design.
    new ed. Columbus, OH: Merrill, 1975.
e. Moore. Mathematical Elements of
    Scientific Computing. New York: HR&W,
    1974. (Gr 11-12)
f. *Oliveri, Peter and Rubin, Michael.
    Computers and Programming: A Neoclassical
    Approach. New York: McGraw, 1975.
g. Sharratt, J.R. Data Control Guidelines.
    Berkeley, CA: 1974. (Gr 11 and up)

Periodicals

a. Business Automation, Elmhurst, Illinois,
    Business Press International, Inc.
b. Computers and Automation, Newtonville,
    Massachusetts, Berkeley, Pub.
c. Computers and Data Processing News. New
    York, N.Y., Nielson Publishing Company, Inc.
d. Computing Newsline. Santa Monica, Com-
    puting Newsline.
e. Data Processing Magazine, New York, N.Y.
    North American Publishing Company.

Manuals

a. Burroughs Corporation
    6071 Second Avenue
    Detroit, Michigan
b. Control Data Corporation
    8100 34th Avenue South
    Mineapolis, Minnesota
c. General Electric Computer Division
    P.O. Box 270
    Phoenix, Arizona

      d. Honeywell Electronic Data Processing
           Division
          60 Walnut Street
          Wellesley Hills, Massachusetts

      e. International Business Machines
          112 East Post Road
          White Plains, New York

      f. RCA Computer Division
          Cherry Hill
          Camden, New Jersey

      g. Univac Division
          Sperry Rand Corporation
          1290 Avenue of the Americas
          New York, New York 10009

B. <u>Audio-Visual Materials</u>
   1. Films 16 mm
      a. <u>Art from Computers</u>. color, NBC, 8 min.,
          1971.
      b. <u>Business Machine Operators</u>. color,
          STERLING FILMS, 7 min., 1970.
      c. <u>The Business Office: Making Things
          Happen</u>. color, JOURNAL FILMS, 10 min.,
          1969.
      d. <u>Computers</u>. color, BAILEY-FILM ASSOCIATES,
          11 min., 1970.
      e. <u>Computers and You</u>. color, JOURNAL FILMS,
          15 min., 1971.
      f. <u>Data Processing: Introductory Principles</u>.
          color, STERLING FILMS, 15 min., 1968.
      g. <u>Data Processing: Printing Card Punch</u>.
          color, STERLING FILMS, 15 min., 1968.
      h. <u>What Is a Computer</u>. color, EB, 19 min.,
          1971.

C. <u>Recordings</u>
   1. <u>Computer Speech</u>. Bell Telephone Laboratories,
      309 W. Washington, Chicago, Illinois. 31 min.,
      33-1/3 rpm.

PLANTS AND HOW THEY GROW

INTRODUCTION

A. <u>Grade Level</u>: 3rd grade; <u>Age Level</u>: 8 to 9 years

B. <u>Duration of Time</u>: 6 to 8 weeks

C. This unit is organized so as to progress from the learning that there are varieties of plants, to the learning of the parts of plants and their function, how plants are reproduced, what products plants give us, and the parts of plants we can eat. This involves basic understandings and the development of skills through various experiments.

OBJECTIVES

A. General Objectives

    1. Student will develop understanding that plants are part of our environment.

    2. Student will experiment in planting various seeds.

    3. Student will develop idea that plants produce their own kind.

    4. Student will learn the parts of plants and their function.

    5. Student will appreciate the various products obtained from plants.

B. Specific Objectives

    1. Cognitive:

        a. To be able to observe that there are different kinds of plants that grow

203

b. To be able to explain the results of red dye in celery experiment involving the function of a stem

c. To be able to relate the function of roots to growth of plants

d. To be able to predict result of plant planted without root portion of plant

e. To be able to identify the parts of plants

f. To be able to identify parts of flower

g. To be able to discover that seed, when planted, will resemble that plant that produced it

h. To be able to predict which seed will grow faster - one with seed coat removed or one without seed coat removed

i. To be able to hypothesize if plant will grow without light, air, water and warmth

j. To be able to draw a conclusion that .parts of plants can create a new plant

2. Affective:

a. To be able to show awareness that plants of various kinds grow around us

b. To be able to demonstrate a belief in the importance of the functions of different parts of plants

c. To be able to show an interest in planting seeds

d. To be able to appreciate the foods we obtain from plants

e. To be able to show concern for the care of plants

        f.   To be able to attend to carrying through
             and drawing conclusions of experiments
        g.   To be able to adhere to the rules to
             be followed in cleaning up work area
             after experiments are completed

   3. <u>Skill</u>
        a.   To be able to collect plants from
             around the school area
        b.   To be able to collect leaves
        c.   To be able to write an experience chart
             about plants observed
        d.   To be able to conduct experiments
             through planting
        e.   To be able to prepare a bulletin board
        f.   To be able to operate a microscope for
             observing roots, etc.
        g.   To be able to dig up plants for experi-
             ments and observation purposes
        h.   To be able to plan for a field trip

III. CONTENT OUTLINE
   A. There are a variety of plants
      1. Flower
      2. Vegetable
      3. Grasses and ferns
      4. Bushes and trees
      5. Weeds
   B. Plants are different in many ways
      1. Size
      2. Shape
      3. Colors (mushrooms have no color)
      4. Places where they grow
      5. Flowering and non-flowering
      6. Seeds, spores

C. Parts of seed plants and their function
    1. Stems
        a. Carry food to plant (water and minerals)
        b. Support leaves, flowers and fruits, putting leaves in position to absorb light
        c. Connect tubes in stems with veins in leaf.
    2. Roots
        a. Absorb water through root hairs
        b. Are passageways for water and minerals to move up plant
        c. Anchor plant
        d. Contain root hairs
        e. Store food made in leaf (carrot, beet, etc.)
    3. Leaves
        a. Contain veins that carry water
        b. Contain cells that manufacture food (chlorophyll in cells)
        c. Contain small openings for absorbing carbon dioxide (gas in the air)
        d. Use water and minerals from ground and carbon dioxide (gas in air)
        e. Manufacture sugar and starch
        f. Use food to make more cells
            (1) Causes plant to grow larger
            (2) Gives plant energy needed for growth
    4. Seeds
        a. Make new plant
        b. Contain many parts
            (1) Seed coat
            (2) Embryo
            (3) Root

        (4) Stem
        (5) Cotyledon (food - like a lunch box)
c. Seeds very in size, shape, and color.
        (1) Coconut largest seed
        (2) Orchid seed is one of smallest
             seeds in the world (1 tablespoon
             could hold 7 million of these seeds)
        (3) Watermelon seed is black
        (4) Rough and jagged seeds
5. Flowers
  a. Produce seeds
  b. Contain many parts
        (1) Petal
              (a) Is a kind of leaf
              (b) Shows where flower is located
              (c) Attracts insects
        (2) Stamen
              (a) Male part of plant
              (b) Grows around center, next to
                   pistils
              (c) Has pollen on the tips
              (d) Fertilizes the ovules (not
                   yet seeds)
        (3) Pistil
              (a) Female part of plant
              (b) Contains stigma onto which
                   pollen falls
              (c) Contains ovary where undevel-
                   oped seeds are stored
        (4) Sepal
              (a) Another type of leaf
              (b) Protects young and delicate
                   parts of the bud

D. Ingredients needed for plants to grow
1. Air
2. Light
3. Warmth
4. Water

E. Parts of a plant can grow another plant
1 Seeds
2. Cuttings (stems)
a. Geranium
b. Rose plant
3. Leaf
a. African violet
b. Ivy
4. Buds
a. White potato
5. Roots
a. Carrots
b. Beets
c. Radishes
d. Sweet potato
6. Bulbs
a. Onions
b. Tulip
c. Lilies
d. Hyacinths
e. Jonquils

F. Parts of plants we eat
1. Roots
a. Carrots
b. Beets
c. Radishes
d. Parsnips
e. Sweet Potato

2. Seeds
    a. Pumpkin seeds
    b. Poppy seeds
    c. Peas
    d. Grains (3 most important--rice, wheat corn)
3. Stems
    a. Celery
    b. Rhubarb
    c. White potato
    d. Asparagus
4. Fruits
    a. Apple
    b. Oranges
    c. Cherries
    d. Any other fruits
5. Leaves
    a. Lettuce
    b. Spinach
    c. Kale
    d. Cabbage

Plants produce important products for man's use
1. Food
    a. Oil, fat (seeds) soybeans, peanuts, cotton, corn
    b. Spices (seeds) dill, mustard, poppy, celery, caraway
    c. Coffee (seeds) cola drinks
2. Lumber, paper
    a. Trees
3. Cloth
    a. Cotton plant (fine hairs of cotton grow out of seed coat of cotton seed)
4. Linen
    a. Flax plant

5. Drugs
   a. Molds

Vocabulary

flower	veins	sepal
vegetable	embryo	leaf
stem	cotyledon	bud
roots	petal	bulb
leaves	stamen	fruit
seeds	pistil	

IV. ACTIVITIES
   A. Initiatory Activities
      1. Introduce song - "Oats, Peas, Beans and Barley Grow"
      2. Have students collect some plants from a local prairie or from around their home. Have students discuss how you would dig up a plant before starting this activity. Respect for growing things can be part of the social studies area.
      3. Collect seeds from various plants or trees for a display. Here the idea that plants produce something will initiate later learning that plants can reproduce themselves.
      4. Class discussion or experience chart about what we have observed about the plants and seeds collected
      5. A visit to a greenhouse can offer an opportunity for observing the numbers of different kinds of plants
      6. Estimated length of time: 1 week

Developmental/Integrative Activities

1. Language Arts
   a. Prepare a science notebook or dictionary of new terms.
   b. Prepare a bulletin board labeling different parts of plants.
   c. Read stories:
      (1) How Plants Travel by Joan Elma Rahn
      (2) A Tree is Something Wonderful by Elizabeth Cooper and Padraic Cooper
      (3) Watch Out, It's Poison Ivy by Peter R. Limburg
   d. Poetry: Favorite Poems for Children's Hour
      (1) The Daisy   Page 233
      (2) The Dandelion   269
      (3) The Violet   244
      (4) Baby Seeds   141
      (5) Two Apple-Howling
      (6) Songs   143
      (7) Flower Chorus   220
      (8) The Voice of the Grass 228
   e. Listen to the story Plant Sitter - Gene Zion
   f. Prepare students for scientific approach to doing an experiment.

2. Social Studies
   a. Collect pictures of parts of the plants we eat.
   b. Collect pictures of things we use from plants.
   c. Walk and observe types of plants that grow around school area.
   d. Walk and compare size and color of plants and flowers.

211

        e. Note variety of leaves through collection
           of them.
        f. Research and find what countries produce
           products from plants.
        g. Show filmstrip: <u>Parts of a Plant</u>
3. <u>Science</u>
        a. Conduct celery experiment using red dye
           for purpose of discovering the function
           of the stem. Set up hypotheses and
           detail the results.
        b. Use microscope, observe root hairs.
           Plant 2 plants but remove the root hairs
           of 1 plant and see if it will grow.
        c. Sprout beans on blotter and look for
           root hairs.
        d. Gather plants with large roots (carrot,
           parsnip).
        e. Tear root section off one plant and test
           to see if it will grow.
        f. Examine leaves for veins and cells with
           microscope.
        g. Remove leaves from a plant and see if
           plant will grow.
        h. Cover leaves with foil and uncover in
           about a week to see if leaves will lose
           their color.
        i. Cover leaves with petroleum jelly for
           observing that plants breathe.
        j. Examine parts of a tulip if possible.
           Otherwise, use commercial model to
           identify parts of a flower.
        k. Examine flower for pollen grains and
           sticky stamen.

l. Plant seeds (mustard, radish) in wooden
    box to observe if plant resembles the
    plant that produced the seed. Organize
    a report evaluating the results.

m. Test students on materials presented.

n. Observe parts that seeds contain 1) seed
    covering, 2) fat halves (cotyledons),
    3) tiny new plant.

o. Show film: How Seeds Are Scattered

p. Observe that seeds are also different
    in sizes and shapes.

q. Collect seeds - nuts, fruits, etc. Find
    seeds in apple, pumpkin, etc.

r. Soak bean to remove seed coat. Plant
    one seed with covering removed and
    another with seed covering. Observe
    which plant grows first.

s. Perform experiment to see if plant can
    live out of ground.

t. Observe if plant can live without air
    by covering leaves with black paper.

u. Experiment to see if plant needs light
    to grow by putting one plant in darkness
    and exposing the other to light.

v. Experiment to see if plant needs warmth
    to grow by putting one plant in a cold
    area and one in a warm area.

w. Perform experiment to observe if plant
    can be grown from a geranium stem.

x. Plant African violet and ivy leaf to
    observe if plant can be produced from this.

4. Mathematics

a. Prepare a chart or graph comparing the
    length of time it took for various seeds
    to grow.

213

        b. Given x number of seeds to grow, prepare
            a rectangular chart stating how many
            rows would be planted and how many seed
            would be planted in each row.
        c. Solve mathematics problems dealing with
            seeds, flowers, etc.
    5. Fine Arts
        a. Sing songs - Discovering Music Together
            (1) The Seasons
            (2) Autumn
            (3) Leaves Party
            (4) Under the Spreading Chestnut Tree
        b. Collect seeds and prepare a collage.
        c. Collect leaves and make a leaf booklet.
        d. Prepare a notebook of leaf screening.
        e. Make a bracelet out of seeds.
    6. Physical Activities
        a. Dramatize the song "Leaves Party" and
            develop sound effect for the dramatization.
        b. Dramatize the song "Under the Spreading
            Chestnut Tree."
        c. Do combination of dramatization and
            fingerplay for poem "Seeds."
C. Culminating Activities
    1. Hold an art show displaying the projects
        made by the class during this unit. Committees
        can be formed for preparing invitations,
        refreshments, and display set ups. This can
        be incorporated in the area of social studies.
    2. Visit the Garfield Park Conservatory or
        Natural History Museum. This will lend an
        opportunity for the students to summarize
        what they have learned.
        (The length of time for the culminating
        activity would be about 1-1/2 weeks.)

V. EVALUATION
  A. Beginning the Unit
     1. Before the unit begins, discuss with the students the things they know about plants and flowers.
     2. Ask students if there is anything of particular interest they might like to study or resource.
  B. Measuring Student Progress
     1. Before the unit begins, discuss with the students the things they know about plants and flowers.
     2. Keep a progress chart on each pupil for reference.
     3. Have students keep a progress chart on how their experiments are progressing.
  C. Teacher Evaluation
     1. Have children developed an interest in growing things?
     2. Do students understand the parts of plants and their function?
     3. Have students shown an interest in the various experiments?
     4. Have students been willing to participate in the various experiments?
     5. Did students seem motivated during class?
     6. Do students understand that plants require certain things in order to grow?
     7. Do students understand that plants can be grown from parts of plants?
     8. Do students understand that fruits, vegetables and other products come from plants?
     9. Do the slow learners participate in the various jobs assigned to them during the science projects?

10. Do the students handle the equipment
    carefully?

VI. MATERIALS AND RESOURCES
    A. Reading Materials
        1. Student texts
            a. Cooper, Elizabeth and Cooper, Padraic.
               A Tree is Something Wonderful. Chicago:
               Golden Gate, 1972. (Gr 2-4)
            b. Gallop, Edward. City Leaves, City Trees.
               Totowa, NJ: Scribner, 1972. (Gr 3-5)
            c. Limburg, Peter R. Watch Out, It's
               Poison Ivy. New York: Messner, 1973.
               (Gr 3-6)
            d. Rahn, Joan Elma. How Plants Travel.
               Paterson, NJ: Atheneum, 1973. (Gr 4-6)
            e. Selsam, Millicent E. The Apple and
               Other Fruit. Caldwell, NJ: Morrow.
               (Gr 3-5)
        2. Teacher texts
            a. Bates, Arthenia. Seeds Beneath the Snow.
               Washington, D.C.: Howard U Pr., 1975.
            b. Grae, Ida. Nature's Colors: Dyes from
               Plants. Riverside, NJ: Macmillan, 1974.
            c. Heady, Eleanor B. Plants on the Go:
               A Book About Reproduction and Seed
               Dispersal. New York: Parents, 1975.
            d. Jaques, H.E. Plants We Eat and Wear.
               New York: Dover, 1975.
            e. Wach, Natalie. Seeds, Leaves, and Flowers.
               Norwalk, CT: Gibson, 1975.
            f. Victor, Edward. Science for the Elementary
               School. 3rd ed. New York: Macmillan,
               1974.

g. White, Laurence B. Jr. Science Games.
    Reading, MA: Addison-Wesley, 1975.

Audio-Visual Materials

1. Films 16 mm
    a. How Seeds are Scattered. black and
        white, McGRAW-HILL TEXTFILMS, 10 min.,
        1958.
    b. Plant Motions: Roots, Stems, and Leaves.
        color, ENCYCLOPEDIA BRITANNICA EDUCATIONAL
        FILMS, 13 min., 1962.
    c. Plants That Have No Flowers or Seeds.
        color, CORONET, 11 min., 1967.
    d. Reproduction in Plants. color, CORONET,
        14 min., 1967.
    e. Secrets of the Plant World. color,
        WALT DISNEY, 15 min., 1965.
2. Filmstrips with records or cassettes
    a. Plants and How They Grow. color,
        #407-2, Chicago, SVE, 58 frames, 13 min.
    b. The Wonderful World of Plants. color,
        #407-1, Chicago, SVE, 48 frames, 12 min.

Facilities and Materials In and Outside the School

1. Obtain plants and flowers from the Garfield
    Park Conservatory, 300 N. Central Park,
    Chicago, Illinois 60624.
2. If an empty classroom is available, obtain
    permission to set up a greenhouse for the
    pupils to make their own garden patches.
3. Set up cold water aquariums in the classroom.
4. Set up warm water aquariums in the classroom.
5. Set up a semiaquatic terrarium in the classroom.
6. Set up a woodland terrarium in the classroom.
7. Order monthly display materials of mounted
    fossil, mineral, and herbarium samples

217

from the Chicago Natural History Museum,
Roosevelt and Lake Shore Drive, Chicago,
Illinois.

8. Secure materials for the unit: plants,
   seeds, flowers, pots, jars, soil, fertilizer,
   humus, etc.

D. Community Resources and People
   1. Visit the Chicago Natural History Museum.
   2. Visit Chicago Zoological Park.
   3. Visit Garfield Park Conservatory.
   4. Visit Lincoln Park Conservatory.
   5. Visit Forest Preserve District of Cook
      County, Little Red Schoolhouse Nature Center.
   6. Have resource people from the Morton
      Arboretum speak to the children.
   7. Invite resource people from the Trailside
      Museum of Natural History to visit the class.

E. Pupil Participation in the Community
   1. Have pupils suggest and plan field trips in
      the local community:
      a. Local parks
      b. Local nature centers
      c. Neighbors or parents flower displays,
         gardens, or yards
   2. Have pupils bring in materials for the unit:
      a. Seeds
      b. Plants (weeds, flowers, etc.)
      c. Bottles
      d. Pressed leaves
      e. Flower pots, jars, and boxes
   3. Bring in resource people from the neighbor-
      hood that are knowledgeable about growing
      plants.

TEACHING UNIT

Format Two

SIMPLE MACHINES MAKE OUR WORK EASIER

. INTRODUCTION

A. Grade Level: 3rd grade; Age Level: 8 to 9 years

B. Duration of Time: 6 weeks

C. This unit is correlated with the Curriculum
Guide of Science from the Chicago Public
Schools with the over-all science outline for
the primary grades.

D. The six simple machines to be covered in this
unit are:
1. The lever
2. The inclined plane
3. The wheel and axle
4. The pulley
5. The wedge
6. The screw

E. The working procedure for this unit will consist
mainly of demonstrations and individual experimentation. It is hoped that the students will
be able to comprehend the principles involved
through their own experiences with each of
the machines.

. OBJECTIVES

A. General Objectives
1. To know that there are different kinds of
machines that can produce work.

2. To know that machines make our work easier.
3. To understand that many complex machines are made up of the six simple machines.
4. To participate in individual and group experiments using the six simple machines.
5. To appreciate the work machines perform for society.
6. To gain skill in using and spelling scientific words presented in this unit.
7. To be able to recognize every day objects used in the home as a certain type of simple machine.

B. Specific Objectives
   1. Cognitive:
      a. To understand that work is done whenever an object is moved.
      b. To be able to discuss the different sources of energy that can be used to move an object.
      c. To be able to list the names of the six simple machines.
      d. To know the lever as a simple machine that can lift and pry.
      e. To know that the wheel and axle is a simple machine that makes turning and pulling easier.
      f. To comprehend that the pulley is a simple machine which can change the direction of a pull.
      g. To recognize an inclined plane as a slanting ramp to make pulling and pushing easier.
      h. To be able to comprehend that a wedge is made from an inclined plane.

i. To know that the screw is a simple
    machine that winds around a center.

2. <u>Affective</u>:

    a. To learn the importance of co-operation
        when working within a group, experi-
        menting with the simple machines.

    b. To gain personal satisfaction from
        participation in group discussions and
        individual experiences with the machines
        and related equipment.

    c. To develop interest in using the
        different simple machines.

    d. To enjoy participating in the discussion
        and demonstration of the various simple
        machines.

    e. To follow rules of safety using the
        simple machines.

3. <u>Skill</u>

    a. To be able to collect and classify
        pictures of the machines.

    b. To be able to use art materials that
        will be used to construct simple models
        of the machines.

    c. To be able to work and use each of the
        machines manually.

    d. To identify the fulcrum as the balancing
        point of the lever.

    e. To know when less force is needed when
        using a longer and lower plane.

    f. To recognize gears as wheels with teeth
        that turn about each other.

    g. To gain skill using the pulley's action
        in reversing the direction of a pull.

    h. To gain skill in classifying the six
        simple machines according to their functions

221

III. CONTENT OUTLINE
    A. Orientation
        1. Man's early development of machines
        2. Man's use of machines through the ages
        3. Different kinds of machines that produce work
        4. Definition of work
            a. Energy
            b. Force
        5. Everyday experiences with objects in the home and school that are simple machines
    B. Lever
        1. Essential parts of the lever
            a. Fulcrum
            b. Lever arm
        2. Functions of the lever
            a. Lifting
            b. Prying
        3. Kinds and types of levers
            a. Seesaw
            b. Crowbar
            c. Scissors
            d. Can opener
            e. Shovel
            f. Broom
            g. Pliers
            h. Screwdriver
    C. Inclined plane
        1. Definition of a plane
            a. Slanted and smooth surface
            b. Flat and slanted surface upon which objects can be moved to a higher point with more ease than straight lifting

2. Use of more or less force in relation to amount of slanting or inclination of the plane
3. Kinds and types of planes
   a. Ramps
   b. Conveyors
   c. Stairs
   d. Escalators
   e. Slides
   f. Ladders
   g. Bridges
   h. Hills
   i. Inclined driveways
D. Wheel and axle
   1. Movable wheels vs. fixed wheels
   2. The need for the axle to make turning easier
   3. Ball bearings
      a. Ball bearings are tiny steel wheels
      b. Ball bearings are usually fixed between two wheels
   4. Gears
      a. Gears are wheels with teeth all around
      b. Gears can be made up of two or three of these wheels
      c. The action or turning of one wheel turns the next wheel
   5. The uses of the wheel, axle, ball bearings and gears in bikes, cars, and more complex machinery
E. Pulley
   1. Function
      a. Lifting
      b. Reversing direction of a pull
   2. Uses and examples of pulleys

3. Observation of flagpole pulley
F. Wedge
    1. Function
        a. Used to split things apart
        b. Used to brace one object next to another
    2. Types of wedges
        a. Single
        b. Double
    3. Classes of wedge
        a. Sharpened
            (1) Ax
            (2) Knife
            (3) Nail
            (4) Pin
        b. Jagged
            (1) Handsaw
            (2) Drill
G. Screw
    1. Function is to hold things together
    2. Composition
        a. Winding center
        b. Inclined plane
    3. Uses of screws
    4. Different types of screws and bolts
E. Complex machines
    1. Definition
    2. Composition in relation to the six simple machines
    3. Function
    4. Common examples
        a. Cars
        b. Diesel engines

c. Large factory machines
d. Motors on electric lawn mowers and kitchen appliances

<u>abulary</u>

ax	lever	machine
pin	plane	movable
saw	screw	pulling
axle	slide	lifting
flat	wedge	inclined
hill	wheel	crowbar
jack	energy	conveyer
nail	hammer	fulcrum
work	ladder	scissors
broom	pliers	slanted
drill	pulley	ball bearings
fixed	seesaw	can opener
force	shovel	escalator
gears	smooth	pencil sharpener
knife	stairs	screw driver

ACTIVITIES

A. <u>Initiatory Activities</u>

   1. To know there are different kinds of machines that can produce work

     a. Read story: <u>Machines</u> by Jerome S. Meyer, Cleveland, OH, Collins-World, 1972. (Gr 4-6)

     b. Bring in objects that are simple machines and pictures showing their common use.

     c. Discuss what part of the object they think is considered a simple machine and speculate on how it works.

Afterwards, hold brief demonstration
using each of the objects. Then once
again, ask children to describe in their
own words, how they think the object
works. Ask if they think the object or
machine makes work easier.

d. Invite children to bring in pictures or
examples of machines found around the
house, or in construction and industry.

e. Discuss that a machine is an object
that produces work and makes our work
easier.

f. Read book: <u>Wheels: A Book to Begin On</u>.
by Eleanor Clyner, New York, HR&W, 1965.

2. To know that machines help make our work
easier

a. Show film: <u>How Simple Machines Make
Work Easier</u>. color, CORONET, 11 min.,
1964.

b. Initiate discussion about various kinds
of machinery used by fathers at work or
at home. Have them look through display
and pick out and identify those objects
that they think are the ones their
fathers might use.

c. Continue discussion about various kinds
of machinery used by their mothers at
work or at home. Have them look through
display and pick out and identify those
objects that they think are the ones
their mothers might use.

d. Tell children scientific meaning of work
and force, "When an object is moved,
work is accomplished."

e. Have children name some things they use
   to do "work" (scissors, crayons, pencils,
   sharpeners, and see-saw, etc.).
f. After discussing use of machinery and
   work, suggest that the children closely
   observe their parents using machines
   at home. Have them be aware of themselves using objects to do work.
g. Select examples of some machines - stress
   that the children describe them by using
   verbs like dig, pull, press, crush,
   slice, roll, mash, etc. If capable,
   have children act out the machine while
   using descriptive words above.
h. Introduce the idea that there are six
   simple machines and that many big
   machines are made up of some of the
   simple machines. Stress that we will
   be studying and working with each of
   the six simple machines in this unit.
i. Worksheet: Complex and simple machines
   scrambled on paper. Have children
   circle the six simple machines and label
   them.

To know that there are six simple machines:
Lever, pulley, wheel and axle, inclined
plane, wedge, screw

a. Review of ideas presented in the topic:
   "Machines help make our work easier."
b. Pick up examples of each of the six
   simple machines. Have small groups
   examine each machine.
c. Discuss the physical features of each
   machine (weight, color, depth, length,
   basic construction).

227

d. Briefly demonstrate use of each object.
e. Have children draw each of the six
   simple machines. Have them select one
   they especially like and write short
   story: "If I were a wheel, I...."
4. To know that a lever is a simple machine,
   that can pry and lift.
   a. Put example of small see-saw in front
      of class.
      (1) Explain that a see-saw is an
          example of a simple machine called
          a lever.
      (2) Stress that the board is called
          the lever and the stand is called
          the fulcrum.
      (3) Draw a diagram on board and add a
          lever and fulcrum to vocabulary
          list.
   b. Have two children draw each of the six
      objects and come up and try to push a
      medium sized box.
      (1) Explain that the children must work
          to push the box.
      (2) Ask them how they think they can
          make a lever and fulcrum to make
          their work easier.
      (3) Use a piece of plywood and a rolled
          up rug as fulcrum and have some
          children demonstrate that a lever
          can lift and make our work easier.
   c. Have each child make a lever on his
      desk by using a book as object, pencil
      as lever and finger as fulcrum. Discuss
      convenience and construction of a lever.

d. Divide children into small groups. Let
    each child try to pry the lid of an
    empty paint can with his fingers -
    then with a screwdriver.
    (1) Discuss which was easier.
    (2) Stress that a screwdriver is a kind
         of a lever that can pry and lift.
e. Have children add phrases onto riddle
    about the lever.

5. To know that the wheel and axle is a simple
    machine.
    a. Simple machines that make turning and
        pulling easier
        Read book: _Wheels_ by Ellie Simmon (Gr K-3)
    b. Fill box with books. Have a child try
        to push it across floor using one hand.
        "Was it easy?"
    c. Place dowel rods or pencils under box.
        Have some child push the box again with
        one hand. "Was it easy?" "Is the work
        getting done?" "Are we using a wheel?"
    d. Have 2 or 3 children lift box into a
        small wagon. Have the smallest child
        push the wagon across room.
        (1) Ask if the small child could have
             done this without the wagon.
        (2) Ask if this is more convenient than
             having to keep moving the dowel
             rods under the box. Why?
        (3) Introduce concept that the wheels
             stay with the load because of the
             axles - put on vocabulary list.
        (4) Explain that an axle is a rod around
             which a wheel turns.

e. Show pictures of different things with wheels - have them try to pick out the axle and explain its use.
f. Bring in example of a door knob catch assembly or a faucet handle.
   (1) Try to make the latch move by turning the axle with a few fingers - "Can you do it?" "Is it easy?"
   (2) Allow several children to try above and then let them try to turn door knob on the classroom door, "Does it move?" "Is it easy to move the latch now?"
   (3) Ask where is the wheel and the axle in the door knob.
g. Introduce ball bearings by placing them in two cans (grooved lids) on top of each other. Have children try to turn top can. Then place marbles in groove of bottom can, then turn. Let them discover that ball bearings are a type of wheel that helps to turn things easier.
h. Introduce simple gear - some wheels can make other wheels turn.
   (1) Stress the chain belt.
   (2) Bring in egg beater and mounted examples of a bicycle chain belt.
   (3) Explain how teeth help force of 1 wheel turn wheel 2. Have them speculate what will happen when wheel 2 is turned, etc.
6. To know that the pulley is a simple machine which can change the direction of a pull.

a. Hold up an assimilated model of pulley. Tell child it is a simple machine. Ask if they recognize anything about this simple machine. It has a wheel and axle in it.

b. Briefly review the construction and operation of the wheel and axle.

c. Explain that the pulley is a grooved _wheel_ mounted on an axle. Put new words on vocabulary list.

d. Let class carefully examine a real pulley. Show rope fits around the wheel, when the rope is pulled, the wheel turns.

e. Have them look around room for examples of a pulley. (shades, outdoor flag pole, etc.)

f. Arrange for school custodian to demonstrate how he uses pulleys to raise and lower the school flag. Discuss how the flag went _up_ when he pulled _down_.

g. Have children go home that night and observe how we pull down on drapery cord and the drapes move across.

h. Discuss how a pulley changes the direction of a pull.

i. At a height easily reached by children, attach two pulleys to opposite side of room and thread them with rope wire. Next day have children take turns hanging any of their art work or their pictures using clothes pins or paper clips. When the picture is hung, pull the rope or wire toward him so that the paper moves away from him and makes room for another child's paper.

231

      j. Worksheets on parts of wheel and axle
          and pulleys.
7. To know that the inclined plan is a simple
    machine that makes pulling and pushing easier.
      a. Ask who knows what a ramp is - describe it.
      b. Ask where they might see it.
      c. Show pictures of industrial ramps used
          to load and unload boxes.
      d. Explain that hills are examples of an
          "inclined plane."
          (1) Put inclined plane on board and
              explain that it is a flat, slanting
              plane or hill along which a heavy
              object may be pulled or pushed to
              move it to a higher level.
          (2) Add words to vocabulary list.
      e. Have children suggest some common
          examples of planes. (slides, ladders,
          stairs, escalators.)
      f. Have children fold a piece of paper to
          look like steps. Then pull the paper
          stairs out tight to show that steps
          form an inclined plane.
      g. Put a box of books on a table. Have a
          few children try to take the box off
          and on. Then give them a piece of wood
          and have them try to discover how they
          can make an inclined plane and take box
          on and off the table easier.
      h. Worksheets: Have examples of objects
          with wheels and pulleys mixed in with
          pictures of inclined planes. Have them
          circle the planes and draw a line under
          the other types of simple machines
          studied so far.

To know that a wedge is a simple machine
made of inclined planes to make lifting
and cutting easier.

a. View film <u>The Inclined Plane Family</u>.
   black and white, CORONET, 6 min., 1954.

b. Discuss how lumberjacks use an ax to
   chop and cut a tree and trunk.

c. Discuss that an ax is an example of the
   simple machine the wedge. Add to
   vocabulary list.

d. Bring in large picture of an ax. Ask
   how many planes the wedge is made of. (2)

e. Ask if they can think of any utensils
   in the kitchen that can be used as a
   wedge.
   (1) Stress knife which can split
       things apart.
   (2) A pin which can move through
       something.
   (3) A needle which can cut and move
       through something.
   (4) A saw which can cut something apart.

f. Bring in examples of the above. I will
   demonstrate the use of each for safety
   reasons.

g. Have children try to cut an apple apart.
   Then cut the apple apart with a wedge
   (knife) for them. Let them compare which
   is easier, then have an apple eating
   party.

h. Let children guess the riddle below or
   have them compose their own:
   > This is a wedge
   > Could be used north or south

233

Its full of sharp teeth
But has no mouth (a saw)

9. To know that the screw is a simple machine
   that can wind around a center and can be
   used to hold things together.
   a. Have children pretend they are a screw
      and act out with movement.
      (1) Explain that a winding staircase
          is a winding ramp.
      (2) Explain that this is an example of
          the sixth simple machine, called
          the screw.
      (3) Add screw to the vocabulary list.
   b. Integrate math and art lesson by making
      a screw.
      (1) Make paper inclined plane about
          6" long with a 3" side.
      (2) Math - have them use rulers to
          measure the paper and draw a slanted
          line to form the 3rd side (slanting).
      (3) Color a band along the long slanting
          side with crayon.
      (4) Have children cut little snips
          along the slanted side with scissors.
      (5) Starting at the hight point (end) of
          the slant, wrap the slant around a
          pencil.
   c. Ask if the finished product looks like
      something their fathers might use. (screw)
   d. Have them unwrap the screw and observe
      what they started with an inclined plane.
      (1) Should respond it started with an
          inclined plane.
      (2) Discuss that a screw is an inclined
          plane that winds around and around
          a center.

(3) Explain that a screw holds things together better than a nail. Why?
- e. Bring in examples of different types of screws and a screw wedge and a cork screw for demonstration.
- f. Worksheets: pictures of objects. Have them draw a circle around all the plain wedges. Then have then draw a box around all the screws.

Culminating Activities
1. Individual
   - a. Make dittos of science word unscramble as a review.
   - b. Have one column with different names of some type of simple machines - letters scrambled.
   - c. Have them unscramble words and match with list in second column.
   - d. Have children draw and color a simple picture of the machine in the space provided to the right of second column.
   - e. Have each row decide on a simple machine they would like to describe and demonstrate to the class.
   - f. Show filmstrip on complex machines and engines.
   - g. Have pictures of different kinds of simple and complex machines
   - h. See if they can pick out the simple machines in each.
   - i. Set up groups for science show.

Developmental - Integrated Activities
1. Social Studies
   - a. Discuss history of man's early use of simple machines.

235

b. Discuss how machines can affect our lives.

c. Discuss how development of complex machines from small ones has created automation and is responsible for the great growth of industry in America.

d. Discuss how machines have made our lives easier so we have more leisure time to spend with our families and friends.

e. Bring in pictures of people and communities where there are few modern versions of machines. Compare their homes and lives with ours.

2. Language Arts

a. Read stories and poems.

b. Have children construct riddle chart for each machine.

c. Make experience charts - stressing new vocabulary words about the machine parts. The experiences for the chart will be gained from demonstrations and class participation with the experiments.

d. Develop classification and association skills:

(1) Classification according to like-nesses and differences in size. parts, uses and importance

(2) Association skills gained by using descriptive words that describe the sound and function of the machine

e. Develop listening skills - children will be able to hear the sounds the machines make (scissors, eggbeaters, can opener, hammer).

f. Discuss use of movement and body
      awareness when acting out a machine.
   g. Discuss ideas while performing an
      experiment.
   h. Exchange of conversation and ideas when
      working at display table.
3. <u>Mathematics</u>
   a. Measure distances when pushing boxes or
      cartons across room.
   b. Discuss weight when using lever or plane
      for lifting heavy objects.
   c. Measure boards used for inclined plane.
   d. Measure rope when discussing pulleys.
4. <u>Science</u>
   a. Classify machines according to simple
      or complex.
   b. Perceive likenesses and differences of
      machines.
   c. Perceive relationships between parts
      and a whole.
   d. Use scientific terminology.
   e. Use scientific method and inferences;
      set up problem and find solution from
      inferences and final experimentation.
   f. Develop analytical thinking.
4. <u>Health and Safety</u>
   a. Point out that some machines are
      dangerous and must be handled carefully.
   b. Discuss safety when using screws, nails,
      scissors, knives, and needles. They can
      be swallowed or they can cut.
   c. Discuss first aid for accidents with
      machines.
   d. Show how simple machines make up many

237

complex machines that give us milk,
water and food much quicker and fresher.

6. Art
   a. Draw pictures of different machines and
      pictures of different people using them.
   b. Make a collage.
   c. Construct simple machines from paper,
      balsa wood and milk cartons.
   d. Draw a screw.
   e. Draw or paint pictures of each machine
      for the pulley rack in topic 6.

7. Physical Education
   a. Perform movement exercises when acting
      out the machines.
   b. Explain the muscle movement involved
      when pulling, pushing, lifting and
      stretching are used for the lever, plane,
      pulley and wheel.
   c. Develop manual skills when working the
      machines.

V. EVALUATION

   A. Measuring Student Progress
      1. Can the children name and label the different
         kinds of machines that can produce work?
      2. Do the children understand that machines
         make our work easier?
      3. Do the children know that there are six
         basic simple machines, the lever, wheel and
         axle, pulley, inclined plane, wedge and screw?
      4. Do the children understand that a lever is
         an inclined plane, that can lift and pry?
      5. Do the children understand that a wheel and
         axle is a simple machine that makes turning
         easier?
      6. Do they understand that an axle is important
         for keeping a wheel turning?

7. Do the children understand that a pulley is a simple machine that can change the direction of a pull?

8. Do the children understand that an inclined plane is really a ramp, that makes pushing and pulling heavy objects easier?

9. Do the children understand that a wedge is a simple machine that is made up of one or more inclined planes?

10. Do the children understand that a screw is a simple machine that winds around a center and can be used to hold things together better?

11. Give the children a picture identification on the simple machines.

12. Have them draw each of the six types of levers from memory.

13. Have them list at least three places where each machine may be found or used.

3. Teacher Evaluation

1. Did I use scientific books and movies at the proper level to motivate the children?

2. Did I use each topic so that the children recognized the scientific method of stating a problem, experimentation and solving?

3. Did I organize each topic so that the children could formulate the problem and make inferences?

4. Did I use materials that were on the children's level?

5. Was each child involved in the experiments so that he had experience with each machine?

6. Did the children enjoy the topics and demonstrations?

7. Did significant behavioral and expected outgrowth take place?
8. Will the children be able to transfer the learnings about simple machines to their daily lives?

VI. MATERIALS AND RESOURCES
   A. <u>Reading Materials</u>
      1. Student texts
         a. Hellman, Hal. <u>Lever and the Pulley</u>. Philadelphia: M. Evans, 1971. (Gr 2-6)
         b. Larrick, Nancy. <u>Wheels of the Bus Go Round and Round: School Bus Songs and Chants</u>. Chicago: Childrens, 1972. (Gr 3-7)
         c. Meyer, Jerome S. <u>Machines</u>. Cleveland, OH: Collins-World, 1972. (Gr 4-6)
         d. Navarra, John G. <u>Wheels for Kids</u>. New York: Doubleday, 1973. (Gr K-3)
         e. Pine, Tillie S. and Levine, Joseph. <u>Simple Machines and How We Use Them</u>. New York: McGraw, 1965.
         f. Scott, John M. <u>What Is Science?</u> New York: Parents, 1972. (Gr 2-4)
         g. Zim, Herbert S. and Skelly, James R. <u>Machine Tools</u>. Caldwell, NJ: Morrow, 1974. (Gr 4-6)
      2. Teacher texts
         a. Althouse, Rosemary and Main, Cecil. New York: Teachers College, 1975.
         b. Dixon, Bernard. <u>What Is Science For?</u> Scranton, PA: Harper & Row, 1974.
         c. Hailey, Arthur. <u>Wheels</u>. New York: Doubleday, 1971.
         d. Nelson, Leslie W. and Lorbeer, George.

Science Activities for the Elementary
Children. 5th ed. Dubuque, IA: Wm. C.
Brown, 1972.

e. Zlot, William et al. Sourcebook of
Fundamental Mathematics, Arithmetic,
Elementary Algebra, Elementary Geometry.
Chicago: Aldine-Atherton, 1971.

Audio-Visual Materials

1. Films 16 mm

   a. How Levers Help Us. color, CORONET,
   11 min., 1970.

   b. How Machines and Tools Help Us. color,
   CORONET, 10 min., 1954.

   c. How Simple Machines Make Work Easier.
   color, CORONET, 11 min., 1964.

   d. Let's Look at Levers. black and white,
   JOURNAL, 10 min., 1961.

   e. Lever (The). color, BAILEY-FILM
   ASSOCIATES, 11 min., 1971.

   f. Schools and Sharing: Let's Share a
   Seesaw. color, McGRAW-HILL TEXTFILMS,
   10 min., 1967.

   g. Simple Machines: Levers. color, CORONET,
   6 min., 1954.

   h. Simple Machines: The Inclined Plane
   Family. black and white, EB, 11 min.,
   1960.

   i. Simple Machines: Wheels and Axles. black
   and white, CORONET, 6 min., 1954.

2. Filmstrips

   a. Finding Out About Simple Machines. S.V.E.

   b. Finding Out About Wheels and Pulleys.
   S.V.E.

C. Community Resources and People
1. Visit the "Museum of Science and Industry."
2. Visit industries and manufacturing companies:
   a. Pepsi-Cola
   b. Campbell Soup
   c. International Harvester
   d. Local machine shops
3. Have manufacturing representatives visit the class and demonstrate various products ...indicating the simple machine principles.
4. Have children bring to school items from home that represent each of the six principles of the lever.
5. Take a field trip through the neighborhood to locate examples of simple machines we see everday.
6. Write for free materials of pictures, posters, and other items from industry and business.

TEACHING UNIT

Format Two

HOW NEWSPAPERS SERVE US

INTRODUCTION

A. <u>Grade Level</u>: 6th grade; <u>Age Level</u>: 11
B. <u>Duration of Time</u>: 4 weeks
C. Unit planned to be correlated with the 5A semester Social Studies work on <u>Communication</u>. Other
   social study units to be worked on this semester
   include:
   1. How the post office serves us
   2. How telephones serve us
   3. How radio and television serves us

OBJECTIVES

A. <u>General Objectives</u>
   1. To understand that newspapers help to bring
      a better understanding about all the people
      all over the world
   2. To be able to write a well organized theme
      or article
   3. To be able to interpret the opinions
      expressed in the editorials
   4. To be able to use maps efficiently
   5. To appreciate the significant role of the
      newspaper in our daily lives
   6. To develop a variety of reading interests
   7. To understand that modern machines have
      improved the methods of printing and distrib-
      uting the newspapers

243

B. Specific Objectives

Cognitive

1. To describe the ways in which modern machines are used in every step of newspaper production from gathering the news to distributing the papers

2. To list the main workers on a newspaper staff, describe their duties, and their importance to the newspaper

3. To explain in simple terms how paper is made as demonstrated by each child composing an in-class composition entitled "From Trees to Newspaper"

4. To know that the process of gathering, printing and distributing of the news requires the work of many people

Affective

1. To appreciate the content and value of the daily newspaper

2. To appreciate the importance of world news in everyday affairs

3. To respect the efforts of people who write, gather, and distribute the news

4. To recognize the need for responsible and balanced presentation of information and news

Skill

1. To be able to use reference material in obtaining information

2. To participate in planning and organizing a class newspaper

3. To locate on a map areas in the Great Lakes Region where forests supply paper for our city newspapers

         4. To list the various kinds of information a
             newspaper contains
III. CONTENT
      A. Kinds of information in the newspaper
          1. News
          2. Special
          3. Advertisements
          4. Pictures
          5. Editorials
      B. Work of the newspaper staff
          1. Gathering the news
          2. Printing the paper
          3. Distributing newspapers
      C. How news is obtained and printed
          1. Reporting news and information
          2. Writing and editing the story
          3. Setting type
          4. Making mats and lead castings
          5. Running the presses
      D. How newspapers are distributed
          1. Assembling the parts of the paper
          2. Counting and wrapping into bundles
          3. Loading trucks
          4. Delivering to newsstands and agencies
      E. Why depend on newspapers
          1. Interdependence of people all over the world
          2. Need for rapid communication
          3. Special training of newspaper workers
          4. Special equipment and services of newspaper
              companies
      F. Unit Vocabulary
          editor   advertisement   type
          editorial   cartoon   machinery
          reporter   comic strip   distribute

245

article   printing press   publish
print   staff   publisher
printer   communication   forest
                                                headline

IV. ACTIVITIES
   A. Initiatory Activities
      1. A class trip to the Chicago Tribune at
         435 N. Michigan. Involve students in all
         stages of planning the trip.
      2. Class discussion of all aspects of the trip
         and initial discussion of the work of the
         newspaper staff including:
         a. News reporting
         b. News writing and editing
         c. Type setting
         d. Making mats and lead castings
         e. Running the presses
         f. Assembling the parts of the paper
         g. Counting and wrapping into bundles
         h. Delivering to newsstands and agencies
         i. Did they enjoy the trip?
         j. Which process particularly interested
            them?
         k. Do any of them have a paper route?
      3. Make and discuss an experience chart about
         the trip dealing with some of the above
         topics.
      4. Make a bulletin board about the trip and
         the things they have seen.
   B. Developmental/Integrative Activities
      1. Language Arts
         a. With the children's help draw up and
            chart a list of new vocabulary words

246

such as editor, reporter, etc. Have
each child keep list for reference.
b. Have each child bring a copy of the
previous days' paper (preferably the
Sun-Times because its size would be
easier to handle) and discuss the kinds
of information in it and the special
sections.
  (1) News
  (2) Special Features
  (3) Advertisements
  (4) Pictures
  (5) Sports
  (6) Cartoons, etc.
c. Discuss news articles that come from
all over the world and their effect on
or similarity to our own daily lives.
d. Make a class collection of these
articles in a scrapbook, bulletin
board, or display.
· Have each child pretend he works on a
newspaper. Have him write either a news
article, a special interest article,
interview, editorial, etc.
· Read aloud selections from the book,
Ben Franklin, Printers Boy, which tells
about Franklin working on his brother's
newspaper.
  (1) Discuss the kinds of work which
      Ben did in helping to print the
      paper.
  (2) Have the children act out what Ben
      Franklin's job might have been like.

g. Contribute original stories and pictures to be mounted in a special place in the room under "News of the Day."

h. Make an experience chart or class story about "How We Depend on Newspapers."

i. Have the children conduct and write interviews. Have them interview each other, you, other teachers, their parents, the principal, janitor, school nurse, etc.

2. Mathematics

a. Introduce rulers and measuring concepts along with the idea of column divisions, type height, etc.

b. Have each child construct his own measured newspaper layout including columns, mast, etc.

3. Science

a. Obtain the booklet, How a Modern Newspaper Goes to Press from the Chicago Sun-Times.

(1) Have the class study the pictures and along with what they have seen on the field trip, note and discuss the ways in which modern machines are used in every step of newspaper production.

(2) Have them make a bulletin board on this subject or even cardboard miniatures of some of these machines.

b. Have individuals or a committee of students report and explain to the class how paper is made.

248

c. Show film <u>Paper and Pulp Making</u>. color,
   CORONET, 11 min., 1955.
d. Show film <u>Conservation and Our Forests</u>.
   color, FILM ASSOCIATES OF CALIFORNIA,
   16 min., 1966.
   (1) Discuss what can be done to save
       our forestland.
   (2) Have the students write slogans
       and illustrate posters with this
       theme.
e. In connection with their art work have
   pupils make a mural "From Trees to
   Newspapers."
f. Locate areas in the Great Lakes Region
   where forests supply paper for our
   city. (i.e. newspapers)

Social Studies

a. Examine pictures from the Communication
   Series published by Creative Educational
   Society to learn more about the workers
   on a newspaper staff.
   (1) Discuss the duties of each
   (2) Have each child pick the one he
       would like to be and explain why
       and/or make a bulletin board on
       this subject.
b. Invite some of the staff of the school
   newspaper or of the neighborhood newspaper to talk to the class about the
   various duties that they perform on the
   paper.
   (1) The day after the talk have the
       class compose a thank-you letter to
       thank the speakers for coming.

249

c. Discuss the duties of a news reporter.
   (1) Read the story, <u>I Want to be a News Reporter</u> by Carla Greene.
   (2) Have the children write or tell why they think this might be an interesting job. Show the filmstrip <u>You and Your Newspaper</u> (Popular Science Publishing Company). Compare the activities with those observed during the day's tour.
d. Collect and have children collect articles from newspapers that show how a newspaper serves the community by sponsoring community events, sports events, youth achievement contests, and other things of interest to the children or their families. (The Sun-Times Fun Club is a good example.)

5. <u>Arts and Crafts</u>
   a. Let the children experiment with different methods of printing. For example, potato prints, string prints, leneoleum printing.
   b. Have children draw pictures of the activities observed in the production and distribution of newspapers.
      (1) Do a bulletin board or display on the subject.
   c. Have children illustrate the news story they have written.
   d. Have the children illustrate their mural. (Mentioned above)
   e. Have children compose and illustrate their own cartoon or comic strip.
   f. Have pupils make a bulletin board or mural -- <u>How Newspapers Serve Us</u>.

250

6. Physical Activities
   a. Take part in a paper drive.
   b. Have small groups of children perform skits, make up stories about some imaginary event or occurence or have them simulate an interview. Then have all children compose their own news story of what they had seen and heard. Compare all the different ways that the children described the same events.
   c. Have small groups of children act out the events described in a news story.
   d. Role playing--editor, reporters, newspaperboys, printers, Ben Franklin, etc.

Culminating Activities
1. The class will create (write, illustrate, edit) their own newspaper.
   a. Let the students vote on a name for the paper.
   b. Each pupil will have certain duties on the paper.
      (1) Let them suggest each job.
      (2) Editors
      (3) Reporters
      (4) Cartoonists
      (5) Illustrators
      (6) Students in charge of lay-out, etc.
   c. The teacher will do the duplication work (try to keep to about a four page copy).
   d. The finished newspaper can be distributed to the pupils' parents, other teachers, other third grade classes, or even sold for a penny or two to pay for duplicating cost if any, or have the proceeds contributed to charity.

V. EVALUATION
   A. Beginning the Unit
      1. Have the students bring in a local news-
         paper and select a section of it (sports,
         editorials, want ads, comic sections).
      2. List on the blackboard the various sections
         of the newspaper and have each pupil con-
         tribute information to each section of the
         outline.
      3. Have pupils relate their personal experiences
         and those of relatives and friends who work
         for a newspaper.
      4. Have the students write down all they know
         about the newspaper including such infor-
         mation as:
         a. Importance of newspaper
         b. Responsibilities of workers and staff
         c. Gathering of news
         d. Source of news
         e. Distribution
         f. Costs
   B. Measuring Student Progress
      1. Have pupils keep a weekly log, notebook,
         and/or scrapbook of the unit and individual
         activities.
      2. Have pupils keep a folder of news items,
         editorials, entertainment, sports, cartoons,
         etc.
      3. Have them evaluate their reporting, writing,
         and editing by comparing it.
      4. Hold conference with pupils to show them
         how to evaluate their own work.
      5. Have pupils make different types of graphs
         depicting their scores on the weekly quizzes.

252

6. Hold class discussion of various aspects of the newspaper produced by committees putting together the newspaper.

C. Teacher Evaluation

1. Evaluate pupils' knowledge of unit through discussion and projects and weekly quizzes.

2. Evaluate individual pupil's contribution to the newspaper.

3. Have pupils write an essay on what they learned from the newspaper unit on a weekly basis and at the culmination of the unit.

4. Observe how individual pupils participate in small and large group activities.

5. Record progress of individually assigned projects and activities.

6. Observe cooperativeness of pupils in committee work and share activities.

7. Note the ideas, activities and projects initiated and implemented by individual pupils and groups.

8. Record the interest of the class by their level of participation.

9. Evaluate each pupil's development in the following skill area through observation and written work:

   a. Improvement in written communication-- reporting, rewriting, and editing.

   b. Taking a responsibility and following it through to the end

   c. To be able to give an oral presentation to the class

   d. To be able to participate in skits and take the role of various newspaper staff

253

  e. To be able to use reference materials
    and conduct research on an assigned
    topic

  f. To develop skill in measurement in
    relation to newspaper layouts, columns,
    etc.

  g. Improvement of vocabulary and reading
    skills

  h. To develop and use interview techniques

VI. MATERIALS AND RESOURCES

  A. <u>Reading Materials</u>

    1. Student texts

      a. Drabkin, Marjorie, and Zlotnik, Harold.
        <u>Understanding Words: A Guide to</u>
        <u>Vocabulary</u>. new ed. Woodbury, New York:
        Barron, 1975. (Gr 5 and up)

      b. Evans, Harold. <u>News Headlines</u>. New York:
        HR&W, 1974. (Gr 5 and up)

      c. Goamna, Muriel. <u>News and Messages</u>.
        North Pomfret, VT: David & Charles,
        1973. (Gr 3-8)

      d. Longgood, William. <u>Write with Feeling</u>.
        New York: School Book Service, 1974.
        (Gr 6-8)

      e. Smith, and Smith. <u>Newsmakers: The Press</u>
        <u>and the President</u>. Reading, MA: Addison-
        Wesley, 1974. (Grades 5 and up)

    2. Teacher texts

      a. Dagher, Joseph P. <u>Writing: A Practical</u>
        <u>Guide</u>. New York: Houghton Mifflin, 1975.

      b. Evans, Harold. <u>Newsman's English</u>. New
        York: HR&W, 1972.

      c. Kennedy, Larry. <u>Teaching the Elementary</u>
        <u>Language Arts</u>. Scranton, PA: Har-Row,
        1975.

d. Lutz, William W. _News of Detroit: How a Newspaper and a City Grew Together_. Waltham, MA: Little, 1973.

e. McCrimmon, James M. _Writing with a Purpose_. 5th ed. New York: Houghton Mifflin, 1975.

f. Rucher, Frank W., and Williams, Herbert L. _Newspaper Organization and Management_. 4th ed. Ames, IA: Iowa St U Pr, 1974.

3. Magazine Articles

a. Lewis, C. Courses by newspaper. _Phi Delta Kappan_, 56:60-62, 1974.

b. Newton, Bryan. Writing to communicate. _Times Educ Supp_, 3095:63, 1974.

c. Salama, N. Use the newspapers! _Eng Lan Teach J_, 28:336-343, 1974.

d. Stratton, L. What's black and white and moves all over? _Teacher_, 92:20-23, 1974.

· _Audio-Visual Materials_

1. Films 16 mm

a. _Critical Thinking: Making Sure of Facts_. color, CORONET, 11 min., 1972.

b. _Journalism: Mirror, Mirror, On the World_. black and white, NET, 52 min., 1968.

c. _Propaganda Techniques_. black and white, CORONET, 11 min., 1950.

d. _Your Communication Skills: Writing_. color, CORONET, 11 min., 1969.

· _Facilities and Materials In and Outside the School_

1. Acquire the use of a ditto or mimeograph machine.

2. Obtain some blank newsprint to display in the class.

3. Obtain day-old newspapers from local and neighborhood publishers for reading material and display purposes.
4. Obtain recent and also dated posters, want ads, news items, newspapers, and other materials from newspaper publishers that would be of interest to the class.
5. Locate an old and small printing press.
6. Locate resource people in the school staff that could be used as resource persons.

D. Community Resources and People
1. Locate community resource people who have or are working on a newspaper to speak to the class.
2. Visit Museum of Science and Industry to see the exhibit on the "Historical Development of the Newspaper."
3. Visit neighborhood and city newspaper publishing offices--e.g. Chicago Defender, Lerner News, Sun-Times, etc.
4. Locate and obtain free printing materials from parents and local newspapers and printing firms.
5. Visit a neighborhood printer.
6. Visit a local book publisher, e.g. Scotts-Foresman, University of Chicago Press, etc.

E. Pupil Participation in the Community
1. Have students write to other schools to obtain samples of school papers.
2. Have pupils ask older brothers and sisters or relatives to arrange for the class to visit a college or university press.
3. Have pupils write to pen pals in other countries for a copy of class or school

newspapers as well as news items.
Have pupils organize a paper drive with
the cooperation of a parent(s).
Have individual pupils obtain cooperation
of parents to obtain resource materials,
obtain permission to visit printing firms
or to secure resource persons.

Prior to examining a third teaching unit format, let us explore in detail the steps in the development of the teaching unit as indicated in <u>Formats One and Two</u>. These formats should be considered as examples or skeletal outlines. Each teacher should use or develop a format that suits <u>her</u> needs and is applicable to the needs and interest of the students and the demands of the curriculum. The following is an analysis and elaboration of the necessary steps in the preparation and construction of a teaching unit.

Detailed Description for Development of Teaching Unit Formats

I. UNIT PREPARATION AND IMPLEMENTATION
   A. Obtain a tentative list of units expected to be taught from curriculum guides, course of study, pupils experiences, and needs of the community. This includes teacher-pupil planning of content, questions, and objectives.
   B. Establish a time segment for each unit to be taught during the term or year.
   C. Get to know the type of student in school and community.
   D. Get information about the specific students you will be teaching.

II. OVERVIEW OF UNIT
   A. Select a unit title which will be unifying and descriptive. Review the units listed in the bibliography for additional titles.
   B. Include subject area, grade level, and time limit of the unit. These should be balanced between pupil experiences and subject matter. One could generalize that the lower and middle grades place a heavier emphasis on experiences, whereas in the upper grades and high school the greater stress is placed on subject-matter content. The

degree of emphasis depends on the subject matter, maturity of students, their experiential background, objectives, needs and interests.

I. OBJECTIVES AND EXPECTED OUTCOMES*
   A. General objectives
   B. Specific objectives
      1. Cognitive
      2. Affective
      3. Psychomotor

V. OUTLINE OF CONTENT, TOPICS AND PROBLEMS
   A. The subject-matter content of the teaching unit can be organized in two ways.
      1. It can be integrated with the resouce activities as in Format One or
      2. The content can be outlined or organized under a separate section of the unit as in Format Two.
   B. Generally, Format One teaching unit is the extension of a curriculum guide or course of study where the subject matter has been organized in some detail. Therefore, to write the same outline of content into the teaching unit would be redundant work. It is possible, however, to use Format One teaching unit without a resource unit by using a text or simply following a course of study or curriculum guide.
   C. The writers feel that Format Two in which the content is outlined separately is easier to use, particularly for the more disciplined subject areas such as mathematics, science, and history at the middle and upper grade levels.

---

*This was discussed in detail in Chapter II, "Writing Objectives and Activities." Review Chapter III and sample units.

259

D. In Format Two teaching unit the subject-matter content can be organized from simple to complex (mathematics) or hierarchical (history) or in a structural sequence conceptual or structural content of a subject area (science). The outline of content can conform to the dominant activities or structure of the different disciplines, as in the following examples:
   1. Physical education (skills and activities)
   2. Industrial arts (projects)
   3. Science and mathematics (experiments, demonstrations and problems)
   4. History and social studies (topics, events, dates, and personalities)
E. Both formats allow for flexibility in the organization of content according to the structure of the disciplines, and needs of the students and the strengths of the teacher.

V. ACTIVITIES OR LEARNING EXPERIENCES
   A. Initiatory Activities
      This section launches the unit. Its purpose is to create interest in the unit by employing experiential situations that are real to the pupils or through vicarious situations by sharing these latter experiences in discussion and other activities. This can be accomplished through a planned classroom environment by directing the pupils attention to incidents, interesting situations, and important events by announcements and the display of materials such as graphs, pictures, specimens, exhibits, bulletin boards, models, products, books, displays, magazines, newspapers, murals, etc. Other materials that can be used effectively are: motion pictures,

slides, T.V. and radio programs, excursions,
field trips, resource speakers, e.g., former
drug addicts, policeman, fireman, etc. (depending on the grade level, of course). Story
telling, reading, visits and field trips can
also be employed. The teacher should also find
out what the interests and needs of the pupils
are and what they know about the material.

B. Developmental Activities

This is the major part of the unit. The
activities should be varied and extensive,
including intellectual, emotional, and motor
activities. Listed here are different categories of activities in which pupils can be
involved in these three realms. Experiencing
by doing rather than just explaining is more
effective not only in terms of pupil involvement
but for retention as well.

ACTIVITIES BY AREAS OR TASKS[13]

Work with Visual Materials

1. Collect pictures and other illustrative materials.
2. Make and examine exhibits of materials in classroom
   and out.
3. List interesting questions while examining materials,
   films, etc.
4. Select visual materials they themselves can use when
   giving reports.
5. Organize and file materials for future reference
   and use.

---

[13]This is recommended by the course of study bulletin
of the Los Angeles Schools. It has been edited for
presentation here. See Course of Study, Bulletin No. 162.
Los Angeles City Schools) for more detailed information.

Excursions and Trips

1. Visit museums, aquariums, zoos, points of interest.
2. Call on business firms and industries for needed information and materials.
3. See demonstration of manufacturing processes. Expose community, social, welfare, and health services.

Study of Problems

1. Search for information in answer to important questions.
2. Consult encyclopedias and reference books for needed information.
3. Bring books from outside the school to supplement what the schools have.
4. Locate the books in the school which can help solve problems.
5. Write to various sources for needed information and materials.
6. Work from directions prepared by the group, committee, or teacher.
7. Take notes and assemble information for reporting orally and in writing.
8. Interpret maps; locate places.
9. Perform experiments, learn to give demonstrations.
10. Check accuracy of information by looking in several sources.
11. Organize a plan of attack upon a problem as a group or individually.

Appreciation of Literature

1. Make a good bibliography.
2. Read interesting stories for pleasure and information.
3. Read interesting poems for pleasure and stimulation to create.
4. Listen to interesting poems and stores for pleasure and information.

Illustrations and Constructions
1. Prepare charts and diagrams.
2. Make blue-prints.
3. Draw and construct maps.
4. Prepare posters.
5. Make illustrations for books written by the class.
6. Prepare scenery for a play.
7. Prepare a frieze or mural.
8. Make a model for an exhibit or sharing.

Work Involved in Presenting Information
1. Plan ways for presenting information.
2. Edit materials for books.
3. Keep an organized bulletin board up-to-date.
4. Plan and give an assembly program or a program within the classroom.

Review the section under "Activity Unit" for additional suggestions for activities. The reader should also review Chapter II, for writing activities, if needed.

C. Culminating Activities

These are designed to summarize and to focus on central ideas and concepts of the unit. Mehl, Mills, and Douglas, state that the purposes of culminating activities are:[14]

1. Provide a way of sharing experience with others.
2. Provide a group motivation for solving problems.
3. Give recognition to the efforts of every individual who made a contribution to the group project.
4. Provide an audience situation.

---

[14]Mehl, Mills, and Douglas, Op. cit., p. 179.

5. Make it possible for each child to achieve.

6. Provide for the presentation of activities, skills, and understandings acquired during the study of the unit.

7. Bring the unit to a close. Culminating activities can take the form of assembly programs, exhibits, an art show, a tournament, committee reports, science fairs, a dinner or tea honoring parents (e.g. in homemaking).

D. Correlation with Other Subject Areas
   Integration and correlation of subject-matter content is an essential part of the teaching unit. Here subject-matter boundaries are completely obliterated and the unit covers a broad area of studies. Each subject makes its contribution to the unit through the activities. The correlation not only permits the integration and branching of content, but the review and reinforcement of previous unit material and subject areas. The new unit vocabulary can be included in this section as well. (Review the sample units for additional ideas.)

VI. EVALUATION OF THE UNIT AND LEARNING

A. Evaluation is an important aspect of learning. The objectives need to be evaluated to determine if they have been achieved, which includes evaluation of the progress of the class and of each pupil in the class. The teacher should also evaluate himself in terms of the learning environment, teaching effectiveness and techniques.

Sometimes this can be done cooperatively by teacher and students. The following suggestive

264

evaluation procedures can be used:

1. Have students tell what they have learned in the unit.
2. Self-appraisal by students.
3. Teacher's evaluation of pupil.
4. Parent evaluation.
5. Evaluate unit by pupil's success.

B. In organizing the evaluation of the unit, the objectives should be clear and concise so that the class has an advanced understanding of the procedures and criteria for evaluation. Competency-based objectives can be used extensively. (See Chapter II and sample units.) Evaluation is an integral and ongoing process in teaching and learning. Therefore, the teacher should continue to study the pupils' records, to confer, to observe, to measure and evaluate with them. The primary purpose of evaluation is to:

1. Motivate.
2. Guide and direct the learning process.
3. Improve teaching and learning.
4. Diagnose and affect remediation measures where and when needed.
5. Know what has been accomplished.
6. Make for possible review of weak areas of learning.
7. Prepare for individual conferences with pupils and parents.
8. Evaluate the quality and quantity of the activities.

Evaluation can be accomplished through a number of ways; the best way is to have continuous and cumulative evaluation.

Some Evaluative Methods:
1. Evaluation of skills can be accomplished by direct observation of participation in class, writing skills, reading and reference skills, activities, projects, etc. If needed, a rating sheet or check list can be used.
2. Evaluation of subject matter can be accomplished through individual or class discussion, teacher-made quizzes and tests, cumulative assignments, e.g. seatwork, homework, and individual class and small group work.
3. Evaluation of attitudes and interests can be determined through observation, interviews and discussions. Preference scales, anecdotal records and sociometric devices can be employed.

The teacher can also pose such questions as:
1. How well have the unit objectives been accomplished? Here competency or criterion-based objectives can be used most successfully. (See Chapter II.)
2. What grades or marks have been earned by the pupils?
3. Which areas of the unit need reinforcement and which pupils need additional help and in what areas--understandings, skills, social or affective areas?
4. To what extent have certain forms of instruction, e.g. lecture, recitation, demonstration, and other approaches, etc. been most and/or least effective?

VII. MATERIALS AND RESOURCES
Materials and resources are the media for the learning activities, therefore, the materials should be:
A. Appropriate for the age and grade level and related to the unit.

B. Free from bias--particularly books, films, posters, etc.
C. Recent, up-to-date--original or revised.
D. Appealing and attention holding.
E. Good technical quality--simple and workable.
F. Reasonably priced, within the school budget.

The types of materials available are varied. Many n be obtained for free or at a minimal cost. Following a list of the different types of resources and terials:

A. Textbooks
B. Workbooks
C. Teacher guides
D. Reference Books: atlases, world almanacs, dictionaries, encyclopedias, collateral books, readers, stories, etc.
E. Current materials
    1. Pamphlets from different businesses, charities, governments and industries, etc.
    2. Brochures, flat pictures, posters
    3. Newspapers
    4. Magazines
    5. Comics
    6. Charts
F. Teacher-pupil created materials
    1. Poems
    2. Stories
    3. Biographies
    4. Projects--art, math, science, social studies
    5. Music
    6. Writings
    7. Charts
    8. Murals

267

G. Teacher produced materials
    1. Ditto
    2. Xerox
    3. Mimeo
    4. Thermofax
H. Permanent materials
    1. Chalk boards
    2. Felt boards
    3. Magnetic board
    4. Electric board
    5. Maps, charts, globes
    6. Objects, specimens, and models
    7. Exhibits - geometry - science fair
    8. Loan boxes of specimen kits from Board of
       Education, Bell Telephone, Coal Company,
       Edison Electric, Park District
    9. Educational television
    10. Language laboratories
I. Audio-visual resources and equipment
    1. Slides and filmstrips
    2. Motion pictures
    3. Overhead projector
    4. Opaque projection
    5. Tachistoscope
    6. Stereo projector
    7. Radio, T.V.
    8. Tape and record player, recorder, cassette
    9. Language masters
J. Community resources as learning materials
    1. Local field trips to museums
    2. Extended field trips in the state
    3. Resource persons
    4. Native materials, aquariums, terrariums

There are a number of materials which can be
obtained free or very inexpensively. Examples of such

sources are: The curriculum guides and the publications
on free and inexpensive materials for the classroom
teacher. (See appendix for additional sources.)

The task of the teacher is to acquaint the student
with many sources of information and to help him locate
and use accurately the relevant information to the best
advantage.

IX.   BIBLIOGRAPHY:

The bibliography should contain a selected list of
references for both teacher and pupil. This is
derived from the resources unit. It is used to
supplement the materials and resources in the unit.
Included with or appended to the unit could be
sample examinations and tests, evaluative scales,
charts, worksheets, handcharts, word lists, vocabulary, class organization, seating charts, etc. If
possible, text books and reference materials should
be available in the classroom.

We have analyzed the step by step process of
developing a teaching unit using Formats One and Two as
illustrative examples. Let us now examine a third
format for a teaching unit. Format Three is quite
similar to Formats One and Two, and the developmental
procedures are identical. The major differences between
Format Three and the former Formats are the statement
of objectives in the conditional and evaluative forms
(of course, these can be included in any format), the
incorporation of a pre and post test and the inclusion
of a section on remediation as integral part of the unit.
Like Format Two, it is also a type of subject matter or
indepth study unit.

Format Three was especially developed for the QUEST
(Quality Urban Education for Successful Teaching) program
at Chicago State University. It is intended to be used

for the intensive study of a specific subject area
over a brief period of time.

TEACHING UNIT*
Format Three

I. Title of Unit
II. Identification Information
    A. Subject and Grade Level
    B. Date for Initiating the Unit
    C. Date for Terminating the Unit
    D. Room Number and Time
III. Behavioral Objectives
    A. Teacher: Preparation to teach Unit
    B. Pupil: General objectives
    (These objectives can be stated in conditional and
    evaluative form. See sample units.)
IV. Prerequisites: List of information background and
    skills required to be successful with unit.
    A. Informational background
    B. Skills
    (Stated in specific instructional form)
V. Pretest: A test administered for ascertaining
    pupils' background skill and/or achievements for
    judging the appropriateness of planned teaching
    materials and procedures.
    (List and write everything you know about the subject.)
VI. Content Outline
    (List content in descriptive sentence form, denoting
    factual information about the subject area.)
VII. Learning Alternatives: List the instructional
    alternatives (activities) planned in this unit which

---

* Developed by and used with the kind permission of
Dr. Lillian Dimitroff, Professor of Education, Chicago
State University.

will enable your students to demonstrate specific
competencies.

C = class

T = teacher

I = individualized instruction

RSG = reports on small group activities

III. Posttest: A test administered for the purpose of
judging the demonstration of skills and/or achievements stated in your objectives.

IX. Remediation: Prepare an anticipated list of topics
and learning alternatives needed for pupils who are
not demonstrating the competencies expected in your
objectives.

Topics	Learning Alternatives Activities
1. Vocabulary Skills	Flash cards, Phonic exercises, use of vocabulary
2. Reduction of reading skills	Work sheets with reading, vocabulary and tasks
3. Story telling about occupations or other subjects	Draw pictures demonstrating these subjects
4. Workers in the community	Dramatizations

X. Bibliography

A. Textbook(s)

B. Books and reading materials for pupils

C. A. V. Materials

1. Films

2. Filmstrips

D. Special equipment and materials

You may notice that Format Three makes no distinction
between initiatory, developmental and culminating activities, but it could be modified to include them as

separate categories.   Following are two sample units of
the Format Three type: Pages 273-293.

1. A fourth grade unit:
   "Comparison of City and Country Environments"
2. A third grade unit:
   "Becoming Aware of Spring Changes in Plants
   and Animals"

TEACHING UNIT

Format Three

TITLE OF THE UNIT: Comparison of City and Country
Environments

IDENTIFYING INFORMATION

A. Teacher's Name:

B. Subject: Social Studies   Grade Level: Four

C. Date of Initiation and Termination of Unit:
September - December, 1979

D. Room: 209

BEHAVIORAL OBJECTIVES

A. Teacher

  1. Urban

     a. By allowing the children to touch a
         primary globe, the teacher will explain
         that a map is a replica of the globe on
         a flat surface in order to make relation-
         ships from globe to map.

     b. The teacher will locate on a map of the
         United States for the children the state
         of Illinois, Lake Michigan and the city
         of Chicago.

     c. On a Chicago area map the teacher will
         show the pupils the Uptown district where
         Stockton School is located.

     d. The teacher will show the pupils a
         picture of a downtown area of an urban
         community for recognition of places such
         as the post office, shopping sections,
         schools, traffic lights, different types
         of streets, etc. and explain that this

273

information may be conveyed to a map
form.
e. The teacher will show pictures of our
community helpers and other occupations,
in order to make children aware of the
different occupations the city offers.
f. A filmstrip entitled "Different Neighborhoods" will be shown to the class in
order to make the students aware that
Chicago is composed of many communities.

2. Rural
a. The teacher will introduce to the class
a color picture of a modern farm, in
order to start contrasting urban and
country environments by questioning
students. Examples: Do you see sidewalks in this picture? How close do you
think the neighbors are to the farm house?
Do you think one can walk to town from
this place? How do you suppose children
get to school?
b. The teacher will guide the children in
learning classification of pictures
belonging to city, country or both.
c. The teacher will help the class to construct two dioramas, one depicting the
city and the other showing a rural setting.
The children will decide where their
objects belong, the city or the farm.
Animals, buildings, trees, etc. will be
made out of construction paper.

B. Pupils
1. After locating the state of Illinois, Lake
Michigan and the city of Chicago on the map,
the students will mark individually the way

to school from home on a school district map
with 80% accuracy.

2. After a discussion on the community helpers
   and other occupations, the children will be
   able to match on paper the picture of a
   worker in uniform to the name of his occupa-
   tion with 90% accuracy.

3. Given teacher guidance and a worksheet, the
   class will demonstrate with 75% accuracy,
   comprehension of the story book <u>Brian's
   Secret Errand</u>, read by the teacher.

4. The class will observe a picture of a farm
   scene, the new vocabulary will be written on
   the board and the children will use those
   words to complete sentences on a paper with
   75% accuracy.

5. Given paper and pencil, the children will
   circle the correct word under each picture
   with 75% accuracy.

6. With paper, scissors and paste, the children
   will cut out pictures and classify them under
   the proper heading: city, country - both
   with 75% accuracy.

7. Given teacher guidance, the children will
   make buildings, trees of a city neighborhood
   with 95% accuracy.

8. Given teacher guidance, the children will
   make farm animals, people, trees, a barn, a
   silo to build a farm diorama. When a child
   finishes his object he will know if it
   belongs in the city or on the farm with 90%
   accuracy.

. PREREQUISITES

A. <u>Informational Background</u>

1. The child should be able to know and find the name of the street where he lives on a map of the school district in order to trace his way home.
2. The pupil should distinguish the difference between city and state.
3. The student should know where Lake Michigan is located from his home and school.
4. The child should have experienced a trip out in the country in order to trace his way home.

B. Skills

1. The child should have sufficient phonetic skills in order to attack new vocabulary.
2. The child should read with adequate comprehension.
3. The child should be able to print words legibly.

V. CONTENT OUTLINE

This unit contrasts city and country environment and its impact on the life style of the inhabitants.

A. City Characteristics

1. Streets and sidewalks
2. Close housing
3. Public transportation
4. Grocery and department stores
5. Hospitals and doctors
6. Schools for higher education
7. Recreation
   a. Parks and zoos
   b. Beaches (Chicago)
   c. Amusement parks
   d. Theaters
   e. Museums

B. Country Characteristics
    1. Wide open spaces
    2. No close neighbors
    3. Car dependence
    4. Farm animals
    5. Home grown vegetables, fresh milk and eggs
    6. Outdoor activities
    7. Unpolluted country air and no noise

VI. PRETEST

VII. LEARNING ALTERNATIVES

(T) 1. Introduce children to the globe and maps available in the school.

(C) 2. Have children locate Illinois and Lake Michigan on the map and globe.

(C) 3. Have children locate the city of Chicago on the globe and maps.

(C) 4. Have children trace the way from home to school on a map of the school district.

(T) 5. Present city picture with many recognizable buildings, such as a school, post office, Fire Department.

(C) 6. Have children name important places in our Uptown community, such as the Bezazian Library, Post Office, Fire Departments, main shopping area, Boys Club, Hull House and parks.

(C) 7. Have children draw a picture of their own house: single-family home, housing project, apartment building and write their address down.

(T) 8. Have children present finger play, "Ten Firemen."

(T) 9. Read story related to city life entitled "Brian's Secret Errand."

(C) 10. Question class for comprehension of story read.

(C) 11. Have children complete sentences using the new vocabulary on paper.

(T) 12. View the following film: "Different Neighborhoods" - #P8390.

(C) 13. View picture, 3"x2"x2" in color, printed by Field Enterprise Educational Corporation, depicting a modern farm.

(C) 14. Have children cut out pictures of city and farm scenes and paste them classifying them in three categories: city, farm, suburbs.

(C) 15. Have children take a post-test the day before the unit closes.

(T) 16. Bring two cardboards to class: one having artificial grass on the surface to indicate the ground in a rural setting, the other having streets marked, ready to line up buildings for the city.

(C) 17. Have children construct and color pictures of animals, people and buildings to make two dioramas: an urban community and a rural scene.

VIII. POST TEST (See attached sheet)

IX. REMEDIATION

Topics	Learning Alternatives
Vocabulary skills	Integrate with learning activities. Use flash cards and cassettes to increase sight vocabulary and phonic skills.
Map skills	Have more activities that include maps.

278

Speaking and listening   Help individual children
who have verbal problems
and do not respond when
called to take part in
discussions.

. BIBLIOGRAPHY

A. Student Books

1. Baker, Jim. How Our Counties Get Their
   Names. Worthington, Ohio: Heartland Hse,
   1973. (Gr 4-12)

2. Brennan, Matthew J. The Environment and You.
   new edition. New York: Grosset & Dunlap,
   Inc., 1973. (Gr 3-7)

3. Busch, Phyllis S. Exploring As You Walk
   in the City. Philadelphia: Lippincott,
   1972. (Gr K-4)

4. Corcos, Lucille. The City Book. Racine,
   Wisconsin: Western Pub., 1972. (Gr 1-5)

5. Fenton, Carroll L., and Kitchen, Herminie B.
   Animals That Help Us: The Story of Domestic
   Animals. Rev. ed. New York: John Day,
   1973. (Gr 3-6)

6. Halacy, D. S. Jr. Your City Tomorrow.
   New York: Four Winds, 1973. (Gr 3-5)

7. Phillippa, Pearce. What the Neighbors Did
   and Other Stories. New York: T. Y. Crowell,
   1973. (Gr 3-7)

8. Pitt, Valerie. Let's Find Out About the City.
   New York: Watts, 1968. (Gr K-3)

9. Pringle, Laurence. From Pond to Prairie:
   The Changing World of a Pond and Its Life.
   Riverside, New Jersey: Macmillan, 1972.
   (Gr 4-6)

10. Webster, Norman. City People, City Life.
    St. Paul, Minnesota: EMC Corp., 1972. (Gr 3-8)

B. Teacher Texts

1. Birch, David et al. <u>Patterns of Urban Change</u>. Lexington, Massachusetts: Lexington Bks., 1974.

2. Booth, Edward T. <u>Country Life in America</u>. Westport, Connecticut: Greenwood, 1975.

3. Borsodi, Ralph. <u>Flight from the City: An Experiment in Creative Living on the Land</u>. Scranton, Pennsylvania: Harper & Row Pubs., 1972.

4. Chester, Michael. <u>Let's Go to Stop Air Pollution</u>. New York: Putnam, 1973.

5. Cobb, Betsy, and Cobb, Hubbard. <u>City People's Guide to Country Living</u>. Riverside, New Jersey: Macmillan, 1973.

6. Engle, Shirley, and Longstreet, Wilma S. <u>Design for Social Education in the Open Curriculum</u>. Scranton, Pennsylvania: Harper & Row Pubs., 1972.

7. Gillispie, Phillip H. <u>Learning Through Simulation Games</u>. Paramus, New Jersey: Paulist-Newman, 1974.

8. Hoaken, Fran P. <u>Language of Cities</u>. new edition, Cambridge, Massachusetts: Schenkman, 1972.

9. Lee, John R. <u>Teaching Social Studies in the Elementary School</u>. New York: Free Pr., 1974.

10. Ventura, Piero. <u>Book of Cities</u>. Westminister, Maryland: Random, 1974.

C. Audio-Visual Materials

1. Films (16 mm)

   a. <u>Altered Environments: An Inquiry into the Growth of American Cities</u>. color, A BERT KEMPERS PRODUCTION, 19-3/4 min., 1972.

b. <u>Altered Environments: An Inquiry into the American Highway</u>. color, A BERT KEMPERS PRODUCTION, 9½ min., 1971.

c. <u>City, The</u>. color, ENCYCLOPEDIA BRITANNICA EDUCATIONAL FILMS, 11 min., 1962.

d. <u>Changing City, The</u>. color, CHURCHILL FILMS, 16 min., 1963.

e. <u>Climates of the United States</u>. black and white, CORONET, 11 min., 1962.

f. <u>Color of the City Green</u>. color, U.S. DEPT. OF AGRICULTURE, 30 min., 1969.

g. <u>House of Man, Our Changing Environment</u>. color, ENCYCLOPEDIA BRITANNICA EDUCATIONAL FILMS, 17 min., 1965.

h. <u>Using Maps-Measuring Distances</u>. black and white, U.S. DEPARTMENT OF AGRICULTURE, 14 min., 1959.

i. <u>Water Pollution</u>. color, JOURNAL FILMS, 13 min., 1971.

2. <u>Sound Filmstrips with Cassettes or Records</u>

a. <u>City Problems and Alternatives</u>. Series of 6 filmstrips with cassettes or records, color, average frames: 62 each, A CLIFFORD JANOFF PRODUCTION, 1972.

2. <u>Living Environment</u>. Series of 4 filmstrips with cassettes or records, color, average frames: 61 each, A CLIFFORD JANOFF PRODUCTION, 1972.

3. <u>Investigations in Science: Earth Science</u>. Series of 5 filmstrips with cassettes or records, color, average frames: 30 each, A HENRY BARZILAY PRODUCTION, 1971.

<u>Duplicating Masters</u>

. <u>Occupation Word Hunt I</u>. number 357, 10 masters,

Niles, Illinois, Developmental Learning
Materials, 1975.

2. <u>Occupation Word Hunt II</u>. number 358, 10
   masters, Niles, Illinois, Developmental
   Learning Materials, 1975.

3. <u>Word Hunt Puzzles I</u>. number 317, 10 masters,
   Niles, Illinois, Developmental Learning
   Materials, 1975.

4. <u>Word Hunt Puzzles II</u>. number 318, 10 masters,
   Niles, Illinois, Developmental Learning
   Materials, 1975.

POST TEST

1. Match the following words to city or country:

   _____Museum   _____Horse   _____Chicken coo[p]

   _____City Hall   _____Cow   _____Fields

   _____Barn   _____Orchard   _____Parks

   _____Farm   _____Theater   _____Zoo

2. Write the streets that divide Chicago into North and
   South and into East and West.
   a._____   b._____

3. On the city map there are numbers that mark streets,
   parks, buildings, beaches, and so forth. Beside the
   following numbers write the places marked by the
   numbers.

   1._____   4._____   7._____   10._____
   2._____   5._____   8._____   11._____
   3._____   6._____   9._____   12._____

Write five characteristics of the city:

a. _____

b. _____

c. _____

d. _____

e. _____

Write five characteristics of the country:

a. _____

b. _____

c. _____

d. _____

e. _____

TEACHING UNIT
Format Three

I. TITLE OF UNIT: Becoming Aware of Spring Changes in
Plants and Animals

II. IDENTIFYING INFORMATION
   A. Teacher's Name:
   B. Subject: Science   Grade Level: Three
   C. Date of Initiation and Termination of Unit:
      May 19 through June 17, 1979
   D. Room: 215

III. BEHAVIORAL OBJECTIVES
   A. Teacher
      1. Given the science curriculum guide, the
         teacher will be able to explain the orderly
         process of the life of plants and animals.
      2. Given library materials, the teacher will
         review materials that will be helpful in
         teaching the unit.
      3. Given teacher prepared teaching aids, the
         teacher will be able to do demonstrations
         on the subject areas being taught.
      4. Given the knowledge acquired after studying
         resource books and materials, the teacher
         will be able to present the lessons
         adequately.

   B. Pupils
      1. Given various types of seeds to view and
         examine, the students will be able to
         identify a seed with 100% accuracy.
      2. Given a milk carton, radish seeds, water and
         some special soil, the students will be able

284

to plant their own radishes with 95%
accuracy.

3. Given a simple direction sheet, the students
    will be able to read the instructions with
    90% accuracy.
4. Given adequate instructions, the students
    will be able to recall the steps used for
    planting the radishes with 85% accuracy.
5. Given a variety of fruit seeds the students
    will be able to identify each seed with
    85% accuracy.
6. Given a worksheet containing pictures of
    buds, bulbs, and seeds, the students will
    be able to identify them with 100% accuracy.
7. Given an experience in planting seeds the
    students will be able to develop an
    experience chart with 85% accuracy.
8. Given a worksheet with signs of spring and
    other seasons, the students will be able to
    identify the signs of spring with 100%
    accuracy.
9. Given a picture with the parts of a flower,
    the student will be able to cut out the
    parts and paste them to form a picture of
    a flower with 100% accuracy.
10. Given pencil and paper, the student will be
    able to write the three things needed for
    seeds to grow with 100% accuracy.
11. Given adequate instructions, the students
    will be able to define hibernation with
    90% accuracy.
12. Given adequate instructions, the students
    will be able to explain why animals go south
    for the winter with 80% accuracy.

285

13. Given a worksheet with animals, the students will be able to make an "X" on the animals that hibernate with 95% accuracy.

14. Given adequate instructions, the students will be able to explain why some warm blooded animals hibernate in the winter, with 85% accuracy.

15. Given a worksheet, the students will be able to name, by circling the right picture, the two things that enable both kinds of animals (hibernating and non-hibernating) to become active once again, with 85% accuracy.

IV. PREREQUISITES

A. <u>Informational Background</u>
   1. Students should know how plants grow.
   2. Students should know that fruits and vegetables are different classes of food.
   3. Students should know the importance of plants and animals to man.

B. <u>Skills</u>
   1. The students will know that vegetables and fruits are parts of plants.
   2. The students will know that plants need sunlight, water and air to grow.
   3. The students will be able to name common plants.
   4. The students will know that plants grow indoors as well as outdoors.
   5. Students will know that animals need food and water in order to live.

V. CONTENT OUTLINE

A. Plants grow in different ways. Example: seeds, bulbs

B. Some plants grow from seeds. Example: radishes, rice

286

C. Some plants grow from leaves or stems.
   Examples: Pansies, petunias, marigolds, and
   zinnias
D. Buds become flowers, leaves, or stems. Example:
   Forsythia
E. Seeds need water, air, and warmth to gow.
   Example will be shown in experiment.
F. Animals that go south for the winter return in
   the spring. Example: Robin, Monarch butterfly
G. Animals that sleep in the winter wake up in the
   summer. Example: Bears, turtles, frogs
H. Spring is one of the four seasons of the year.

VI. PRETEST (See attached sheet)
II. LEARNING ACTIVITIES

(C) 1. The teacher will discuss the different kinds
       of seeds.
(C) 2. The students will examine different kinds
       of seeds.
    3. The students will plant seeds in milk
       cartons. (RSG)
    4. The students will plant bulbs in milk
       cartons. (RSG)
(C) 5. Students will have a radish tasting party.
(C) 6. Students will have a tasting party comparing
       fruits with vegetables.
(I) 7. Students will write short stories about
       their tasting experiences.
(C) 8. Teacher will help students write experience
       charts.
(I) 9. Students will make a science notebook.
(I) 10. Teacher will read stories to the students
        about plants and animals.
(I) 11. Students will draw pictures of animals that
        hibernate.

287

(I) 12. Students will write stories about animals
that migrate.

VIII. POST TEST (See attached sheet)

IX. REMEDIATION

Topic	Learning Alternatives
Recognizing animals that hibernate	Supply the students with pictures of animals. Discuss the pictures with students.
Understanding the word hibernate	The teacher will have students pretend that they are animals and have them dramatize how they hibernate.
Identifying seeds	Supply seeds taught in the unit and have students separate according to color. Show filmstrip on various kinds of seeds.
Identifying parts of plants	Show the student pictures of plants and have them name the parts.
All concepts taught in unit	Provide instruction for students who need it.

X. BIBLIOGRAPHY

A. Student Books

1. Carthy, John. Animal Camouflage. new ed.
New York: McGraw, 1974. (Gr 2-6)

2. Cartwright, Sally. Animal Homes. new ed.
New York: Coward, 1973. (Gr 2-4)

3. Fox, Charles P. <u>When Spring Comes</u>. Chicago, Illinois: Reilly & Lee, 1964. (Gr 3-6)
4. Jordon, Helene J. <u>How a Seed Grows</u>. New York: T. Y. Crowell, 1960. (Gr K-3)
5. Neigoff, Anne. <u>Now You Know About Plants</u>. Chicago, Illinois: Ency. Brit. Ed., 1973. (Gr K-3)
6. Rahn, Joan Elma. <u>How Plants Travel</u>. Paterson, New Jersey: Athensum, 1973. (Gr 3-6)
7. Reit, Seymour V. <u>Animals Around My Block</u>. New York: McGraw, 1970. (Gr K-3)
8. Selsam, Millicent E. <u>Carrot and Other Root Vegetables</u>. Caldwell, New Jersey: 1971. (Gr 2-5)
9. Tison, Annette, and Taylor, Talus. <u>Animal Hide and Seek</u>. Cleveland, Ohio: Collins-World, 1972. (Gr K-3)
10. Verite, Marcelle. <u>Animals Around the Year</u>. Racine, Wisconsin: Western Pub., 1972. (Gr 3-6)

Teacher Texts
1. Butts, David P., and Hall, Gene E. <u>Children and Science: The Process of Teaching and Learning</u>. Englewood Cliffs, New Jersey: Prentice-Hall, Inc., 1974.
2. Cole, Joanna. <u>Plants in Winter</u>. New York: T. Y. Crowell, 1973.
3. Fisher, Aileen. <u>Animal Houses</u>. Glendale, California: Bowmar, 1973.
4. Gale, Frank C., and Gale, Clarice W. <u>Experiences with Plants for Young Children</u>. Palo Alto, California: Pacific Bks., 1974.
5. George, Kenneth D. et al. <u>Science Investiga-

tions for Elementary School Teachers.
Lexington, Massachusetts: Heath, 1973.

6. Jones, David A., and Wilkins, Dennis A. Variation and Adaptation in Plant Species. New York: Crane-Russak Co., 1971.

7. Marsh, Rober. Seed Picture Making. New York: Intl. Pubns., 1974.

8. Martin, Alexander, and Barkely, William D. Seed Identification Manual. Berkeley, California: U of Cal. Pr., 1973.

9. Munroe, Esther. Sprouts to Grow and Eat. Brattleboro, Vermont: Greene, 1974.

C. Audio-Visual Materials

1. Films (16 mm)

   a. Plants are Different and Alike. color, CORONET, 11 min., 1967.

   b. Plants Live Through the Winter. color, CORONET, 9 min., 1968.

   c. Spring Brings Changes. color, CHURCHILL FILMS, 11 min., 1961.

   d. Spring Comes Again. color, BAILEY FILMS, INC., 11 min., 1962.

   e. Spring Comes to the City. color, CORONET, 11 min., 1968.

   f. Spring Is a Season. color, JOURNAL FILMS, 11 min., 1960.

   g. Spring Is an Adventure. color, CORONET, 11 min., 1955.

2. Sound Filmstrips with Cassettes or Records

   a. How Animals Grow and Change. Series of 3 filmstrips with cassettes or records, color, average frames: 42 each, A NORMAN BEAN PRODUCTION, 1974.

b. <u>Life from Life</u>. Series of 6 filmstrips with cassettes or records, color, average frames: 34 each, PRODUCED BY CENTER FOR MEDIA DEVELOPMENT, 1970.

c. <u>The Story of Birth</u>. 1 filmstrip with cassette or record, average frames: 55, A UNIVERSITY OF UTAH AUDIO VISUAL BUREAU PRODUCTION, 1967.

Super 8 Silent Film Loops

a. Knatt, Robert, and Thier, Herbert D. <u>Animal Behavior</u>. Series of 7 film loops, color, AN EDU-IMAGE PRODUCTION, 1973.

b. <u>Processes of Science: Classifying Animals</u>. Series of 12 film loops, color, A FILM TECHNOLOGY COMPANY PRODUCTION, 1968.

c. <u>Processes of Science: Classifying Flowering Plants</u>. Series of 12 film loops, color, A FILM TECHNOLOGY COMPANY PRODUC-TION, 1968.

Captioned Filmstrips

a. <u>Habitat</u>. color, average frames: 44, A BERT KEMPERS PRODUCTION, 1971.

b. <u>How We See</u>. color, average frames: 41, A HARRY ROBBIN PRODUCTION, 1971.

c. <u>Shapes and Structures in Nature</u>. color, average frames: 35, A JOE AND ANNE BARFIELD PRODUCTION, 1974.

291

P R E T E S T

DIRECTION: Circle the correct answer.

1.	Can plants live with water?	Yes	No
2.	Can plants live without sunlight?	Yes	No
3.	Do some trees grow tall?	Yes	No
4.	Are all plants green?	Yes	No
5.	Do all animals eat plants?	Yes	No

DRAW A TREE | DRAW A BIRD

POST TEST

DIRECTIONS: Write YES or NO on the line.

1. Some animals migrate.   _____

2. Animals grow in the ground.   _____

3. Plants grow in the ground.   _____

4. Some plants grow from bulbs.   _____

5. Some plants grow from seed.   _____

6. People hibernate in the winter.   _____

7. Vegetables are good to eat for
    dinner.   _____

8. Fruit is not good to eat.   _____

9. Can plants talk?   _____

10. Can animals see?   _____

We have examined three different teaching unit formats. The formats are quite similar in many ways, but they differ in terms of emphasis and organizational structure.

The following Format Four unit plan deviates from the conventional unit plan and from unit plans Formats One through Three in that it is a student Study-Work Unit.

A Study-Work Unit is a teacher constructed set or series of lessons included in a unit format which lists activities and work sheets that are given to the student and which he follows, somewhat like a personalized curriculum guide or teacher-made textbook. In a sense, it is a teacher devised programmed text or set of lessons which the student uses instead of relying on a standardized textbook. The Study-Work Unit is a form of individualized instruction, a packaged unit developed by a group of teachers or an academic department that teach the same subject or subject areas. Both teacher and students have a copy of the unit. The Study-Work Unit could best be described, perhaps as a set of "student" lesson plans, an individualized study guide and workbook, a miniature curriculum guide.

The student using the Study-Work Units need not depend upon a single text for information, but can and should use many texts, reference books and related resource materials found in the classroom library and in the school library and curriculum center. The students should also avail themselves of community resources.

The Study-Work Unit has several advantages over the other units:

1. It is given to the students to use as a study guide and workbook in which they can take notes and complete assignments.

2. Students (whether pre or post high school) like to have concrete materials in their hands for study and reference.

294

3. It can easily be substituted for the class text in cases where there are none available or where the material is outdated.
4. The students can keep the units in a spiral notebook as they complete them, thus keeping an organized record of content covered and lessons completed for themselves, the teacher and their parents.
5. It also serves as a good evaluation source for students, teacher and parents.
6. It provides a concrete and practical method of introducing contemporary data and new materials into the curriculum, not found in textbooks.

Following is the format for the Study-Work Unit:

TEACHING UNIT
Format Four

Study-Work Unit

Title of Unit: _____

Department: _____

Classroom Number: _____ Grade: _____

Teacher: _____

Beginning Date:_____ Terminating Date:_____

I. Purpose:

This section should include a statement of goals for the students and/or a list of objectives stated in behavioral terms.

I. Introduction:

This section includes an overview of the content of the unit--knowledge, concepts, processes and cause and effect relationships to be developed in the unit.

III. Vocabulary:
   New or technical vocabulary related to the topic of
   the unit can be listed separately or included in
   each lesson of the unit.
IV. Outline of content:
   The content or topics of the unit can be listed
   sequentially in terms of concepts, topics, processes
   or statements of facts and relationships. This
   could take the form of a table of contents.
V. Materials and Resources:
   This includes textbooks and other reading materials,
   films, filmstrips, diagrams, and other audio-visual
   aids essential for the implementation of the unit.
VI. Assignments:
   The remainder of the unit is organized into a series
   of student assignments or lessons which include
   readings, reports and related activities. As
   stated in the introduction to Unit Format Four,
   each student has a copy of the complete Work-Study
   Unit which he or she follows and completes certain
   assignments and activities. The assignment section
   may include:
   A. Introduction to topic or concept in the form
      of research, reading, discussion, following
      directions and completing a worksheet or viewing
      a film or filmstrip. The student is given an
      outline of content to follow in the form of
      exercises to be completed or questions to be
      answered.
   B. Developmental Activities that reinforce and
      enhance the concepts and facts learned in the
      introduction. The activities are individual
      and group oriented involving the students in
      writing assignments and such as answering questions,

296

writing a report, constructing a project, taking
a field trip, listening to a lecture, etc.
C. Depth Opportunity or Enrichment Activities:
This section provides for individual differences
in ability and interest. The student(s) can
research the topic in greater depth as well as
acquire extra credit for this additional work.
D. Evaluation and Independent Work:
Each of the assignments may include a quiz or
test by which the students can evaluate their
knowledge of the topic. The students can work
individually or in small groups.
E. Appendix:
This section includes resource materials, tests,
diagrams, tables and student worksheets.

The Work-Study Unit may not necessarily include all
he elements in the specific order outlined in the
at. The teacher or department organizes the unit to
the structure of the subject matter and the grade
l, achievement level and interest of the students.
To illustrate this point, the following pages contain
rk-Study Unit developed in Lansing, Illinois. The
le units are entitled:[15]
1. A sixth grade unit:
    "The Human Body"
2. A seventh grade unit:
    "Africa"

---

[5]Developed by the staff of West View Jr. High School,
ville, Ill. and used with the kind permission of
am J. Dragovan, Assistant Principal.

Unit #_____   THE HUMAN BODY
                Prepared For The
                SCIENCE DEPARTMENT

Name:_____
H.R.#_____   Grade:_____
Teacher: _____

Due Dates: _____   Points:_____
           _____   _____
           _____   _____
           _____   _____
           _____   _____
                             Grade: _____

Comments: _____
_____
_____
_____
_____
_____
_____
_____

INTRODUCTION

We are starting a study of the major systems of the
human body. You will be called upon to learn many
new facts and terms. This unit can prove to be one
of the most interesting units because it involves
your own body. In this unit, we will try to understand the following concepts.

* The skeleton serves as the framework of the
  body.
* There are two kinds of skeletons: an endo-
  skeleton and an exoskeleton.
* A bone consists of both organic material and
  matter.
* Bones are connected together by joints.
* Muscle tissues join together to make-muscles.
* Muscles enable parts of the body to move.
* There are three general types of muscles:
  skeletal muscles, smooth muscles, and heart
  muscles.
* The circulatory system distributes blood
  through the body.
* The heart is an important part of the circula-
  tory system; it pumps the blood.
* Arteries carry blood away from the heart;
  veins carry blood to the heart.
* Capillaries take blood to all cells of the
  body.
* The capillaries serve as connections between
  the veins and arteries.
* Air passes through the trachea and the
  bronchial tubes into the lungs.

* Oxygen passes from the air sacs in the lungs
  into the capillaries: these capillaries
  expel carbon dioxide.
* The capillaries in the lungs transfer
  oxygen to the circulatory system.
* The alimentary canal consists of the digestive organs.
* Digestion prepares foods for the body cells;
  it changes solids into liquids.

The main concept we want to understand from the
study of the human body is that the human body is
a "living machine" consisting of interlocking parts.

II. VOCABULARY

A study of the human body involves some words which
may seem difficult at first, but if we understand
the parts which make up the words, it will help us
understand other new terms. The following words
should be spelled correctly when they are used.

alimentary canal	esophagus	respiratory syste
artery	exoskeleton	saliva
auricle	femur	septum
biceps	gland	skeletal system
bile	humerus	superior vena ca
capillary	incisor	trachea
chitin	inferior vena cava	triceps
coccyx	ligament	vein
diaphragm	marrow	ventricle
digestive system	molar	vertebra
endoskeleton	pancreas	
epiglottis	periosteum	

III. OUTLINE OF UNIT

This unit on the human body will be divided into
five sections as follows:

　　1. The Body's Framework

           2. The Muscle System
           3. The Circulatory System
           4. The Respiratory System
           5. The Digestive System
IV. REFERENCES
     Each student will be required to read the following
     material:
           Today's Basic Science, pages 211-240
           Science Problems, pages 140-161
     Following is a list of additional material students
     may refer to for answers to problems or interesting
     reading: The following list may be found in the
     school library:
           Asimon, Isaac Brain. Houghton Co., 1964
           Asimon, Isaac The Human Body. Houghton Co., 1963
           Glemser, Bernard The Human Body. Random House,
           1958.
           Keen, Martin The Human Body. Grosset, 1961
           Lauber, Patricia How Your Body Works. Random
           House, 1962
           Parker, Bertha M. You As a Machine. Row
           Peterson, 1958
           Schneider, Herman How your Body Works. W. R.
           Scott, 1949
           Weyl, Peter Man, Ants, and Elephants. Viking,
           1959
V. DEPTH OPPORTUNITIES
     1. Make a large silhouette, or outline frame of the
        human body, from paper. Hang it on the wall.
        As you study the various parts of the human body,
        draw these parts onto the silhouette. You will
        find it necessary to use more than one silhouette
        to show all the parts. Perhaps this could be a
        group project.

                           301

2. Obtain part of a spinal column from a butcher.
Study it closely. Can you see individual
vertebrae? Can you see discs between the
vertebrae? Is part of the spinal cord in the
spinal canal. Boil the bones until they loosen
up. Remove an individual vertebrae and study
it closely.

3. From a doctor, try to obtain some old X-rays
of normal bones and of bones with fractures.
Observe them closely. Perhaps the doctor can
discuss them with you.

4. What are the basic food groups from which you
should choose your foods for a daily diet?
Talk with our school nurse about this. Read
about it. Prepare a chart with drawings or
cuttings from magazines to show the important
foods you should eat each day.

5. Take a deep breath of air. Blow as much of it
into a balloon as you can. Have an adult do
the same thing. Have a younger and a smaller
person do it. Compare lung capacities in this
manner.

6. Obtain a blood sample. Make a blood smear on
a microscope slide and study it under high
power with the microscope. Can you see the
individual blood cells?

*7. Read about the history of medicine and learn
what you can about the great medical discoveries.
What can you find about the work of such men as
Pasteur, Curie, Lister, Jenner, Reed, Salk, and
others? Prepare a report for the class.

*8. Take your body temperature during different
parts of the day. Make the first reading just

after you wake in the morning. Take a reading
after strenuous exercise. Then rest a while and
take it again. What do you discover about the
body temperature?

*9. Find out the causes of childhood diseases such
as measles, mumps, chicken pox, and influenza,
etc. How can these diseases be prevented? How
are they spread? How are they treated?

*10. Using an opaque projector and a diagram from a
book, make a large chart of one of the body
systems. Project the picture on a piece of
poster paper and trace it. Label the organs.
Your teacher may wish to put your chart up in
the classroom and use it in the study of the
human body.

*11. Make a report on any one of the specific organs
in the body. Arrange a time with your teacher
to make the report.

* The starred reports will take more work but will
receive extra credit.

I. ASSIGNMENTS

A. Introduction and Discussion of Vocabulary Words.
    1. Read pages 211-212 in Today's Basic Science
       and pages 131-139 in Science Problems.
    2. Using your Science Dictionary, write the
       definitions to the vocabulary words on page
       two of your unit plan. You will be required
       to know how to spell these words.

B. The Body's Framework
    1. Read pages 212-222 in Today's Basic Science.
    2. Color the diagram and learn the bones of the
       skeleton on drawing A. Place in your notebook.
    3. Color the bones of the foot different colors
       and enter in your notebook.

303

4. Bring one type of bone into the classroom
   prepared to identify the name of the
   animal from which it came and the name of
   the bone.
5. Color and learn the different parts of the
   tooth in diagram (C).
6. Answer the following questions:
   a. Why is a child less likely to break
      a bone in a fall than an elderly adult?
   b. Do bones serve any other purpose than
      to provide a framework for your body?
      Explain.
   c. Make a drawing of a bone, labeling its
      various parts.

C. The Body's Muscles
   1. Read pages 223-227 in Today's Basic Science.
   2. Read pages 152-157 in Science Problems.
   3. Examine a piece of meat at home. In a
      short paragraph explain what you see.
   4. Answer the following questions:
      a. How is muscle formed?
      b. What are the three types of muscles?
      c. Explain how muscles work in pairs.
      d. Look at the picture on page 153 in
         Science Problems. Answer the questions
         on that page.
   5. Fill in the worksheet on Muscles. Refer to
      your readings for the answers.

D. The Circulatory System
   1. Read pages 227-232 in Today's Basic Science.
   2. Read pages 132-139 in Science Problems.
   3. Label and color the parts of the heart and
      circulatory system in diagrams (E) and (F)
      included in this unit. Color the oxygenated

304

blood red and the non-oxygenated blood blue.
Refer to pages 230-231 for this exercise.
4. During a study period, examine a chart of
   the circulatory system tracing one specific
   organs blood supply.
5. Answer the following questions:
   a. Why do diagrams of the circulatory
      system show the arteries colored red
      and the veins colored blue?
   b. How does the Muscle System depend on
      the Circulatory System?
   c. Name the place in the body where veins
      carry pure blood and arteries carry
      impure blood.
6. Fill in the Crossword puzzle on the
   circulatory system (Diagram G) included in
   this unit.

The Respiratory System

1. Read pages 232-234 in Today's Basic Science.
2. Read pages 158-161 in Science Problems.
3. Study and color the various parts of
   diagram (H) included in this unit.
4. During a study period, examine the model of
   the lung. Also, study the bell jar demonstration of how the lung is inflated and
   deflated.
5. Answer the following questions:
   a. What parts of your body come into action
      when you take a deep breath?
   b. How do the Circulatory and Respiratory
      Systems work together?
   c. How does smoking harm your lungs?
6. Fill in the Take Home Quiz (1) included in
   this unit on the Respiratory System.

305

F. The Digestive System
   1. Read pages 235-238 in <u>Today's Basic Science</u>.
   2. Read pages 146-151 in <u>Science Problems</u>.
   3. Study and label the parts of the Digestive System on diagram (D).
   4. Answer the following questions:
      a. Name the parts of the alimentary canal.
      b. How does the Digestive System work with the Circulatory System?
      c. Describe peristalsis.
   5. Fill in the worksheet on the Digestive System included in this unit.
G. <u>Include one report</u> in this unit on an article in a magazine or a book that has to do with one of the systems of the human body.

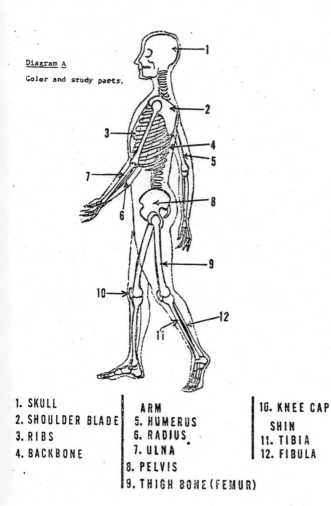

1. SKULL
2. SHOULDER BLADE
3. RIBS
4. BACKBONE

ARM
5. HUMERUS
6. RADIUS
7. ULNA
8. PELVIS
9. THIGH BONE (FEMUR)

10. KNEE CAP
SHIN
11. TIBIA
12. FIBULA

Diagram 8
Color and Label parts.

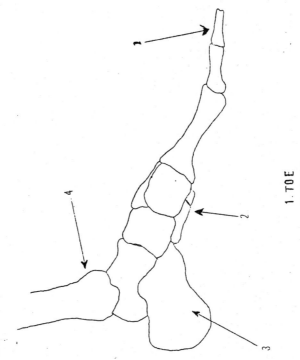

1.TOE
2.ARCH
3.HEEL
4.ANKLE

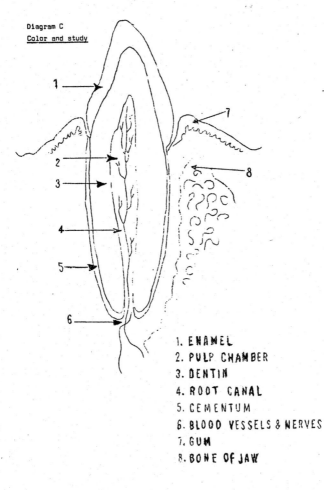

Diagram C
Color and study

1. ENAMEL
2. PULP CHAMBER
3. DENTIN
4. ROOT CANAL
5. CEMENTUM
6. BLOOD VESSELS & NERVES
7. GUM
8. BONE OF JAW

309

Diagram D
<u>Color and label parts.</u>

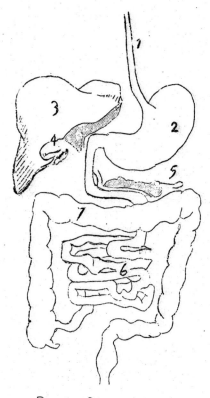

Digestive System of Man

310

Diagram E
Color and label parts.

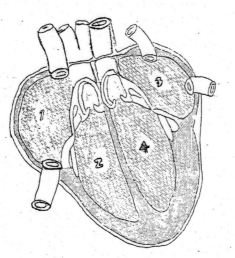

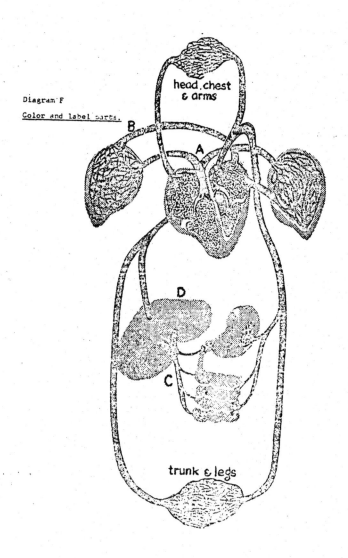

Diagram F

Color and label parts.

B

A

head, chest & arms

D

C

trunk & legs

312

Crossword Puzzle: Circulatory System

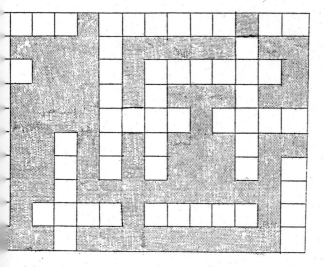

)SS

The blood vessels which carry blood to the heart.
The blood vessels which carry the blood away from
the heart.
Veins carry blood _____ the heart.
The heart does not rest. Yes or No.
The fluid part of the blood.
The smallest unit of the human body.
Blood that has oxygen in it is called _____.
Chambers in the heart. Number.
What stops the blood from backing up in the veins.

313

1. The largest chamber of the heart.
2. The upper chamber of the heart.
5. The beat of the heart felt in the wrist.
11. Blood with carbon dioxide.
10. The name of the liquid in our vessels.
12. Arteries carry blood _____ from the heart.

Muscles   Name _____

Date_____Class_____

o the student: In the blank in each of the following
entences write the word or words that are needed to
ake it a true statement.

_____ is the shortening of the muscles.

Lengthening of the muscles is called _____.

Every movement of the body is the result of the
contraction and relaxation of the _____.

_____ serve to produce voluntary movements
of the body.

The _____ muscles are used in the action
of the heart.

The muscles of the arm are _____ muscles.

Muscles are developed by _____.

Muscular _____ is a disorder of the muscles.

A _____ is a strong white cord, one end
of which is attached to a muscle above a joint, and
the other to a bone or flesh below a joint.

_____ bind bones together at the joints
and _____ attach muscles to the bones.

tching: INVOLUNTARY   LIGAMENTS   FLEXOR   TRICEPS

EXTENSOR   BICEPS   MUSCLE   MUSCULAR RHEUMATISM

RELAXATION   VOLUNTARY   TENDON   INVOLUNTARY

_____ a bundle of fibers that produce
motion on some part of the body.

_____ muscles of the heart.

_____ muscles of the hand and foot.

_____ muscles we cannot control.

_____ muscles which bend the limbs.

_____ muscles which straighten the limbs.

_____ a muscle that straightens the elbow.

_____ act of lengthening the muscles.

315

Science Take-Home Test   <u>Respiratory System</u>   Name _____
                          Date _____   Class _____

To the pupil: In the blank in each of the following
sentences write the word or words that are needed to
make it a true statement.

1. _____ is the process of taking in oxygen
   and giving off the products formed by the oxidation
   of tissues.

2. _____ are usually the cause of mouth
   breathing.

3. The trachea is commonly called the _____.

4. The _____ is really the voice box.

5. Air passing between the _____ produces
   the voice.

6. The _____ are two bright spongy bodies.

7. The membrane surrounding the lungs is called the
   _____.

8. The _____ are hairlike processes which
   line the air passages to the lungs.

9. The _____ are the air tubes in the lungs.

10. The lungs supply the body with _____ and
    remove the _____.

11. Taking air into the lungs is known as _____.

12. Forcing the air out of the lungs is called _____.

13. We breathe in order to take into the body a
    substance called _____.

14. The _____ is a muscle across the bottom
    of the chest cavity which aids in breathing.

15. The best kind of air to breathe is _____.

16. Air should first pass into the body through the
    _____.

17. After passing from here through the pharynx it
    enters the _____ or voice box.

18. From here it passes down through the _____
    which finally divides into the two main branches
    called the _____.

19. From those tubes it enters the _____.
20. The oxygen which is carried into the body is taken
     up by _____.

1. _____ is the process of changing foods into such forms as can pass through the walls of the blood tubes and become a part of the body.

2. _____ is the grinding of the food by the teeth and also mixing it with saliva.

3. Chewing the food thoroughly aids the process of _____.

4. The mouth and the salivary glands belong to the _____.

5. There are _____ teeth in the permanent set.

6. Enamel is the hard white covering of the _____.

7. The hard bone which covers the body of the tooth is _____.

8. The hard white shell which covers the crown of the tooth is called _____.

9. The teeth are fixed in the jawbone by a soft bone called the _____.

10. It is the _____ in teeth which makes them hard.

11. Defective teeth sometimes cause _____.

12. Decayed teeth prevent the proper _____ of the food we eat.

13. The _____ is the muscular tube which connects the pharynx with the stomach.

14. The stomach is a conical enlargement of the _____.

15. The opening into the stomach is called the _____.

16. Gastric juice is secreted by the glands in the _____.

17. The _____ is the opening from the stomach into the intestine.

18. The food is a soupy mass called _____ when it enters the small intestine.

19. The last digestive juice to be mixed with the food is _____.

20. The _____ are fingerlike projections in the small intestine.

AFRICA
GRADE 7

SOCIAL STUDIES DEPARTMENT

Name: _____

Class Room # _____

Social Studies Teacher: _____

Date Unit Began _____ Date Unit Due _____

RODUCTION:

Dramatic and swift has been the political awakening
Africa. History offers no parallel to the onrush of
nts in this great continent, where, in the past ten
rs (1956-1966) we have witnessed the rise of 34
ependent countries. Political transformation, eco-
ic upheaval, and social transition are everywhere at
, as former colonies and territories grapple with
problems of self-government. From the shores of the
terranean to the Cape of Good Hope, a new world is
he making.

The significance of these developments for the
ern democracies is enormous. Already African new-
rs to the United Nations can tip the balance of
r in the General Assembly and have, upon occasion,
so.

Free men watch in suspense and anxiety to see what
of new world will emerge in Africa. Largely
perienced in state-craft, African peoples and their
ers find self-government a formidable challenge. As
consolidate their political independence, will they
in free and democratic? Parliamentary institutions
already given way, in some instances, to strong
man rule with imminent danger of dictatorship.
st every day has brought startling news of political
st in many parts of Africa, and of violence, real or
atened. Meanwhile, Communist influence, Communist
ation, and Communist aid are ever present to mislead
ca's new countries and to lure them into the orbit
oscow or Peking.

Unworkable economics have, in some countries, gener-
popular discontent. This has been further aggravated
eavy population shifts from rural to urban and
strial areas, uprooting family and tribal relation-
s. A social revolution is in progress in Africa,

321

marked by changes in the "stratification" of society
and the appearance of new economic interest groups.
It is a "revolution of rising expectations" in which
any eventuality could develop, from order and prosperity
to total anarchy.

Despite seeming chaos, however, the future holds
bright promise for the peoples of Africa. Long-range
economic planning, with financial and technical aid
from the advanced countries of Europe, Asia, and
America, enable newly created governments to modernize
their economies. Roads, railways, port facilities,
power installations, and irrigation projects are
planned and under way to enable African enterprise to
develop the vast natural resources of the continent.
Improved living standards, prosperity, and wealth are
within the reach of African societies. As their
leaders discuss the possibilities of federation,
emphasis is placed upon non-alignment. Africa is to
be developed for the Africans. Their new world can
aspire to freedom, to dignity, and to leadership.

Purpose

A purpose of this unit is to make the student aware
that Africa is more than just an area where wild
animals roam and primitive people live. Recently,
Africa has undergone many changes that have greatly
affected the entire world. This unit will show the
student the many changes which are taking place in
Africa and the importance of Africa to the world.

The unit is to give the student an understanding
of the importance of colonialism, tribalism, and
nationalism on the developing countries of Africa. It
will show examples of 19th century European colonialism
and the rise of nationalism in opposition to it.

322

so time will be spent on how old tribal loyalties
e in conflict to nationalism.

havioral Objectives

To understand how colonialism has affected Africa.
To understand how nationalism has affected Africa.
To understand how tribalism has affected Africa.
To understand the great changes that have taken
place recently in Africa.
To be able to explain why changes have taken place
so rapidly in Africa.
To understand that the racial policies of the
Republic of South Africa, Angola, Mozambique and
Southern Rhodesia may lead to more violence.
To understand the many problems which face the
developing nations of Africa.
To understand that some black people of Africa in
the past have had very advanced civilizations.

A good way to begin the study of a continent such as Africa is to find out what is already know. The preliminary test here is an attempt to find out what you already know.

DIRECTIONS: On the space on the left, write the letter of the answer which best answers or completes the statements below.

_____ 1. The majority of Africans are dependent for their living on:
        (a) industry
        (b) small business
        (c) farming and cattle raising
        (d) overseas trade.

_____ 2. One of the most important rivers in Africa is the:
        (a) Indus   (c) Ganges
        (b) Nile   (d) Euphrates

_____ 3. The greater part of the African continent has a climate which is:
        (a) ideal for farming
        (b) similar to that of the United States
        (c) temperate
        (d) tropical

_____ 4. Kilimanjaro is:
        (a) one of the earliest known centers of African civilization
        (b) one of the highest mountain peaks in the world
        (c) one of the world's longest rivers
        (d) one of the continent's largest lakes

_____ 5. South Africa is the world's most valuable source of:
        (a) gold and diamonds (c) timber
        (b) oil   (d) cotton

_____ 6. For thousands of years, African society has
        been organized on the basis of:
            (a) tribal groups
            (b) nations
            (c) clans
            (d) occupational groups
_____ 7. Ancient Carthage was:
            (a) a South African kingdom
            (b) an Arab kingdom in South Africa
            (c) an Egyptian City
            (d) a powerful Phonencian city-state
                 on Africa's Mediterranean Coast
_____ 8. During the Middle Ages, a large part of
        North Africa was conquered and settled by:
            (a) Arabs   (c) Persians
            (b) Indians   (d) Europeans
_____ 9. One of the most famous of all 19th century
        African explorers was:
            (a) Jan Christian Smith
            (b) Ferdinand de Lesseps
            (c) David Livingstone
            (d) Paul Kruger
_____ 10. The First Negro republic to be established
        in Africa was:
            (a) Liberia   (c) Ghana
            (b) Algeria   (d) the Republic
                                       of the Congo
_____ 11. In 1966 a crisis developed in Nigeria when:
            (a) Nigerian leaders declared their
                 country independent of Britain
                 without British consent
            (b) the president was assassinated by
                 a crazed farmer
            (c) a military coup aggravated tribal
                 conflicts and set off widespread
                 killing

(d) A Mau Mau uprising took place

_____ 12. Among prominent African leaders today are:

        (a) Haile Selassie

        (b) Jomo Kenyatta

        (c) Habib Bourguiba

        (d) all three

How well did you do? These statements should give you some idea of the complexity of the African question today. Let's begin to find some of the answers.

The basic reference for this unit will be <u>EMERGING AFRICA</u> by Charles R. Joy. Other useful references to use are:

<u>EURASIA, AFRICA, AND AUSTRALIA</u> by Robert M. Glendinning, Marguerite Uttley, and Elison E. Aitchison, pp. 413-508.

<u>BEYOND THE AMERICAS</u> by Paul R. Hanna, Lee L. Jacks, Clyde F. Kohn, and Robert Lively, pp. 174-251.

<u>HOMELANDS BEYOND THE SEAS</u> by Ernest L. Thurston, Grace C. Hankins, and Lawrence C. Haby, pp. 373-443.

You will find other sources in the Humanities Resource Center and the central library.

The following books can be found in the West View Library.

916 Ev15e	<u>Africa</u>	Evans, Lancelot O.
910 L786a	<u>Africa</u>	Lobsenz, Norman
960 C831t	<u>Africa</u>	Coughlan, Robert
960 G229n	<u>Africa</u>	Gatti, Ellen
960 Sa92s	<u>Africa</u>	Savage, Katherine
323.4 Sp33c	<u>Africa</u>	Spencer, Cornellia

967 G958m	<u>Africa, Central</u>	Gunther, John
960.3 D281a	<u>Africa-Civilization</u>	Davidson, Basil
B St25b	<u>Africa-Description & Travel</u>	Benet, Laura
574.9 C23L	<u>Africa-Description & Travel</u>	Carr, Archie
B L763e	<u>Africa-Discovery & Exploration</u>	Eaton, Jeanette
B St25h	<u>Africa-Discovery & Exploration</u>	Hall-Quest, Olga
960 H782e	<u>Africa-Discovery & Exploration</u>	Horizon Magazine
960 M787b	<u>Africa-Discovery & Exploration</u>	Moorehead, Alan
960 M787w	<u>Africa-East</u>	Moorehead, Alan
967 N417a	<u>Africa-Fiction</u>	Nevins, Albert J.

This unit on "Africa" will be divided into ten assignments as follows:

Assignment #1:   The Needs of Man
Assignment #2:   The Land
Assignment #3:   People of Africa
Assignment #4:   Climate of Africa
Assignment #5:   Education of Africa
Assignment #6:   Animals of Africa
Assignment #7:   Transportation of Africa
Assignment #8:   History of Africa
Assignment #9:   Looking at Africa's Problem
Assignment #10: Problems of African Development

"EXTRA CREDIT" WORK

1. The Land
   A. On outline maps of Africa, indicate the principal
      rivers, mountains, and deserts--on another out-
      line map show the tropical belts, the savannas,
      and the fertile farming areas.
   B. Prepare a research paper showing the kind of
      trade carried on between the United States and
      Africa. (You might write to the Dept. of
      Commerce, Washington, D.C. for information.)
   C. Prepare a talk for the class on any one of the
      subjects below:
      (a) a tourist's itinerary through Africa
      (b) Kruger National Park
      (c) the Sahara
      (d) African jungles and rain forests
      (e) African wild life and efforts to
          conserve it
      (f) The Great Rift

2. The People
   A. Prepare a table of the major languages spoken in
      Africa. Beside each language listed enter the
      name(s) of the country (countries) in which it
      is spoken, and indicate the number of persons
      speaking the language.
   B. Form a group of students and do research and
      prepare a classroom exhibit of a typical African
      village in any part of the continent you choose.
      You might use pictorial materials or construct a
      scale model of a village, or both.
   C. Prepare an oral report on the following:
      (a) major tribes or any particular tribe
          such as the Bantus, Swahili, Zulus, etc.

   (b) the distinctive societies of these
     peoples and their importance in the
     new African countries.

Africa's Past

A. Prepare an oral report on any one of the
  following:
   (a) Berber kingdoms of West Africa
   (b) ancient Ethiopia
   (c) Timbuktu
   (d) Nok art
   (e) the ruins at Zimbabwe, or
   (f) the Ashanti

B. Prepare an outline map of Africa showing the
  locations and dates of founding of the chief
  European settlements and trading stations in
  Africa from the 16th to the mid-19th century.

Colonialism and Independence

A. Prepare a biography on Cecil Rhodes, Paul Kruger,
  Louis Botha, or Jan Christian Smuts.

B. Explain this statement: "Nationalism in Africa
  would not have developed without colonialism."

C. Prepare a written report on any of the following
  topics:
   (a) France, England, Egypt, and the
     Suez Canal
   (b) the mandate and trusteeship systems
   (c) African colonialism and World War I
   (d) the French community
   (e) African members of the Commonwealth
     of Nations
   (f) Sino-Soviety rivalry in Africa

North Africa Today

A. North Africa is often referred to as " an
  extension of southern Europe." Explain if you
  agree or disagree - why?

B. Write a biographical sketch on any one of the
    following:
   (a) Houari Boumedienne
   (b) Haile Selassie
   (c) Hassan II
   (d) Habib Bourguiba
C. Report orally on any one of the following topics:
   (a) the oil potential of the Sahara
   (b) the movement for Arab unity in
     North Africa
   (c) tensions between African Nations
   (d) the Suez Crisis of 1956
   (e) strategic importance of North Africa

6. Tropical Africa Today
A. Write an editorial as it might have appeared in
    U.S. newspapers in 1963 supporting or attacking
    the actions taken by the United Nations to end
    the secession of Katanga Province from the
    Democratic Republic of the Congo.
B. Prepare a written or oral report on any of the
    following topics:
   (a) European and Asian minorities in Kenya
     and Tanzania
   (b) the history of Liberia
   (c) the union of Tanganyika and Zanzibar
   (d) Communist influences in Guinea, the
     Congo (Brazzaville) and Mali
   (e) Albert Schweitzer's work in Africa
   (f) tribal conflicts in Nigeria

7. Southern Africa Today
A. Write a research paper on "Operation Noah," the
    transfer of wild animals to safety as the lake
    behind the Kariba Dam was formed.

330

B. Write a biographical sketch of any of these
   people: Albert John Luthuli, Ralph Bunche,
   and Martin Luther King.

C. Get the book <u>Cry, the Beloved Country</u> by Alan
   Paton and read to the class some excerpts or
   write a book report.

D. Hold a round-table discussion in which students
   assume the roles of Kamuzu Banda, Joshua Nkomo,
   and Kenneth Kaunda. Discuss the race problem
   in Southern Africa today.

Problems and Promises

A. What is meant by the statement, "Many of the
   colonies in Africa were merely geographical
   accidents?"

B. Write to the Peace Corps in Washington, D.C. for
   information and then report orally (or in written
   form) to the class on its work in Africa at
   the present time.

C. Write an essay on how you would help Africa
   solve its various problems if you were the U.S.
   Assistant Secretary of State for African Affairs.

Africa Looks at the World

A. Draw up a balance sheet of the factors encouraging
   and discouraging the spread of communism in
   African Nations. Show how these could work in
   Guinea, Ghana, Mali, the Republic of the Congo
   and Tanzania.

B. Suggest a list of principles to govern U.S. policy
   toward Africa.

C. Organize a debate around the question, "Resolved:
   The United States should encourage aid for
   Africa from any source."

331

<u>Maps</u>

   Three maps are included in this unit for your
convenience. Use these maps for the following
assignments.

1. Political map - Identify the following: major
                        cities, capitals, and countries.
    Use <u>Africa</u> by W. D. Allen (Fedeler Co., 1968) p. 53
              <u>OR</u>
    <u>Eurasia, Africa and Australia</u> by Glendenning, Uttley,
                              and Eislen (Ginn and Co.,
                              1958) Part III, page 7
2. Rainfall map - Use a color key code to indicate
                     the amounts of rainfall.
    Use <u>Africa</u>, page 24 <u>OR</u> <u>Eurasia, Africa and Australia</u>,
                        page 12
3. Mineral Resources map - Label the resources and
                             include a key to explain the
                             symbols.
    Use <u>Africa</u>, page 108

POLITICAL MAP

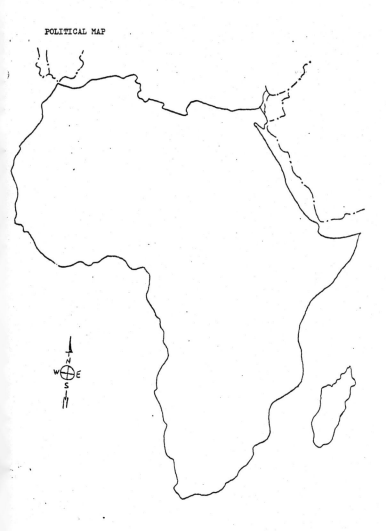

RAINFALL MAP

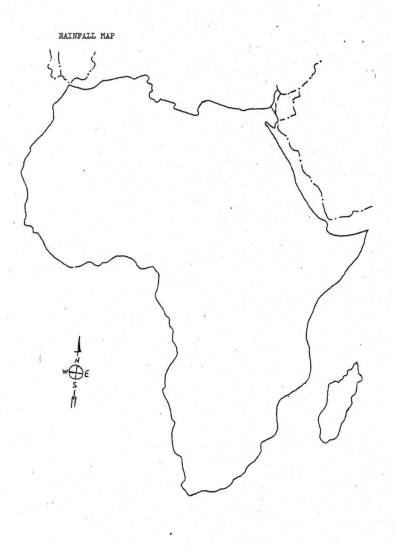

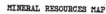

MINERAL RESOURCES MAP

335

The following latitude and longitude readings are only approximates. Clues and symbols are provided, so that you will find the correct answer.

Book: Eurasia, Africa and Australia
       Pages 74 and 75
       Map of Equatorial Africa

	Latitude	Longitude		
1.	$5°N-3°S$	$12°-27°E$	River	_____
2.	$0°-2°N$	$32°-35°E$	Lake	_____
3.	$5°-9°N$	$8°-11°W$	Country	_____
4.	$13°N$	$17°W$	City	_____
5.	$6°N$	$4°E$	City	_____
6.	$10°029°N$	$32°-33°E$	River	_____
7.	$1°N$	$39°E$	City	_____
8.	$16°-19°N$	$28°-37°E$	River	_____
9.	$18°N$	$3°W$	City	_____
10.	$0°-5°N$	$17°-20°E$	River	_____
11.	$3°S$	$38°-39°E$	Mt. 19,340 ft.	_____

Use map of Africa South of the Equator on page 121.

	Latitude	Longitude		
12.	$22°S$	$25°E$	Falls	_____
13.	$30°S$	$31°E$	City	_____
14.	$26°S$	$28°-29°E$	City	_____
15.	$34°S$	$19°E$	City	_____

Use book, Africa by Fideler Publ. Co. map on page 9.

	Latitude	Longitude		
16.	$29°N$	$13°-19°W$	Islands	_____
17.	$30°N$	$31°E$	City	_____
18.	$30°-45°N$	$5°W-35°E$	Sea	_____
19.	$31°N$	$29°E$	City	_____
20.	$12°-28°N$	$32°-42°E$	Sea	_____

The people of Africa, like all other people on the
th, must meet certain basic needs in order to be
lthy and happy. Scientists who study human behavior
l us that these basic needs are almost exactly the
e for every person, whatever his skin color, his
ional origin, or his religion may be. Whether people
rich or poor, they have the same basic needs.
There are three kinds of basic needs. They are:
sical needs, social needs, and the need for faith.

sical Needs

Some basic needs are so important that people will
or become seriously ill if they fail to meet them.
se are called physical needs. They include the need

1. air
2. water
3. food
4. protection from heat and cold
5. sleep and rest
6. exercise

ough all people share these needs, they do not all
them in the same way. How do you meet your physical
s? How do you think people in Africa meet their
ical needs?

al Needs

Each person on the earth also has social needs. He
meet these needs in order to have a happy and useful
. Man's social needs include the following:
1. BELONGING TO A GROUP. Every person needs to
feel he belongs to a group of people who
respect him and whom he respects. Belonging
to a family is one of the main ways people meet

337

this need. What can the members of a family do
to show that they love and respect each other?
How do the members of your family help one
another? Do you think family life is important
to the people of Africa? Why do you think this?

Having friends also helps people meet their
need for belonging to a group. What groups of
friends do you have? Why are these people your
friends? Do you suppose young people in Africa
enjoy doing the same kinds of things with their
friends as you enjoy doing with your friends?
Why? Why not?

2. GOALS. To be happy, every person needs goals
to work for. What goals do you want to accomplish? How can working toward these goals help
you have a happy life? What kinds of goals do
you think young people in Africa have?

3. A CHANCE TO THINK AND LEARN. Every person needs
a chance to develop and use his abilities. He
needs opportunities to find out about things
that make him curious. What would you like to
learn? How can you learn these things? How
can developing your abilities help you have a
happy life? Is it important for people in
Africa to have a chance to think and learn? To
make decisions for themselves? Why? Why not?

4. A FEELING OF ACCOMPLISHMENT. You share with
every other person the need for a feeling of
accomplishment. Everyone needs to feel that his
life is successful in some way. What gives you
a feeling of accomplishment? Can you imagine
what a person's life would be like if he never
had this feeling?

In addition to physical and social needs, every
rson also has a need for faith. He needs to believe
at life is precious and that the future is something
look forward to. A person may have different kinds
faith, including the following:

1. FAITH IN HIMSELF. In order to feel secure,
   each person must have faith in his own abilities.
   He must feel that he will be able to do some
   useful work in the world and that he will be
   generally happy. He must believe that he can
   work toward solving whatever problems life
   brings to him. How do you think a person can
   build faith in himself?

2. FAITH IN OTHER PEOPLE. Every person needs to
   feel that he can count on other people to do
   their part and to help him when he needs help.
   What people do you have faith in? What do you
   think life would be like without this kind of
   faith?

3. FAITH IN NATURE'S LAWS. Another kind of faith
   that helps people face the future with confidence
   is faith in nature's laws. The more we learn
   about our universe, the more certain we feel
   that we can depend on nature. How would you
   feel if you couldn't have faith in nature's
   laws?

4. RELIGIOUS FAITH. Throughout history, almost all
   human beings have had some kind of religious
   faith. Religion can help people understand
   themselves and the world they live in. It can
   bring them joy, and it can give them confidence
   in times of trouble. Religion can also help
   people live together happily. For example,

339

most religions teach people to be honest and to love and help their neighbors. In what ways do people in Africa express their religious faith?

Many People in Africa Are Unable To Meet Their Basic Needs

The people living in Africa must meet the three kinds of basic needs we have explored here. They must meet these needs in order to have happy, useful lives. However, millions of Africa's people do not have a chance to satisfy some of their important needs. For example, large numbers of them do not have adequate shelter or an opportunity to obtain an education.

Why do you think so many people in Africa are unable to meet all of their needs? What is being done to help these people improve their way of life? This book contains much information that will help you answer these questions.

Assignment #2 - THE LAND

Africa is the second largest continent in the world. The only continent bigger than Africa is Asia. The United States could fit into Africa 5 times. Africa is about 4,600 miles wide and 5,000 in length.

Africa's northern boundary is the Mediterranean Sea. To the east of Africa is the Red Sea, to the south is the Indian Ocean, and finally to the west of Africa is the Atlantic Ocean.

Most of Africa is a vast plateau, only a small part of it is mountains and lowlands. The lowlands are near the coastlines and extend in only a few miles.

BASIC UNDERSTANDING: MOST OF NORTHERN AFRICA IS DESERT AREA

The best known of the deserts in the northern area is the Sahara Desert. This desert covers $3\frac{1}{2}$ square miles.

It covers an area from the Atlantic Ocean to the Red
Sea. The Sahara is the largest desert in the world.
Parts of the Sahara are covered with sand piled up by
blowing winds or mountains and rocky plateaus. In
some areas which are very dry it is impossible for plants
and animals to live. In contrast to some areas, there
are oasis. These areas of fertile greenland with
springs, wells, streams, etc. Some of these are small
others large enough for thousands of people to live in
or near them.

In the northwestern part of the African continent
are the Atlas Mountains. This mountain range separates
the Sahara Desert and the Atlantic Ocean. Some of
these mountains are very high, eleven thousand feet or
more above sea level.

BASIC UNDERSTANDING: THE NILE RIVER IS ONE OF THE
                      LONGEST RIVERS IN THE WORLD

The Nile River is in the northeastern part of
Africa. The Nile River is one of the longest rivers in
the world. The Nile River flows northward from Lake
Victoria to the Mediterranean Sea. Near the mouth of
the Nile is the Nile Delta. Many people live in or
near this delta. Also if you would travel up or down
the Nile you would notice wide strips of irrigated land.
They have to irrigate land in order to grow crops in this
region. The Nile Valley in Egypt is one of the most
fertile farming regions in the world.

Also if we follow the Nile River southward we would
come to a region of vast grasslands. Some of the grasslands in this area look much like the western prairies
of America.

In Central Africa we have a vast tropical rain
forest. This area receives a great deal of rain throughout the year. The forest area here is very thick and
dense.

Much of Southern Africa is similar to Northern
Africa. In Southern Africa we have a desert and some
more areas of grassland. The major difference between
Northern Africa and Southern Africa is that most of
Southern Africa is much higher above sea level than the
Northern part of Africa.

Questions for Assignment #2.
1. Where are the deserts of Africa? How much of
    Africa consists of deserts?
2. Which is Africa's biggest desert. What is an
    Oasis?
3. Write a short paragraph about the Nile River? Why
    is it important to Africa? What is irrigation?

Assignment #3 - PEOPLE OF AFRICA
    First of all let's try and answer the question of
where did the African people come from? Different
scientists used to claim that human life or man started
in Asia. Not all scientists agree with this.

    Some people as we have said before used to think
that cradleland of human race was somewhere in Central
Asia. Others think that civilization began in Africa
and people traveled from Africa to other lands. So in
conclusion we cannot tell for sure where man really began.

    Many different types of people live in Africa. Most
of the people who live there are Negroid people. Other
people who live there are Caucasian. For many centuries
these and other people have mingled together. As a
result, the people of Africa are a mixture of people.
These people vary in their languages, customs and
appearance.

    As we travel through Africa we would see great
differences in how the people of Africa live. Some

342

people of Africa live in very primitive ways, like their forefathers had before them. Still other people in Africa live much as we do here in America. They live in cities and work in factories, shops, and office buildings.

We will now look at the people who live in the different parts of Africa.

People of Northern Africa

Most of the people who live in North Africa are either Semitic or are Hamites, or a combination of the two. The Hamitic people live near the western coast of Africa. The Semitics who are the Arabs and the Jews, live in such countries as Egypt, Libya, Ethiopia, etc.

Let's see how the Hamitic people might live. Imagine we are in Morocco, Algeria or Tunisia. This is where most of the Hamitic people live. Most of the Hamitics are farm or sheep or cattle farmers.

Most of the Hamitic people wear long robes for protection against the sun. Also, most of the Hamitic people are of the Moslem religion.

Now let's look at the Semitic people. The Semitic people live along the coast of the Mediterranean Sea. They have lived in this area for many centuries. Arabs mostly are farmers. The Jews are important to business life in the cities.

People of Central and Southern Africa

Most of the people of Central and Southern Africa are Negroes. People in this area live a little differently than people in Northern Africa. Most of the land of Central and Southern Africa is grassland. Grassland is good for raising cattle, sheep, goats, or almost any other kind of animal. Many of these grassland people earn their living raising animals, but some are hunters or farmers.

343

Let's take a look and see how the grassland people live. If we would enter a grassland village, we would see that the houses the people live in are made out of mud. The houses have hard-mud walls and thatched roofs. The house on the inside has little or no furniture, because the people only sleep in the houses, they really don't live in the houses.

Most of the activities of the family who lives there are carried on outside the house. All cooking and other related activities are done outside.

Now let's visit some tribal people in Africa. The first we will visit are the Masai in Kenya. The Masai are cattle, sheep and goat farmers. Their principle food is cattle blood and milk. They draw blood from the neck veins of cattle and mix it with milk.

Next we will visit the Watusi. These people are the tallest people in Africa. They are nearly seven feet tall. They are farmers and cattle raisers.

These are what some of the people of the grasslands are like and how they live.

People of the Low Wet Regions of Africa

The people of the low wet regions live mostly in the tropical rain forests. Most of the people of this region either raise cattle or become farmers to raise crops.

Most of the people who live in this area also live in villages. They are mostly Negro people. Many of these people have been tattooed to show that they belong to a certain tribe.

The people in the village are ruled by a chief. Most of the villages have wise men to help the chief rule. These villages also have what are called "Medicine Men," who is the doctor and religious leader of the village.

344

In the village, everyone has a certain job. Some
get water from a nearby river, some may hunt for
d, still others may be farmers for the village.
IC UNDERSTANDING: MANY EUROPEANS AND ASIANS LIVE
IN AFRICA
We have mentioned the different types of people
where they live. Let's talk about the Europeans
Asians who live there.
There are several million European and Asiatic
ple in Africa. They make up only a small part of
population. Most of the Europeans live in the
thern, southern, or eastern parts of Africa. Most
them work in the cities or own great farms called
ntations.
The Asians are often traders or businessmen. They
e along the Mediterranean Sea and various other
ts of Africa.
The French people are found in Tunisia, which the
nch had once controlled.
The British government once controlled great
tions of Africa. Some of the governments in Africa
1 to be under the control of the British Empire.
countries that were controlled by the British
e called British Colonies. These colonies were
posed to help the British get rich. The British
1 to exploit the people of Africa. Eventually many
these colonies broke away from British rule and
ame free or independent.
In the Republic of South Africa, we found more
opeans than any other part of Africa. Most of the
ole who live here are of Dutch ancestry. Some people
live there are also British and of French decent.
The white people control also most everything in
ch Africa. The white people believe and the South

345

African government believe in a separation of black and white people who live there. As a result, the black and white people live in separate areas. The black people of South Africa do not have equal rights with the white people of South Africa. (We will talk more about this fact later in the unit.)

Questions for Assignment #3.
1. Where did the people of Africa come from?
2. Where do the Hamitic and Semitic people live?
3. How do some of the people of the grasslands or Central Africa live? Why do they live like that?
4. Where do the Europeans live in Africa?

Assignment #4 - CLIMATE OF AFRICA
Much of Africa is hot throughout the year. Why is most of Africa hot the year round? Because the equator passes through the Central part of Africa. Look on a map of Africa to see! You'll remember that it is hot near the equator all year round because the sun's rays hit most directly at this point.

Of course, with a continent as big as Africa, there will be differences in climate in different parts of Africa.

Climate of the Tropical Rain Forests

The climate of the Tropical Rain Forests is hot and wet all year round! Because the climate is hot and wet, plants and trees grow very well in the area.

Climate of the Desert Regions

The climate in the desert regions is hot and dry. Because of the climate, very little will grow in these areas. During the day, the temperature can go well over 100° degrees, but can drop as much as 50° degrees when the sun goes down.

346

The climates of Northern and Southern Africa are
very much alike. The summers are very dry and the
winters are very wet, but mild. Because of this
climate, many Europeans have settled in Northern and
Southern Africa. The only real difference between
Northern and Southern Africa is that the seasons are
different for example. If it is summer in Southern
Africa, it is winter in Northern Africa!

Questions for Assignment #4
  Why does much of Africa have a hot climate year
  round?
  Are the climates of Northern and Southern Africa
  the same or different?

Assignment #5 - EDUCATION IN AFRICA
  In Africa today about 8 out of 10 people cannot
read or write. So 80% of the people in Africa need to
learn how to read and write. Even though many of these
people want to learn how to read and write they cannot,
a reason for this is that there are not enough
schools or teachers in Africa.
  If we were to travel through some of the African
countries, we would see why the people of Africa must
have more education. Many of the people of these
different African countries are sick and very poor.
They do not have in their countries enough doctors,
teachers, engineers, and other trained workers. As a
result, many of the people are sick and some of these
countries are underdeveloped. They are underdeveloped
because they do not have properly trained people to
develop them. Also, if the people who cannot read and
write now, learn how to, it would improve their ways
of living and improve their lives. They must learn

347

how to farm scientifically to produce more crops to
feed the people of Africa.

There are three types of schools that the African
children go to. They are as follows: 1) Tribal
educator schools, 2) Moslem schools, 3) Public schools.
Let's talk a little about each.

TRIBAL EDUCATION - Many African children who do not go
to regular schools, learn the history and laws of their
tribe from old people of their village. Boys are
taught to be honest and brave and to have respect for
their ancestors, parents, and neighbors. They learn
much through songs, stories and dance. Women teach the
girls special songs and dances that are for women only.
The tasks of daily living are taught to the children
by their parents. As they work with their parents, the
children learn how to hunt, fish, farm, and keep house.

MOSLEM SCHOOLS - Many people in Africa who are Moslems
send their children to special religious schools. Let
us visit one of these schools in Morocco. Here we see
boys sitting cross-legged on mats on the tiled floor.
They bend over their tablets as they learn to read and
write the Arabic language, in which the Koran, the holy
book of their religion, is written. These children
study Moslem law and religion as well as reading and
writing.

PUBLIC SCHOOLS - The number of students in African public
schools has increased greatly the last few years. But
still many children in some countries do not attend
school, because of the lack of materials and trained
teachers.

TECHNICAL SCHOOLS - Africa needs more technical schools
to train more African people to become more useful workers.
Only this way can Africa improve itself.

UNIVERSITIES - Again Africa needs more colleges and
universities to help train the people who are needed
in Africa.

Questions for Assignment #5

1. List some of the reasons why more Africans need to receive an education.
2. Would the tribal children receive the same type of education you do? Why? What do they study?

Assignment #6 - ANIMALS OF AFRICA

If you were to travel through Africa, you would see many of the animals you have seen in a zoo or circus. Many of the animals you have seen in the zoo or circus, are natives to the land of Africa.

For example, if we look at the desert lands of Africa we might find an animal called a <u>dromedary</u> or camel. Camels are very important to the people in the desert lands. They are important first of all because they can carry heavy loads or people for long distances. They are also well suited for lands that get little or no rainfall. He is able to store great quantities of water in his stomach. This makes it possible for the camel to travel long distances without drinking. The hump or humps you see on camels also helps him to go long periods of time without eating. The hump is stored up fat that is used when there is little or no food available. If the camel goes for long periods of time without eating, his hump may also disappear!

ANIMALS OF THE GRASSLANDS - If we traveled through the grasslands, one of the animals you would see would be the <u>lions</u>. Lions are usually a light brown in color, and usually weigh from 400 to 600 pounds.

Also, in the grasslands you will see a strange looking animal called a <u>giraffe</u>. The giraffe has a very long neck which enables him to eat leaves and twigs off of the very top of the trees. Some giraffes grow to the height of 18 feet. The giraffe can defend himself with his powerful hind legs.

349

The <u>antelopes</u> are probably the most interesting animal of the grasslands. There are many kinds of antelopes, big and small, but they are all very fast and graceful.

The next animal we see in the grasslands is the great horned <u>rhinoceros.</u> The "rhino" can be a very dangerous animal. He stands about 5 feet 8 inches tall and weighs about 2 or more tons! He has a thick, blush gray hide, and two horns on his snout. He uses these horns to dig up the roots of plants and trees to eat. Many people fear these "rhino's" because they will often charge without warning.

ANIMALS OF THE GREAT RAIN FORESTS - In the rain forests, you will find many types of <u>monkeys</u>. You will find small ones, about as big as a squirrel, to much larger ones.

Also in the rain forest you find <u>apes</u>. Apes are animals like monkeys only they are much bigger. They have long powerful arms and short legs. Like monkeys they live mostly in the tree tops, and feed off of fruits and nuts. Most of the time, apes are shy animals but if attacked they can be very dangerous. Some of the largest apes are called gorillas. Some gorillas weigh as much as 500 pounds.

Along many of the rivers of the rain forests, we may see <u>crocodiles</u> and <u>hippopotamuses</u>. The crocodile is a very large reptile. It eats fish and animals and will sometimes even eat people. The hippopotamus is a very large animal, he swims about in the rivers and lakes. The hippopotamus may weigh well over 2 tons. He can stay underwater for five to ten minutes without breathing. The hippopotamus eats as much as 6 to 8 bushels of water plants or grass to fill their huge stomach.

One animal we have not yet talked about that everyone knows comes from Africa is the <u>elephant</u>. The elephants come mostly from the wooded highland area. Elephants are usually the biggest animals in the world. Elephants usually feed on plants. They reach high into the trees to get tender leaves to eat. They use their trunks for weapons as well as for feeding.

Hunters along with other wild animals as well as progress, have helped to make some of the animals of Africa and of the world in danger of <u>extinction</u>. Extinction means that the animals will all die out and none of a certain kind of an animal will be left on earth. For example, dinosaurs are extinct, that is there are no longer any living dinosaurs. To help keep some of the animals from going extinct, large game reserves have been created. On these game reserves, the animals can wander and feed and multiply to help increase their number. On these game reserves, the animals cannot legally be hunted and thus are protected.

Questions for Assignment #6
1. What is a dromedary?
2. Name some of the animals that live A) in the grasslands, B) tropical rain forests, C) wooded highland regions.
3. Why have wildlife reserves been provided in some African countries?

Assignment #7 - TRANSPORTATION OF AFRICA
Africa naturally is a very large continent. There are various means of transportation ranging from very primative such as walking, or traveling by camel caravan to such modern means as railroads, modern black-top roads and airplanes.

351

Let's go back in time and see how transportation was in Africa long ago. By as late as 1900, Africa had no modern means of transportation. The paths between villages used to be just plain dirt paths. The main routes between villages were footpaths where people often walked single file. On the grasslands, people used to use oxcarts as a means of travel.

The first modern means of transportation introduced into Africa was the bicycle. It proved to be an excellent means of transportation on the footpath.

Many of the footpaths and oxcart trails have been widened into roads. Truck lines have been established to carry goods to and from different areas. Most of Africa's roads are still very poor, even today when it rains, cars and trucks get stuck in the mud. When it is dry, cars form dust clouds.

Airlines have done the most to improve transportation in Africa. Airplanes can move from one part of Africa to another in just a few hours. Whereas before it took many days and/or weeks to travel the same distance.

Even though there have been many improvements made in transportation, Africa still has many areas that need to be improved.

Questions for Assignment #7.
1. Why has Africa had so many problems with transportation?
2. Why is transportation important to any nation?

Assignment #8 - HISTORY OF AFRICA
If we could travel back through time to an ancient Africa, we would see a vast ancient land. The people of ancient Africa used weapons made of stone and wood.

Yet at the same time in Northern Africa in Egypt was a very great civilization. The civilization of the

ptians was one which built great temples, stone
ldings, palaces, and great pyramids. These early
ptians were skilled at growing crops and raising
mals.

If we could travel down the Nile River five
usand years ago, we would pass villages, farms,
cities. We would pass huge temples and pyramids
lt by slaves. These pyramids were built as tombs
kings and queens of ancient Egypt.

The ancient Egyptians were people who believed in
e after death. The climate of Egypt which is hot
dry had preserved many of these pyramids and tombs
t by the Egyptians. From these tombs and pyramids,
ch had writing in them which told of life in ancient
t we have learned many things. We have learned how
Egyptians lived, worked, what food they ate, how
dressed and how they worshiped their gods.

Egypt and Africa were invaded many times over
ral hundred years. Among the people who invaded
ca were the Greeks and the Romans. Africa was
rolled by these various groups until the fifteenth
ury or 1400's.

Beginning in the fifteenth century, the Europeans
ted to settle Africa. The first of the European
tries to set foot on Africa was <u>Portugal</u>. This
try first had people settle in Southern Africa
the Cape of Good Hope.

Later in the 1600's, people from Holland settled
outhern Africa. Later, the French also settled in
same areas as the people from Holland had. If you
there about that time, you could probably see
h and French ships stopping at Southern Africa on
e way home from India and China.

Europeans also settled along the western coast of
ca. During the 1600's and 1700's, the Europeans

353

started slave trading. Many African people, men, women and children, were taken from their homes and treated very badly. They were sent many different places in Europe and European colonies without being asked to go. Later in the 1800's, England and many other European countries made slave trade unlawful.

European countries came to look upon Africa as a vast continent with rich mineral deposits and other valuable items they could use. European businessmen wanted to take these natural resources from Africa to use in Europe. In 1885, many European countries signed agreements dividing Africa among themselves. These European countries claim the right to do this because their explorers had explored the lands they claimed. Today many areas of Africa are under European control but many have also become independent nations.

Questions for Assignment #8.
1. What do you think life was like in ancient Egypt? Can you compare it to your life today?
2. Why were many Africans taken from their homes during the 1600's and 1700's by the European people?
3. Why did many Europeans want to establish settlements or colonies in Africa?

Assignment #9 - LOOKING AT THE PROBLEMS OF AFRICA
Apartheid - What is it?
How does it operate?
Is it good or bad?

Apartheid - A Dutch word for separateness

To the white people of the world it means segregation of the races. This means keeping people separate from one another. In South Africa, it means keeping the

ck Europeans, Asians separated. The South African
tes feel that each so called race must develop its
f separately in government, race, education,
ially, etc.

Now let's look at how a white South African looks at
problem of the <u>apartheid</u>. The Prime Minister of the
ublic of South Africa is Mr. John Vorster, these are
views on <u>apartheid</u>.

"I believe in the policy of separate development,
only as a philosophy but also as the only practical
ution in the interest of everyone to eliminate
ctions and to do justice to every population group
well as every individual."

"I say to the colored people, as well as to the
ians and the Bantu that the policy of separate develop-
t is not a policy which rests upon jealousy, fear,
hatred. It is not a denial of the human dignity of
one nor is it so intended. On the contrary, it gives
opportunity to every individual within his own ·
ere, not only to be a man or woman in every sense, but
also creates the opportunity for them to develop and
ance without restriction or frustration as circum-
nces justify, and in accordance with the demands of
elopments achieved."

"My appeal therefore to every leader of every
ulation group is this: the best of service to
anity lies in service to one's own people. Every
ulation group has what is its own, which is beautiful
which can be developed."

"There is more work for every leader among his own
ple than he can do in his lifetime. I believe that
the whites, the coloreds, the Indians, and the Bantu,
l show the world that we do not only have in principle
answer to the race question, but that we will also
ve it in practice."

"I am aware that we are a small country, and that our population is small. But the greatness of a people does not lie in its numbers but in the character, the drive, the ability to work, the self-respect and the faith of its people."

This is the view of a white man on how the apartheid is supposed to work.

Let's ask this question first of all. Even if the apartheid did work fairly for all the people involved, is it right to segregate people and make them develop separately according to their race or skin color? This is a basic question we must answer.

First of all, let's examine the apartheid to see if it really works like Mr. Vorster says it does.

Does the non-white population of Africa allowed to have a separate but equal government? The non-white population of South Africa is allowed to participate in the government. But this is only in certain areas, such as the so called "homeland" where most Bantu's and non-whites live. For example, Capetown has an all white parliament even though blacks live in the city.

Let's look at some of the laws blacks must live under. The policy of separate development - a term the South African Government prefers to "apartheid" - has been relentlessly pursued since 1948 when the National Party came to power. Its goal is the eventual creation of national states for South Africa's tribes through a staged process bringing more autonomy at each step.

The Transkei, homeland of the Xhosa, is farthest along this path, it now has a parliament. Until the promised day comes, however, blacks cannot <u>vote</u>, own property except in their homelands, or move about without supervision. Let us look at this movement with supervision. In black ghetto's, the blacks are allowed to travel to work in the white man's factories, offices and shops. But in the evening, they are packed into trains and buses and trundled back to dimly lit, violence-ridden areas which they cannot leave until the next work day begins. Every African over the age of 16 must carry a pass book, and failure to produce it to the police can lead to jail, a fine or removal from an urban area to some distant "homeland" he may have never known. What Mr. Vorster called in his opening statement "I believe in the policy of separate development not only as a philosophy but also as the only practical solution in the interest of everyone to eliminate frictions and to justice to every population group as well as every individual." Does treatment or laws such as are listed above do justice to every person in South Africa? He also said that "I say to the colored people as well as to the Indians and the Bantu that the policy of separate development is not a policy which rests on jealousy, fear or hatred? Again are such laws as not having the right to vote, own property, or not being able to move about without permission, based on equality? In the average year, 500,000 Africans are arrested and jailed on such laws as were listed above. The questions asked above are still unanswered.

NATIONS OF AFRICA

The following puzzle contains the names of 31
African nations.

```
E O G N O C S U D A N A B T
T T C M A L I A Y N E K C A
H N O H A N G O L A D E F N
I O G G A L I B E R I A A Z
O B H I O D I F I N J N T A
P A E G Y P T K L M A N U N
I G A I B M A Z O H P U N I
A A L G E R I A G Q G R I A
S W A Z I L A N D A S T S U
D I V W G R X Y N Z A B I C
A D M A U W D D E F G H A I
H N A I I A A L E S O T H O
O U L B N N C A M E R O O N
M R A M E D A N A W S T O B
E U W A A A J S E N E G A L
Y B L G R H O D E S I A K L
```

Algeria	Ethiopia	Liberia	Swaziland
Angola	Gabon	Libya	Tanzania
Botswana	Gambia	Malawl	Togo
Burundi	Ghana	Mali	Tunisia
Cameroon	Guinea	Rhodesia	Uganda
Chad	Ifni	Rwanda	Egypt
Congo	Kenya	Senegal	Zambia
Dahoney	Lesotho	Sudan	

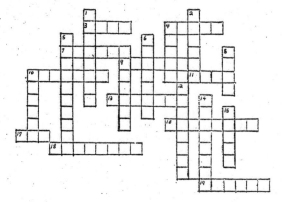

DOWN

1. capital of the Sudan
2. the _____ Ocean borders Africa on the east
5. a large island east of Africa
6. capital of Algeria
8. a famous canal
10. until recently most of Africa was controlled by nations from _____.
12. the second largest fresh water lake in the world
14. South Africa is famous for this mineral
15. Africa's largest mountain range

ACROSS

3. the southern tip of Africa is the Cape of Good _____
4. both a river and a nation have this name

7. the second largest continent
9. Lagos is the capital of this nation
10. runs through the middle of Africa
11. the world's longest river
13. capital of Kenya
16. the _____ Ocean borders Africa on the west
17. the _____ Sea borders Africa on the northeast
18. most of Africa has a _____ climate
19. the world's largest desert

The student or reader will find it helpful when
ting a teaching unit to compare the detailed format
h the sample units. <u>Format One</u>, is an example of
elaborate unit plan, outlining the procedures of
nning a teaching unit. As indicated, these initial
ps are not necessary if a resource unit has been
viously prepared.

<u>Formats Two and Three</u> teaching units are concise
ns of <u>Format One</u> in which the preparatory steps
eliminated. <u>Format Four</u>, which could be designated
a lesson plan-type unit, could very easily replace
usual class text or be an excellent supplementary
rial to the textbook. The Study-Work Unit allows
student to work independently as well as to provide
with up-to-date knowledge and information in certain
s that may not be covered in textbooks.

The teaching unit is a relatively simple method of
nizing an instructional program. It is, however,
rative that the teaching unit be compatible to and
able for the particular class with which the
her is working. The teaching unit should be flexible
gh to:

1. Meet the needs, interests, abilities, and
   experiences of the pupils.
2. Include terminology, concepts, skills and
   expectations the children can understand and
   meet.
3. Limit activities and problems to a reasonable
   length of time.

361

4. Include a variety of activities and materials
    so that every pupil can succeed.

The sample units included in this chapter should be
self explanatory. They vary according to format, subject
matter and grade level. The next chapter will deal
with lesson plans an essential extension of the
teaching unit. For additional samples of teaching units,
review the bibliography of teaching units in the appendix.

CHAPTER V

DEVELOPMENT AND CONSTRUCTION OF LESSON PLANS

The reader has been guided through the process of
classroom curriculum planning via the resource and
teaching unit. Planning is an essential part of classroom teaching. The resource unit is used to assist the
teacher to organize her planning; the teaching or
experience unit is used for classroom implementation.
Both are long range or general planning organizational
schemes. However, teaching must advance from the
general to the specific, from the yearly plan to the
daily plan. Similarly, the effective teacher must
advance from unit to lesson planning. In essence, the
lesson plan is the "daughter" of the teaching unit and
the "grand daughter" of the resource unit, so to speak.
The lesson plan is not only a specific segment of the
unit, but an expanded and more detailed portion of the
unit plan. Although the lesson plan includes all of the
elements of the unit, it is the sections on activities
and materials that are developed in greater detail.

The lesson plan generally covers a single period,
but it could be expanded to cover several periods. In
many school systems, the teacher is supplied with a
commercially prepared lesson plan book. There is a
series of lesson plan boxes (see Lesson Plan Format One)
which covers five days (horizontally) and five to six
class periods per day (vertically). This is more or less
a form of memorandum or agenda for the teacher. The
rather small squares provide little space for detailing

363

aims, content, activities, materials and evaluation of each lesson. This form of lesson planning can be considered a tentative weekly schedule, to be modified in terms of detail and elaboration. How long and detailed should a lesson plan be? This depends on the teacher, the class and the subject matter. Alcorn, Kinder and Schunert state:

> Long enough and complete enough to be of definite help, yet not so detailed as to be confusing. The written plan should serve as a simple ready reference that can be easily read and that will, at the same time preserve continuity of the lesson without unnecessary duplications or undesirable omissions.[1]

Some teachers may find a more detailed lesson plan more desirable. Others may prefer brief outlines or notes on objectives, content, activities, procedures, materials and evaluation. Nevertheless, the written plan provides a practical and tangible record for the teacher since it provides continuity and a basis for future planning. On the other hand, one's memory is generally ephemeral; it provides little in the way of present and future continuity and reference.

Should the lesson plan be rigidly adhered to? Hoover and Hoover state:

> Planning, like map making, enables one to predict the future course of events. In essence, a plan is a blueprint--a plan of action. Although even the best laid plans sometimes go awry, they are necessary for effective (classroom teaching).[2]

---

[1] Marvin D. Alcorn, James S. Kinder, and Jim R. Schunert. _Better Teaching in Secondary Schools_. New York: Holt, Rinehart & Winston, 1970, p. 133.

[2] H. Hoover and Helen M. Hoover. Lesson planning: key to effective teaching. _Clearing House_, 42:41, 1967.

In the same manner, it is neither possible nor probable that one could or would desire to rigidly follow a lesson plan without some deviation. There may be a change in class scheduling, increased absenteeism, individual differences, conflicting activities, expanded activities of the lesson plan and the unpredictable amount of time it takes to implement and complete an activity. The variable of daily classroom interaction, discussion and extra curricular activities preclude inflexible lesson planning. In fact, the experienced teacher will probably find that she has too many activities planned. It is only the novice or student teacher who will feel compelled to adhere rigidly to the preplanned lesson. It gives security and a time-organized structure needed for a well prepared lesson. It keeps the teacher and the class from deviating from the topic and holds them to the essential and major points of the lesson.

The following suggestions for lesson planning are given by parochial educators.

LESSON PLAN

DIRECTIONS TO TEACHERS[3]

Planning in any successful endeavor is not only praiseworthy, but indispensable. It is unlikely that a person would want to be the patient of a doctor who operated by guess or a dentist who practiced his profession using outmoded methods. Every good workman has a plan. A teacher without a plan is like a ship without a rudder. Careful planning prevents haphazard,

---

[3]The Educators Plan Book, Educators Paper and Supply, Skokie, Illinois, n.d., p. 1. Used with permission of the Sisters of Holy Family of Nazareth, Desplaines, Illinois.

indefinite work. A teacher who plans the work carefully, a week in advance, is assured of a greater success than is the one who merely teaches from day to day.

A good lesson plan does the following things for the teacher:

1. Careful planning solves the problem of discipline.
2. Systematic planning prevents haphazard teaching.
3. It makes the teacher the "master of the situation."
4. It helps the teacher to interpret and use the manual correctly.
5. It organizes the teacher's work.
6. It insures more efficient teaching.
7. It facilitates conscientious preparation for each subject.
8. It puts the teacher at ease in the presence of visitors.
9. It helps the teacher to understand the subject more thoroughly.
10. An hour of careful planning is worth two hours of remedial teaching.
11. Know exactly what you are to emphasize in each subject, and you will prevent loss of valuable time and energy for both your pupils and yourself.

Keep your Lesson Plan Book on your desk all the time and USE IT. This book is a guide to your work and a means to an end. The results of your teaching will depend largely on the care and thoroughness in making your plans. While detailed lesson planning is essential for the beginning teacher, there is absolutely no justification for any teacher to prepare for a class in an off-the-cuff manner.

366

THE LESSON PLAN

The basic elements of a lesson plan are: to plan, to teach and to evaluate. The teacher poses such questions as: What?, How?, and When? The following table shows the basic elements and the procedures a teacher can follow in devising any lesson, regardless of the format employed. All lesson plans will include the three major elements. A comprehensive lesson plan will include most of the subelements.

THE BASIC ELEMENTS OF
A LESSON PLAN[4]

Major element: I. <u>WHAT ARE YOU GOING TO TEACH?</u> <u>PLAN</u>
Sub-elements:
    1. Facts to be........learned
    2. Skills to be.......developed
    3. Abilities to be....acquired
    4. Interests to be....aroused
    5. Problems to be.....solved
    6. Thinking to be.....stimulated
    7. Attitudes to be....cultivated

Major element: II. <u>HOW ARE YOU GOING TO TEACH?</u> <u>TEACH</u>
Sub-elements:
    1. Methods to be......employed
    2. Technique to be....used
    3. Strategy to be.....implemented
    4. Materials.........required
    5. Correlations to be.developed
    6. Questions to be....asked
    7. Interests to be....maintained

---

[4]Alcorn, Kinder, and Schunert, <u>op</u>. <u>cit</u>. (revised and adopted)

Major element: III. WHEN IS IT TAUGHT? EVALUATE

Sub-elements:

1. Evidence of...............appreciation
2. Indications of continuity..interests
3. Application of............skills
4. Intelligent use of........facts
5. Thinking.................stimulated
6. Attitudes................acquired
7. Evaluation of.............results

The major elements of a lesson plan can be expanded. How much depends on a number of factors--purpose, subject matter, teacher, grade level, students and classroom organization. There are probably as many lesson plan formats as there are school systems.

For example, the three major elements of the lesson plan can be translated into the following basic lesson plan.

BASIC LESSON PLAN FORMAT

SUBJECT - write the Title of the unit that you are teaching.[5]

TYPE OR APPROACH - Use any of the following methods that is directly applicable to the subject matter you are presenting:

    Development Lesson - (introduction and amplification of present lesson)

    Appreciation Lesson - (artistic and creative activities)

    Preview Lesson - (transition from previous lesson and overview of new lesson)

---

[5]The Educators Plan Book, op. cit.

<u>Practice or Drill Lesson</u> - (reinforcement and review)
<u>Summary</u> - (review of previous or present lesson
         or unit)
<u>Supervised Study</u> - (individualized work or study)
<u>Socialized Discussion</u> - (student involvement in
                  development, review and
                  evaluation of lesson)

CTIVE - See that all your work has a definite aim to
ttained. Know what your goal is for every lesson.
s attention upon one thing at a time and work
gently to accomplish that purpose.

EDURE - Analyze your procedure step by step to
rmine if you have set up the correct procedure to
ize your objective. You may write out your procedure
reater detail on an extra sheet of paper and use it
. guide in your presentation.

GNMENT - Assignments should be so clear and definite
every pupil will know exactly what is expected of
Do not give homework when the dismissal bell rings,
explain it carefully and correlate it with the
ect matter being taught.

Following are ten sample lesson plans in English
Arithmetic[6] of the basic format above. It will give
reader a basic idea of the lesson plan format.

---

[6]<u>Ibid</u>.

SAMPLES OF A BASIC LESSON PLAN

ENGLISH		ARITHMETIC	
S ubject:	Oral Story Telling	**S ubject:**	Combination of Six
T ype:	Development	**T ype:**	Project lesson
O bjective.	To teach children how to keep to the topic.	**O bjective:**	To help children understand the process of addition.
P rocedure:	Call six children to the front of the room. The first child begins an interesting story, while the others continue using the same basic idea.	**P rocedure:**	1. Place 12 objects on the desk 2. Use crayons for addition signs 3. Pupils handle objects and show what $3 + 3 =$; $2 + 2 + 2 =$; $4 + 2 =$.
Assignment:		**Assignment:**	Workbook exercise
S ubject:	Group Paragraph Writing	**S ubject:**	Table of Four
T ype:	Appreciation	**T ype:**	Development
O bjective:	To correlate writing with creative art.	**O bjective:**	An understanding of the multiplication table.
P rocedure:	The children choose any phase of the paragraph above ("Zip and the Jet Plane") and draw a picture of it in class.	**P rocedure:**	1. Show how the table is made by addition; 2. Use practical problems to explain the process.
Assignment:		**Assignment:**	Write the table twice at home.
S ubject:	Descriptive Composition	**S ubject:**	Multiplication of Fractions
T ype:	Development	**T ype:**	Development
O bjective:	To motivate a composition on "Sounds I Hear."	**O bjective:**	To develop skill in solving problems.
P rocedure:	Develop the vocabulary according to the following outline: 1 Sounds I hear, 2 Description of them, 3. To what they can be compared.	**P rocedure:**	Analysis of problem as to: 1. Given 2. Process 3. Statement of Result.
Assignment:	Write a good beginning sentence. The best ones will be written on the board.	**Assignment:**	Compose three problems that can be applied to life situations.
S ubject:	Good ending sentences	**S ubject:**	Problem Solving
T ype:	Development	**T ype:**	Development
O bjective:	To stress the importance of challenging and satisfying ending.	**O bjective:**	To determine the solution to specific problems.
P rocedure:	Read aloud the accepted ending sentences and select the three best.	**P rocedure:**	Pupils discuss the operation of each problem separately at the chalkboard.
Assignment:	Revise the paragraph on a description of a person.	**Assignment:**	Five Problems from the text to solve at home.

370

The above format is basic to most lesson plans.
e type or approach of the lesson plan is influenced
 the specificity and type of subject matter, grade
vel, teacher's teaching style and, perhaps most impor-
ntly, the purpose of the lesson. The activities of
e lesson plan are similarly influenced particularly
 the subject area. For example, if it was a lesson
an on science it could include mainly laboratory
periences, or one on industrial arts would include
nstruction of projects. (The sample lesson plans in
is chapter include examples and descriptions of
fferent lesson presentations and approaches.)

sson Plan Formats

Let us now examine several lesson plan formats and
mple lesson plans. Each format is followed by a
mple lesson plan.

Lesson Plan, Format One is generally used by
achers in large city school systems, such as Chicago
 New York. A series of weekly lesson plan formats
 published in a spiral notebook, covering 40 weeks,
tember through June. This type of format, which is
milar to the basic lesson plan, serves as an outline
 the teacher in which objectives, content, and
erials (page number of texts, names of films and
mstrips, etc. are indicated). It serves as a general
de for the daily and weekly lessons and classroom
ivities--a type of teacher agenda.

The boxes are blank; the teacher fills in the boxes
 each subject area. The sample Lesson Plans of Format
 differ from those of the basic format in that the
cher indicates the text, page numbers, and audio-visual
erials. Here the teacher is using the lesson plan as
aily guide and supplement to the texts in each

371

subject area. Whereas with the basic lesson plans,
the teacher appears to be using the lesson plan, independent of a text, except for assignments. The point
is that the teacher has a great deal of flexibility as
to how to apply a lesson plan in the daily curriculum
of the classroom.

DEVELOPMENT OF A LESSON PLAN
FORMAT ONE

	ENGLISH	SOCIAL STUDIES	SCIENCE
Monday			
Tuesday			
Wednesday			
Thursday			
Friday			

DEVELOPMENT OF A LESSON PLAN (continued)
FORMAT ONE

	SPELLING	ARITHMETIC	MUSIC/ART
Monday			
Tuesday			
Wednesday			
Thursday			
Friday			

SAMPLE LESSON PLAN
FORMAT ONE

	ENGLISH	SPELLING	ARITHMETIC
DATE:	Subject Matter: "Kinds of Sentences," p. 85. Objective Students should write two declarative and interrogative sentences from "Chicago Sun-Times," comic section. Vocabulary: See p. 85. Procedure: Read and discuss p. 85. Dramatize sentences found in comics.	Subject matter: Syllables Unit 13, p. 42. Objective: Students are to pronounce two syllable words and use each word properly in a sentence. Vocabulary: p. 43, #3 orally; p. 43 # 3, 4, 5 written. Procedure: Listen to words used in sentences. Write words with "ns and ss."	Subject matter: "Adding and Subtracting, "p.78. Objective: Students should be able to subtract and add with imitation coins in denominations of pennies and dimes. Vocabulary: pennies, collections, and dimes. Procedure: manual - p. 102.
DATE:	Subject matter: "Extension Exercise," man. 85. Objective: Students are to rearrange and write declarative and interrogative sentences from groups of words on board. Vocabulary: Write four groups of words on board. Discuss procedure. Give independent help to others.	Subject matter; Spelling Words Correctly p. 42. Objective: To have students score a 100% on final unit test, students should check and master errors made on trial test. Procedure: Dictate unit 13 words for trial test. Have students check and master their errors.	Subject Matter: "Exercises" p. 79; manual 103. Objective: Students should be able to solve problems on p. 79 using imitation coins. Vocabulary: addends, sum, and difference. Procedure: Have children work independently. Give individualized instruction.
DATE:	Subject Matter: "Sentences That Tell," p. 86 Objective: Have students write a story using the two types of sentences discussed thus far. Vocabulary:earned & errand. Procedure: Discuss questions on p.86. Have pupils give answers orally. Assign. #4 on p. 86.	Subject matter: Learning to Spell p.17 in English text Objective: To have students use the six steps listed on p.17 to master misspelled words. Vocabulary: individualized spelling errors. Procedure: Follow procedure listed in Language for Daily Use p. 17.	Subject matter: "Value of Coin Collections." Objective: Have students record various total amounts of coin collections on each student's desk. Vocabulary: see above Procedure: Employ use of musical chairs to record total amounts.
DATE:	Subject matter: Imperative Sentences p. 87. Objective: Students should be able to write sentences on the board giving someone directions. Vocabulary: imperative, order, and directions. Procedure: Follow suggested procedure as presented in manual p. 87.	Subject matter: "More Spelling Power," p.44. Objective: Students are to write words in which the letter "y" can spell the vowel sound at the end of words like "only." Vocabulary: Part D, p.44#1,2,3 4 & 5. Procedure:Discussion of rule and writing words.	Subject matter: "Exercises," p.81-manual 105. Objective: Students should be able to complete independently p. 81,#1,2,3, & 4 Vocabulary: nickel Procedure: Review value of coin assign written work; give individualized instruction.
DATE:	Subject matter: Exclamatory Sentences, p.88. Objective: Examine cartoons noting the use of the exclamation mark; have students contrast the exclamation sentence from the declarative, imperative and interrogative sentence. Vocabulary: See p. 88. Procedure: Consult p. 88	Subject Matter: Final Test and Dictation Objective: Student's are to be able to write words discussed with at least 80% accuracy. Procedure: Dictate words and sentences. Check according to usual procedures listed in manual p. iii, "Fifth Day-Part E"	Subject Matter: "Think, Think," p. 82, man.106. Objective: Students should be able to read the exercise, discuss it, and give correct answers after sufficient time was given for practice. Vocabulary: See p. 82. Procedure: See man. 106.

375

	SCIENCE	SOCIAL STUDIES	REFERENCES
Monday	Subject Matter: "What Makes Up the Surface of the Earth? p.85; man. 82. Objective: Children are to tell where they have gone on trips, how they traveled and what land features they have seen. Vocabulary: surface Procedure: Follow suggestions on p. 82 in man.	Subject Matter: "Sweet Foods," text p. 69; man. 34. Objective: Students are to watch a film entitled, "Bees Backyard Science," and note the operations of a honeybee colony. Vocabulary: See film Procedure: Discuss film; consult World Book Encyclopedia for illustrations.	ENGLISH TEXT: Dawson, Mildred A. et al.: Language for Daily Use. New York, Harcourt, Brace & World, 1965. (Grade 3)
Tuesday	Subject Matter: "Exploration," manual p. 82. Objective: Students are to compare and contrast the variety of physical features characteristic of the earth's surface. Vocabulary: earlier, our, world, and country (p.86) Procedure: Follow "Preliminary Development," p.82.	Subject Matter: Same man. TG35; text 69. Objective: Students should be able to describe orally how bees make honey as well as their importance to both man and the blossoms that they visit. Vocabulary: nectar, fertilize, pollen, colony, drones. Procedure: Oral discussion.	SPELLING TEXT: Madden, Richard; Carlson, Thorsten, and Yarborough, Betty H.: Sound and Sense in Spelling. New York, Har Brace World, 1964. (Grade 3)
Wednesday	Subject Matter: Music Teacher: Mrs. Olive Williams Time: 1:50 - 2:15 Plan Period	Subject Matter: Same Objective: Students are to read pp. 69-70 independently and should be prepared to state orally how bees aid the farmer by pollinating many crops. Procedure: Mount pictures of fruits and vegetables which would die if not fertilized by the bees.	MATH TEXT Eicholz, Robert E., and O'Daffer, Phares G.: Elementary School Mathematics. Palo Alto, Addison-Wesley, 1964. (Grade 3)
Thursday	Subject Matter: Earth's Surface, p. 86-87 text. Objective: Students should be able to summarize what has been read and discussed as to how the earth and a ball are alike and different. Vocabulary: see above Procedure: Follow guided questions on p. 82 manual.	Subject Matter: Art Teacher: Mrs. Anna Mead Time: 2:15 - 3:00	SCIENCE TEXT Marshall, Stanley J.; Challand, Helen J., and Beauchamp, Wilbur L.: Science is Exploring. Dallas, Scott F., 1968. (Grade 3)
Friday	Subject Matter: Maps p. 88 Objective: After sufficient practice, students should be able to locate large bodies of water on a wall map or globe. Vocabulary: globe, the Great Lakes, the Atlantic and Pacific Oceans, etc. Procedure: Follow guide in manual on . 83-84	Subject Matter: Same Objective: A selected group of students shall dramatize the story of bees making honey. Vocabulary: liquid Procedure: Assign the part of Tom and another of Grandfather. Select two narrators for 69-70	SOCIAL STUDIES TEXT McIntire, Alta, and Hill, Wilhelmina: Working Together, new revised ed. Chicago, Follet, 1965. (Grade 3)

The basic elements of the lesson plan can be
ended and organized in different ways to fit the
ject area, the achievement level of students, the
ference of teacher and objective of lesson. Some
chers need only a summary to refer to, others feel
e comfortable with a more elaborate lesson plan to
low. Lesson Plan, Format Two is of the latter type.
suggests ways of organizing content for the most
ective presentation. You will notice that this
nat includes a section on evaluation and references.

DEVELOPMENT OF LESSON PLAN
FORMAT TWO

SUBJECT _____
GRADE _____
TEACHER _____
TIME _____

SUBJECT OF LESSON: General Subject area to be
covered, an overview.

OBJECTIVE: (specific)   Specific details of subject
should be in terms of what
the student is expected to
learn or do.

TRAINING AIDS AND   List all aids, blackboard,
PRINTED MATERIAL: motion pictures, slidefilm,
diagrams, mock-ups, equipment,
etc., as well as printed
material, to be used in
teaching this lesson. Listing
these items is like tying a
string around your finger to
remember.

REVIEW LAST LESSON: Review major points of last
lesson and refresh memories
for instruction of present
lesson.

PRESENTATION: Depending on grade level, list
all subject matter points in
order of presentation.

Use outline or more complete
style as you require for your
own use.

The effectiveness of your
presentation depends on what
you present to the student.
The more concretely you have
defined just what your objective for the lesson is, the
easier it is to collect the
right material to achieve it.

Arranging your information to
strike home with the proper
emphasis is at the core of
good instruction.

Phrase your points in language
that is clear and concrete to
the students. Plan to deliver
your points in terms they
understand.

Keep in mind your students'
experience level of developmental background, and the
atmosphere of the class.

Use repetition as a learning
tool. Summarize as you go.
Repeat key ideas in different
words or from different points
of view, intersperse with
questions.

Use a change of pace. Indicate
methods of PRESENTATION:
lecture, demonstration activities, group discussion,
blackboard sketch, etc., that
you will use in presenting various points. Change of pace
increases the student's interest
and involvement. Vary the
activities and methods.

Use Audio-Visual aids. In
explaining complex ideas, or
to create and hold interest,
or to provide a means for
increasing "rememberability,"
consider use of visual aids.
Films, slides, overlays,
charts, etc., can help the
group see the ideas more
clearly.

Use questions: Write down all
questions you will ask to get
students participation and to
check on learning--at the
points in your presentation
where you will ask them.

Make a large "Q" opposite each
question to indicate it clearly.

Key points of the lesson can
be listed in question form.
Questions will secure student
participation and serve as a
check on how well the objectives
have been reached.

EVALUATION:

At the sixth grade or higher
level a quiz of not more than
5 or 10 minutes can be used
to reinforce the information.

REFERENCES:

List on board for students
references, books, and materials
in which they can find additional
information.

ASSIGNMENT:

Include what, how, when, and
why for every assignment that
is made. Be sure all students
understand.

PREVIEW:

Tell what is coming up at the
next lesson; make it interesting.
Be enthusiastic.

The organization of the lesson plan and the material included will vary according to the class and the teacher. But a plan including items similar to the one above should always be worked out on paper before hand.

Following is the Sample Lesson Plan for Format Two.

SUBJECT: CLOTHING CONSTRUCTION: BODY MEASUREMENT
GRADE: 10th
TEACHER: A. Doines
TIME: 1:00 - 2:15

SUBJECT OF A LESSON: The purpose of this lesson is to acquaint the student with the basic techniques of clothing construction; and introduction to measuring, pattern sizes and figure types.

OBJECTIVES:
1. To understand the facts about measurements to determine pattern sizes and figure types.
2. To gain skill in using the tape measure
3. To discover individual pattern sizes and figure types

INSTRUCTIONAL
MATERIALS AND AIDS:
1. Tape measure
2. Silhouette chart
3. Simplicity Pattern Books

383

PRESENTATION:
1. Illustrate basic principles of designing a dress.
2. Demonstrate some basic
   techniques of designing
   for figure types and
   problems.
3. Have students select and
   match patterns by size
   and figure type.
4. Have students prepare,
   lay and pin easy-to-make
   patterns.
5. Using a tape, have students
   measure different figures
   and cut paper patterns.
6. Show students how to lay
   patterns on fabrics that
   require matching vertically
   and horizontally.
7. Summarize lesson - empha-
   sizing the following points
   a. Selection and matching
      of patterns
   b. Preparation, laying
      and pinning patterns
   c. Use of tape measurements
   d. Laying patterns on
      fabrics

EVALUATION:
Have students review the steps
of pattern making.

Discuss the principles of and
problems of dress designing.

FERENCES: Simon, Natasha *Sew It Today,*
Wear It Tonight. New York:
Bantam, 1975.

Sommer, Joellen, and Sommer,
Elyse. *Sew Your Own Accessories*.
New York: Archway, 1973.

SIGNMENT: Have students make a pattern
for a skirt for themselves to
be completed in three days.

EVIEW: Tell them that each student
will be evaluating the skirt
patterns of every other student.
In the following lessons that
pattern will be laid on fabric
and a skirt constructed.

The reader has examined two different formats and samples of a lesson plan. Each is an approach to a systematic preparation which a teacher makes prior to teaching. It incorporates not only the concepts and subject matter to be taught, but also the activities and materials which enhance and give meaning to the lesson.

Now that the reader is familiar with the basic elements of the lesson plan, it would be appropriate to introduce and review some of the finer points of implementing the lesson.

IMPLEMENTATION OF LESSON PLANNING

Other suggestions could be added in terms of implementation. Procedures of the lesson plan should meet individual needs. Following are suggestions developed by the student teaching personnel of Chicago State University.

Perhaps one of the most important aspects of planning a lesson is the preservation of continuity and review. As indicated, the lesson plan is a segment of a teaching or experience unit. The sequential daily lessons should reflect the unit plan. This can be achieved by means of "cyclical teaching," which includes the review of yesterday's lesson, and introduction of new, but related materials, summarization of the lesson, evaluation and review.

PLANNING A LESSON IN TERMS OF A TEACHING CYCLE[7]

Review of Yesterday's Lesson
.Plan five minute review.
.Clarify questions pertaining to last lesson.

Introduce Today's Lesson
.Plan for demonstration - do not hurry.
.Consider use of visual materials.
.For mathematics - use problem solving techniques.
.For social studies, give a brief talk about the topic
 or unit of learning to build background and interest.

Summarize the Lesson
.Stress central ideas -- cause and effect relationship --
 note supporting detail.

Sample Class Before Drill
.Sample to determine how much learning has taken place.
.Sample bright students first, followed by average
 and then question the slow learners.
.Re-teach if you find that the class has not learned
 the main concepts. Be patient and helpful to your
 students. Insight to a new idea is, psychologically
 speaking, a slow process.

Drill and Guide
.Spend much time on drill.
.The purpose of drill is to secure mastery.
.Circulate among students and observe work.
.Aid those who are found to have difficulty.

---

[7]Used with the permission of the student teaching
personnel, Chicago State University.

387

Evaluate Learning Product

...Classroom discussion

...Informal oral testing - short quizzes

...Formal testing. Study mistakes--then re-teach.

Make an Assignment for Tomorrow

...If a lesson involves reading (other than problems
   in mathematics) instruct the students to read the
   assigned lesson twice. Make an outline.

Write Summary in Own Words

...Explain importance of assignment.

...Do not make it too long.

...Instruct students to check their problems.

...Insist on orderly, clean, complete, and well organized
   papers.

DO'S OF GOOD LESSON PLANNING[8]

(1) Plan lesson at least two days in advance.
(2) Set reasons for a particular lesson.
(3) Organize a small "workshop" for slow learners - usually in front seats and help them in their learning problems.
(4) Provide differentiated materials for learning; one book for all will not suffice. Use charts, graphs, globes, maps, pictures, etc. Vary your presentation and method.
(5) Be sure that in lesson presentation you <u>create</u> enthusiasm for the lesson. That's the heart of all instruction.
(6) Whenever possible - show <u>differences</u> and <u>similarities</u> in developing a concept in a lesson - This reinforces perception.
(7) Require organized notebooks from students (grade level permitting). This is <u>organized knowledge</u>. It is good reinforcement.
(8) Re-teach your class if test data reveals that too many students failed in one or two problems or failed to secure the central ideas. <u>Students</u> should never be permitted to continue making the same mistake. <u>That's a sign of poor teaching</u>. "Nip mistakes in the bud."
(9) Never throw away test papers. Mark and grade all test papers and return them to students with appropriate suggestions for improvements. Follow up on this.

---

[8]Used with the kind permission of the student teaching personnel, Chicago State University.

(10) Re-evaluate your teaching to <u>test effect on the</u> learner.

DON'TS OF LESSON PLANNING[9]

(1) Indifference to lesson planning.
(2) Forgetting to review yesterday's lesson.
(3) Rapid presentation to today's lesson.
(4) Assuming that all had been learned because we taught the lesson once.
(5) Hurrying to drill - nothing can be mastered by drill unless something is learned before.
(6) Forgetting to guide slow learners.
(7) Becoming satisfied because students memorized a lesson - <u>Stress understanding</u>.
(8) Setting objectives too broadly.
(9) Assignment forms as: Take ten pages for tomorrow."
(10) Work the next 10 problems.
(11) Sending the entire class to the blackboard to work problems the entire period.

Let us examine another lesson plan format. Lesson Plan, Format Three is quite elaborate in that it includes a listing of different methods and approaches and a set of guidelines for timing and pacing. It could easily be used as a weekly lesson plan.

---

[9]Used with the kind permission of the student teaching personnel, Chicago State University.

390

DEVELOPMENT OF LESSON PLAN
FORMAT THREE

OBJECTIVES: Statements should be made from the
               standpoint of expected outcomes. They
               should be expressed in terms of student
               behavior and expected outcomes. (See
               Chapter II for examples of specific
               objectives.)

MATERIALS: What materials will help me to achieve
               my teaching purposes?

               Which materials will I select for my
               preparation and use?

               Which materials will I select for my
               students?

               Suggestions:
               Film, study guides, equipment, charts,
               text, tests, etc. (Give titles of films
               and/or filmstrips.)

METHODS: What techniques seem suitable for using
               these materials to achieve my purposes?

               Procedures:
               Not every lesson will make use of all
               the procedures listed below and not
               every procedure for teaching is listed.

391

The listed techniques are representative
for a typical class. On occasion,
several may be used in all single
lessons.

Lecture Presentation:
Consider major steps in the development
or the listing of ideas and materials,
including some detail.

Discussion: Teacher Directed
Overview of lesson
Key questions

Grasshopper Approach: Pupil Directed
Enhance student interest and list
responses and questions on the subject
or a branching subject area. (Works very
well with poorly motivated or slow
learners.) It generates class participation. May be difficult to keep class
discussion on the topic.

Committee Work Approach:
Preparation for selection of committee,
definition of problems, work plans.

Laboratory: (or directed study period)
Provision of time for students to
practice newly acquired skills or to
discuss ideas presented.

<u>Discovery Approach</u>:
This approach can be used in areas of:
science, social studies and mathematics.
To increase pupil's interest by decreasing :
generalizations or relating through an
inductive approach. For example,
students watch a radiometer revolving
and ask questions as to what makes it
turn. The student is led to find things
out for himself, discover principles,
relations, and similarities.

<u>Problem Solving or Inquiry Approach</u>:
This approach is wide open. The learner
gathers the data, analyzes and experiments
with it. For example, a bimetal object
that bends in only one direction when
heated involves the student in the
whole process of problem solving through
data gathering, analysis and experimentation. The learning process is under
the control of the learner.

<u>Audio-Visual Presentation</u>:
Principal method of presentation involves
the use of audio-visual material. In the
use of films, steps in preparation of
the class participation, and follow-up
should be employed. This applies to
group and individual use of audio-visual
aids.

<u>Eclectic Activities</u>
See the section on activities in Chapter II.

Any of the above approaches can also be reviewed in the activity section.

Use of Time:
An approximate statement of time (in minutes) should be given in the left margin of the lesson plan for each part of the period.

Getting Work Started:
(a) Relate activities to the past and/or future.
(b) Show the "why" of the activity to students if not apparent to them and get them involved in the development of the activity.
(c) Provide for routine matters, as attendance checks so as not to interfere with opening learning activity.
(d) Make announcements.
(e) Note physical arrangements of the room.

Changing Pace:
How will I change pace from one activity to another without confusion and disorder?

How will I decide on-the-spot when the time is ripe for such changes?

ASSIGNMENT: Provision for time (time allotment and statement on when, during the lesson, the assignment will be made,) content and application.

List of Key Points as Follows:

What: (A statement of subject material
        followed by page numbers.) Write
        statement and pages on board for
        clarity and reinforcement.

Why: (A statement of the relations of
        the assignment to the expected
        outcomes of the lesson being
        studied; or, a statement of a
        motivational nature leading into
        new material.)

How: (Principal points of difficulty.)

When: (The specific time the assignment
        is due.)

EVALUATION:
EXPECTED
STUDENT
OUTCOMES
List day activities or procedures that
provide a daily checkup on the learning
during a class period. These may be
already included in the procedures listed
but should be restated in brief form as
a reminder on how learning outcomes will
be evaluated. For example:
(a) Evaluate written work and projects.
(b) Circulate in room giving attention
    to individual students.
(c) Ask question and discuss lesson.
(The statement given above will enable
the teacher to answer authoritatively
the question: "How do you check to see
if your teaching is effective--other than
a test at the end of the unit?")

Evaluate Teaching Outcomes:

This portion of the prepared lesson
plan should be left blank, of course,
to be filled in as soon as possible
after the lesson is taught. This post-
lesson analysis should be written in--
not typed--and should contain comments on:

A. Desired modifications, if any, for
   further planning.
B. Impressions on why the lesson was
   very good (or bad).
C. Comments, if any, of reactions of
   students to lesson and cooperating
   teacher.
D. Other, e.g. timing and length of
   lesson.

Special Items:

What will I do with a few minutes of
extra time if we finish our work before
the end of the period? If some students
finish the test before others?

Routine Matters:

Have I provided for them?

Discipline:

What positive forms of behavior control
can I employ?

Further Considerations:

What test or other form of evaluation,
should I use to check on what has been
taught?

Lesson Plan, Format Three is a broad and comprehensive plan. It provides suggestions for the implementation of almost all aspects of planning a lesson. Following is a sample lesson plan of Format Three entitled, "Plants and How They Grow."

SAMPLE LESSON PLAN
FORMAT THREE
PLANTS AND HOW THEY GROW

OBJECTIVES: 1. Students will review on the blackboard yesterday's material on roots
through discussion.

2. Students will review pictures of
roots we eat which was yesterday's
assignment.

3. Students will measure water on bottle
from yesterday's experiment.

4. Students will be able to test and
see that a root anchors a plant in
the ground or soil.

5. Students will plant a radish seed
(radish is a root).

6. Students will discuss ways of
measuring growth of radish seed.

MATERIALS: 1. Teacher materials: Reference book -
Plants and How They Grow - blackboard,
chalk.

2. Materials for pupil use: blackboard,
chalk, plants, soil, seeds, water,

                    tape, ruler and reference material
                    that could be found in the school
                    library.

METHODS: Discussion
                    Teacher will lead children in a general
                    discussion of what was discovered the
                    day before such as: roots have different
                    sizes and shapes, they contain root hairs;
                    root hairs absorb moisture and minerals;
                    and roots which we eat in our diet.

                    Presentation:
                    Students will show class yesterday's
                    assignment on roots we eat. This will
                    lead into today's lesson which is a
                    continuation of the study of roots.

                    Other Activities:
                    Approximately 5 students in a group
                    will have a plant and will try to pull
                    the plant out of the soil - this
                    showing that the roots are really an
                    anchor.

                    Each child will plant a few radish seeds
                    (radish is a root we eat).

                    Children will discuss ways of measuring
                    the growth of the radish. How soon
                    before it can be picked to eat?

                    Pace of Time: 40 minutes
                    5 min.   Discuss previous day's lesson.

                              399

8 min.	Show pictures to class on yesterday's homework assignment.	
8 min.	Prove that roots anchor a plant.	
15 min.	Plant radish seeds.	
4 min.	Discuss how they will measure plant growth.	

Changing Pace:

One activity at a time will be covered and the next activity will be undertaken when the previous one is understood. If lesson takes a longer time it may be necessary to postpone some activities. Each activity must be understood before the next one is begun.

ASSIGNMENT: At end of the lesson the teacher will tell students:

What: Prepare a graph onto which you will record the growth of the radish seed.

Why: So we can learn how to plot a graph and by doing so see how much a seed will grow in a day.

How: We will measure growth in inches and we will record this daily. You may prepare a bar or line graph.

When: Assignment will be started in

class and will be completed at home. It should be ready within the next 2 days.

Student Outcomes:
Teacher will check on students' understanding of material covered the day before through observation.

Teacher will have groups gather around students who are pulling the plant out of the soil and will observe if the students understand why this is being done.

Teacher will walk about room checking on the planting of the radish seeds.

Teacher will check to see if students understand ways the growth of the seeds can be measured.

Teaching Outcomes: To be answered after lesson is taught.

Were students interested in the lesson?

Did they enjoy the planting of the seeds?

Did students appear to understand the concepts of the lesson?

Were students able to draw inferences from the lesson?

401

The motto of lesson plan construction should be "let the lesson plan fit the situation." Some learning situations call for an elaborate and highly detailed lesson plan. Other situations call for a concise lesson plan. It depends on the experience and teaching style of the teacher, the length of the lesson and the grade level of the subject matter and the students.

Lesson Plan, Format Four is an example of a brief, but comprehensive lesson plan.

DEVELOPMENT OF LESSON PLAN
FORMAT FOUR

GENERAL OBJECTIVE: This is what the teacher is going
to do. The general objective
justifies the specific aim and gives
continuity to the unit.

SPECIFIC OBJECTIVE: This is what the teacher is going
to do and what the students are
going to learn or accomplish.

CONTENT: This is the material the teacher
will teach and/or the learner is
expected to learn. This could be
outlined on the board (e.g. science
concepts, arithmetic problems,
historical events, etc.) or on a
mimeographed sheet distributed to
the students.

PROCEDURE: A. Motivation:
This is what the teacher and/or
the students are going to do.
This will include all or some
initiatory developmental, and
culminating activities. This
involves introducing the lesson,
motivation, creating or developing
a need for the lesson and setting
the learning mileau. A good

method of doing this is through discussion of leading questions.

B. Development of leading questions: (List the major questions in sequence of use that will promote discussion and interest by which to clarify the responses.)

C. Activities: Follow up discussion with pupil involvement.

EVALUATION: This could include evaluative questions (orally or written in terms of a brief quiz) covering the major points.

MATERIALS: Commercially, teacher and/or pupil-made equipment and materials.

ASSIGNMENT: This is to facilitate continuity and reinforcement and to be integrated with the following day's assignment.

COMMENTS ON LESSON PLAN
FORMAT FOUR

Lesson Plan, Format Four uses an inquiry approach, which involves the formulation of initiating questions by the teacher. This plan, like other lesson plan formats, should be carefully planned and the questions well organized. It is helpful in planning if the teacher would pose the following questions for herself:

1. What is the purpose of the lesson?
2. What statement or questions am I going to use to open the class session?
3. What are the various possible responses I can expect?
4. How will I deal with each of the responses?
5. Which responses should I emphasize?
6. Where will the questions/or responses lead the discussion?
7. At what point in the lesson should I terminate the discussion?
8. How can I bridge the gap from one phase of the lesson to the next?
9. What will I do if the materials are not present or do not work?
10. At what point shall I end the lesson and assign homework?
11. Will I have reached the point from which I can go on tomorrow's lesson?

Following is an example of Lesson Plan, Format Four entitled "Working With Levers" developed from the teaching unit, "Simple Machines Make Our Work Easier." The unit was developed for the second grade.

SAMPLE LESSON PLAN
FORMAT FOUR
WORKING WITH LEVERS

GENERAL AIM: To know that the lever is a simple
                machine that can be used to lift
                and pry.

SPECIFIC AIM: To identify the fulcrum as the
                balancing point of two levers.

CONTENT: Use demonstration, individual and
                group experiments with various types
                of levers. Have each child work
                with each example of the lever to
                insure his understanding that levers
                are used to lift and pry and that
                every lever must have a fulcrum upon
                which the whole lever is balanced.
                Types of levers to be used include:
                crowbar, pliers, screwdriver, seesaw,
                small boulder and plank, automobile
                jack, hammer, shovel, and broom.

PROCEDURE: A. Motivation:
                    1. Have children recite and act
                        out up and down motions from
                        poem: "On A Seesaw."
                    2. Explain that a seesaw is a
                        lever.

406

3. Ask class what would happen if there was no pipe under the middle part of the seesaw board. Explain that the pipe is called the fulcrum.

4. Add the words lever and fulcrum to the vocabulary list.

5. Have science "brain-teaser" - ask children to find at least two levers on their body (mouth, arm, leg).

B. Leading Questions

1. What do you think makes the seesaw go up and down?

2. What would happen to the two children on the seesaw if the pipe was not right in the middle of the board? Would the children be able to go up or down?

3. What would happen to the two children on the seesaw if there was no pipe under the board?

4. Would your father be able to lift up the car and change a flat tire if his jack had no stand?

5. The pipe on the seesaw and on the car jack is called a fulcrum. Can you find the fulcrum on the pliers, the hammer?

        6. Can you find the fulcrum on
            the shovel, broom, and
            crowbar?
    C. Activities
        1. Have class make a lever and
            fulcrum with a pencil and
            their finger and try to lift
            up a book on their desk.
        2. Divide the children into
            small groups. Let each child
            try to pry the lid off the
            top of an empty paint can
            using their fingers, then
            with a screw driver or can
            opener.
            a. Discuss which method was
                easier.
            b. Stress that the screw
                driver and a can opener
                are two kinds of levers
                that can be used to lift
                and pry.
        3. Have children lift a heavy
            box one inch off the floor
            with their hands and then
            with a crowbar. Ask how they
            think a lever can make our
            work easier.

MATERIALS: See saw   Screw driver
                Carjack   Several empty paint cans
                Pliers   Two or three medium size
                             boxes
                Crowbar   Hammer and nails
                Can opener   Pipe, plank, small boulder

IGNMENT: Have class look through magazines
                    and cut out pictures of different
                    types of levers. Have them draw
                    a picture of one member of their
                    family using a lever.

LUATION: Have the children demonstrate each
                    of the levers in the covered lesson.
                    Have children draw the different
                    types of levers and color them.
                    Draw pictures of the levers on
                    large flash cards and have the
                    children name them.

The following Lesson Plan, Format Five is a
riation of Format Four. It is more general and can
used to fit most of the methods of teaching and
ibject areas.

DEVELOPMENT OF LESSON PLAN
FORMAT FIVE*

Identifying data to appear on each daily lesson plan:

Name of Student teacher
Title of Unit
Subject and Grade
Unit Plan Number _____   Daily lesson plan number ____

Suggested Daily Lesson Plan Outline

I.   OBJECTIVES: (These should implement the unit
                    objectives.)

     What teacher and pupils hope to accomplish in the
     class period.
     One achievement objective
     One pupil-personality objective

II. SUBJECT MATTER
     Brief statements or listing of content

III. PROCEDURES
     A. Introduction
         Arousing interest, reviewing, pre-testing,
         teacher-pupil planning.
     B. Work period (activities of children and teacher)
         Suggested types of activities:
             Presenting and explaining new material
             Conducting class discussions

---

*Reprinted with permission of student teaching personnel,
Chicago State University.

Lesson Plan, Format Five presents a slightly
different format. The procedure section includes
introduction (initiatory activities) and work period
(development activities).

Following is the sample Lesson Plan, Format Five
entitled, "Southern States."

SAMPLE LESSON PLAN
FORMAT FIVE
SOUTHERN STATES

I. OBJECTIVES
   A. To gain knowledge of the settlement of the Southern States and the states which comprise this region.
   B. To develop social effectiveness through an understanding and appreciation of individual and cultural differences and similarities.

II. SUBJECT MATTER
   A. The names of the states comprising this region.
   B. Historical points of interest.
   C. The settlement of the Southern States.

III. PROCEDURES
   A. <u>Introduction</u>
      1. Review briefly the previous lesson on major rivers in the Southern States.
      2. Prepare for the reading by discussing:
         a. The names of the states comprising this region.
         b. The historical points of interest.
         c. The early settlement of the Southern States.
   B. <u>Work Period Activities</u>
      1. Read pages 192 through 194 of the text on the settlement and names of the Southern States
      2. Discuss the reading by asking questions and having the pupils verify their answers by reading pertinent content material.

C. Concluding Activities

    1. Have the pupils list the names of the Southern States in alphabetical order. (To help the pupils become familiar with the names and spelling of these states have them write a sentence indicating the states each of them border.)

    2. Ask for volunteers to make oral reports on the settlement and famous historical events which occurred in this region.

IV. EVALUATION

A. Did the pupils understand how the conditions of the early settlements caused the development of so many institutions which still exist today in the Southern States?

B. Were the pupils interested enough to volunteer for the oral reports?

C. Do the pupils now understand how we study the geographical aspects of a region?

V. INSTRUCTIONAL MATERIALS

A. Textbook: *Your Country and Mine*.

B. Map of the United States

C. Blackboard and chalk

Another variation of a lesson plan format that is quite useful is the mid-summary form. Lesson Plan, Format Six allows for a mid-lesson summary. It can readily be used as a transition-type lesson plan in which two different subject areas or major points are being taught, or as a transition between previously taught content and the introduction of new content.

DEVELOPMENT OF LESSON PLAN
FORMAT SIX

MOTIVATION: Write down the specific objective
                       of the lesson and how you are going
                       to interest the students in the
                       lesson. This section would be
                       similar to the introductory
                       activities in the lesson plan. A
                       number of approaches, materials,
                       and media can be used.

AIMS: State the specific purpose of the
                       lesson, developed from the motiva-
                       tion section. Indicate how you are
                       going to convey the objective(s)
                       of the lesson to the pupils. Your
                       aims must be definite and clear. It
                       could be in the form of statement,
                       question or problems.

FIRST DEVELOPMENT: The development of the lesson
                       should be relevant to the background
                       and experiences of your pupils. The
                       more concrete the planned experiences
                       and activities the more relevant it
                       will be to the pupils. This section
                       is similar to the developmental
                       activities in the teaching unit. The
                       subject matter should be logically
                       sequenced and the sequence of the

activities should reflect this logic. The activities should be varied and rich, providing meaningful learning experiences for all levels of academic achievement and maturation.

MIDSUMMARY: The midsummary has several purposes:
1. It unifies the divisions in a lesson.
2. It provides continuity between several subject areas.
3. It reviews the essential points of the first half of the lesson.

By questioning (oral or written) the teacher has an evaluation of pupils' understanding which could lead to a teacher test-reteach sequence of reinforcement of the lesson.

SECOND DEVELOPMENT: This section could be a review on the introduction of new but related material and content. It's better to have too much prepared material than not enough. This is somewhat like beginning a new lesson, except the subject matter is the same as or similar to that which was covered in the first half of the lesson. This section is similar to the initiatory and developmental activity section of the unit.

FINAL SUMMARY: This is a summary of the entire
                        lesson. Method of evaluation can
                        vary according to the grade level
                        of students and the subject area.
                        This includes reinforcement as well
                        as evaluation in which audio-visual
                        aids, illustrative materials, reports
                        and questions by students and teacher
                        summary of major points can be
                        employed. This section is similar
                        to the culmination and evaluation
                        section of the unit.

ASSIGNMENT AND   Explain what the lesson will be
HOMEWORK: about for the following day. Write
                        the assignment on the board or
                        distribute ditto sheets outlining
                        the homework. Be sure that you
                        explain the assignment fully with
                        sufficient guidance. Motivate the
                        student to do the assignment by
                        illustrating its importance, how
                        it ties into the lesson and giving
                        reasons for the homework. Be sure
                        you take enough time to explain the
                        assignment thoroughly. [10]

---

[10]Adopted version of lesson plan from: Melvin Keene,
Beginning Secondary School Teacher's Guide. New York:
Harper & Row, 1969, pp. 41-42. Reprinted by permission of
Harper & Row, Publishers, Inc.

Lesson Plan, Format Six is very useful for extra
g or double periods that may cover one and a half to
hours. The midsummary or mid review period breaks
the extended lesson. The midsummary can be used in
or more places in the lesson, depending upon the
dents, content, etc.

Following is an example of a daily lesson plan on
mple Machines," using Format Six.

SAMPLE LESSON PLAN
FORMAT SIX

MOTIVATION: 1. Show film - <u>How Simple Machines
                    Make Our Work Easier</u>.
                 2. Initiate discussion about various
                    kinds of machinery used by
                    fathers at work or at home.
                    Have children look through class-
                    room display or various machines
                    and see if the children can pick
                    out and identify those objects
                    that they think their fathers
                    might use.
                 3. Continue above discussion by
                    having class look through the
                    display to pick out those objects
                    their mothers use at home.
                 4. Have children discuss and pick
                    out objects in the display or
                    elsewhere in the classroom that
                    they use.
                 5. Tell children scientific meaning
                    of "work." Explain that when an
                    object is moved, "work" is done.
                 6. Then have children tell the class
                    how work is done with machines
                    they picked out from the display.
                 7. Tell the class that we will be
                    using all sorts of machines to
                    do "work" - tell them to closely

observe themselves and their
parents from now on to see what
kind of machines they used and
how the machines make their
"work" easier.

AIMS: To introduce the children to the
                       ideas that there are six simple
                       machines and that machines make our
                       work easier. The children should
                       understand and appreciate the work
                       which machines can be made to do
                       for us.

DEVELOPMENT I: Discuss the types of machines
                       presented in the film. Afterwards
                       have children freely tell the class
                       what machines they have seen and used
                       before, as well as those they have
                       never seen or used before.

                       Show examples of some machines that
                       were in the film. Have children
                       describe them by using verbs like dig,
                       pull, press, crush, slice, roll, mash,
                       etc. If capable, have children act
                       out the machine while using the
                       descriptive words above.

ENDSUMMARY: Review the meaning of "work."
                       Worksheet: Have all types of machines
                       scrambled on a paper. Have children
                       circle the machines they saw in the
                       film.

DEVELOPMENT II:	Pick out examples of each of the six machines that will be studied in this unit. Ask questions: Did you see any of these machines in the film? Do you or your mother and father use any of these six simple machines? Did you know that a straight pin is a simple machine? Did you know that your mouth is an example of a simple machine we call a lever?
	Have each child pick up and examine each of the six simple machines. Discuss the physical features of each machine (weight, color, depth, length, basic construction).
SUMMARY:	Let volunteers come to the front of the class and demonstrate the use of each machine. As each is demonstrated, ask the class if they think the machine is best for lifting, prying or holding things together. Explain that all the children will have an opportunity to work with each of the machines as we work each one individually.
ASSIGNMENT:	Have children draw one example of a simple machine presented in the lesson. Have them select one they especially like and write a short story entitled, "If I Were a _____, I _____."

For illustrative purposes, an additional sample
unit of Format Six has been included. This following
sample lesson plan entitled, "Halftone Photography"
was developed out of a secondary level unit on
photography.

SAMPLE LESSON PLAN
FORMAT SIX
HALFTONE PHOTOGRAPHY

MOTIVATION:	Show the students the film <u>Cavalcade of Color</u>. Ask various questions when the film is over. What was it from the film you learned for the first time, and how can this be applied to our class? How does halftone photography differ from line photography?
AIM:	The students should understand the principle behind halftone photography. The students should understand that this principle is so important to the whole idea of offset printing.
DEVELOPMENT (first half)	Discussion of the film. Guide students in the area of the theory involved in halftone work. Ask them the following question. What difference is there in a glossy picture and one that is printed by the offset method? This should cause much thought. Afterwards, ask the following question. Why is there gradation of tone? Demonstrate to

the students how to obtain different density in a halftone.

MIDSUMMARY: Review the main points in the film about halftone work. Make sure students understand this fully. A way of making sure the students really do understand these points is to ask five true and false questions on a short quiz. After the quiz, once again review the questions they had the most trouble with.

DEVELOPMENT: Have each student examine, through (second half) a magnifying glass, a halftone print or negative which was made with a coarse screen. Have them make a sketch of the shape of the dots in the highlight area, the mid-tone area, and the shadow area. Demonstrate to the students the outcome of a halftone, with and without the flash exposure.

SUMMARY: Ask students the following question. (final) How does halftone photography affect your everyday life? Review the principle behind halftone photography once again.

ASSIGNMENT: At the end of the class tell students to go home and write a short paper (100 words or less) on the principle

423

of halftone photography. Tell them
to use the knowledge gained in class
today, as well as any material taken
from their textbook.

Lesson Plan, Format Seven is one that is used in
the Business Department at Chicago State University.[11]
It is a more elaborate plan in that the activities or
techniques section is detailed and expanded.

---

[11]Used with the permission of the Business Department, Chicago State University.

DEVELOPMENT OF LESSON PLAN
FORMAT SEVEN

ACHER: _____ SUBJECT: _____ DATE: _____
TLE OF LESSON: _____
MS: (List specific purposes of the lesson; what you
     expect the students to get out of this lesson.)

_____
_____
_____
_____

IVATION: (List points that will arouse interest and
          create students' desire to learn the lesson.
          Include WHY the lesson is important. HOW
          WHEN, and WHERE students can apply it:
          Illustrative stories, personal experiences,
          etc.)

_____
_____
_____
_____

SENTATION: (List all subject matter points in order
            of presentation. Use outline form.)

            (Write all questions you will ask -- to
            get trainee participation and to check for
            learning to the points in your outline where
            you will ask them.)

425

```
  NEW SUBJECT MATTER              TECHNIQUES
_____        _____
_____        _____
_____        _____
_____        _____
_____        _____
_____        _____
```

SUMMARY: (Write out the key points of the
                    lesson in a short positive statement.
                    After summarizing the lesson, oral
                    questions and written or performance
                    tests are very valuable in making
                    certain that the objectives of the
                    lesson have been attained.)

ASSIGNMENT: (Include WHAT, HOW, WHEN, AND WHY
                    for every assignment. Do not merely
                    give page or chapter numbers.)

TRAINING AIDS: (List all aids - blackboard, motion
                    pictures, film strips, diagrams,
                    mockups, equipment, etc., to be used
                    in teaching this lesson.)

Following are two sample lesson plans using the
format of the Lesson Plan, Format Seven -- "Bookkeeping
& Accounting" and "Simple Machines."

SAMPLE LESSON PLAN
FORMAT SEVEN

Bookkeeping &
TUDENT: _____ SUBJECT: Accounting ___ DATE: 9/23/75
ITLE OF LESSON: Understanding the Trial Balance _____

IMS:

. To know the difference between a debit and credit
  balance.
. To know the difference between an open and closed
  account.
. To understand equality of debit and credit balances
  in the ledger.
. To know how to prepare the ledger accounts for the
  trial balance.
. To know the significance of the trial balance.
. To understand why the trial balance is taken so
  frequently.

OTIVATION:

. What would be wrong if your daily cash deposit total
  did not coincide with your total ledger credit?
. How would you determine where the error is if your
  cash in the bank (per bank statement) after reconcil-
  iation, did not coincide with book value of "cash in
  the bank"?
. What would it imply if a statement sent to a customer
  showed him owing to your company more than he says
  he does -- give one possibility?

427

PRESENTATION:

NEW SUBJECT MATTER	TECHNIQUES
1. Debits & credits	Discussion
2. Debit & credit balances	Chalkboard, using "T" accounts
3. Open & closed accounts	Chalkboard, using "T" accounts
4. Equality of debit and credit balances in the ledger	Discussion and chalkboard usage
5. Preparing the ledger accounts for the trial balance	Discussion with reference to text book
6. Frequency of the trial balance	Discussion and demonstrations
7. Accounting groups in the trial balance	Chalkboard using a Balance Sheet to show grouping

SUMMARY: Review the definition and application
                         of the terms: debit and credit
                         balances and open and closed accounts.
                         Recapitulate the reason for and use
                         of trial balances.

                         Using "T" accounts, taken from text,
                         have students post the journalized
                         entries to the ledger. Collect
                         exercise and discuss it.

ASSIGNMENT: Assign students two "T" account
                         problems from text (pp. 38-40) and
                         ask them to journalize the entries
                         to the ledger. Explain that the
                         assignment is to reinforce the lesson,

to give them additional practice
journalizing entries and will be
discussed in class tomorrow.

TRAINING AIDS: Text: Brock, H. et al. Accounting
                   Basic Principles. 3rd ed. New York:
                   McGraw, 1974.

SAMPLE LESSON PLAN
FORMAT SEVEN

TEACHER:_____ SUBJECT: <u>Simple Machines</u> DATE: <u>1/6/76</u>
TITLE OF LESSON: <u>Pushing, Pulling, and the Wheel</u>

I. AIMS:

A. The student should know that the wheel and axle is a simple machine.

B. The children should understand through demonstration and experimentation that the wheel makes pushing and pulling easier.

C. The children should comprehend that an axle is a rod around which the wheel turns and stays in place.

II. MOTIVATION:

A. Read story, <u>Wonderful Wheels</u> by Feenie Ziner, to the children.

B. Ask children to discuss objects they have used that have wheels.

C. Show pictures of man's early attempts to use the wheel.

D. Discuss how our lives would have to change if we didn't have wheels - imply the importance of the wheel.

E. Have children try to think of ways a wagon or car could move with just four wheels and nothing to keep the wheels together.

430

III. PRESENTATION:

NEW SUBJECT MATTER   TECHNIQUES

A. The wheel is a simple   1. Experiment
   machine that can make   a. Fill box with
   pulling and pushing   books have a child
   easier.   try to push it
                                         across the room
                                         using one hand.
                                         (1) Was it easy?
                                      b. Have 2 or 3 children
                                         lift a heavy box
                                         into a small wooden
                                         wagon. Have the
                                         smallest child in
                                         the class push the
                                         wagon across the
                                         room.
                                         (1) Could Debbie
                                             have moved
                                             the heavy box
                                             without the
                                             wagon?

B. Axle is rod.   1. Experiment
                                      a. Place a few pieces
                                         of different sizes
                                         of dowel rods. Tell
                                         the children that
                                         these are rods.
                                         (1) Are the rods
                                             round and smooth? .
                                         (2) What do you
                                             think we will
                                             use the dowel
                                             rods for?

C. Axle is rod around   1.   Experiment
    which wheels turn   a.   Place dowel rods
    and are kept in place.   under the box.
                                              Have some child
                                              push the box.

(1) What must Tom keep doing to the rods while he pushes the box?

(2) Does it take a long time to keep moving the rods as the box moves?

b. Slip four wooden wheels over the dowel rods. Have the rods turn the wheels.

(1) Do the rods or axle help the wheels turn?

IV. SUMMARY: A. The wheel is a simple machine because it rolls and enables man to move heavy objects easily. The axle, on which the wheel rotates, is a rod. The rod, or axle, keeps the wheels in place. There are generally two wheels on a rod, e.g. automobile; sometimes one wheel on a rod, e.g. a wheelbarrow; sometimes four wheels on an axle, e.g. a large truck, a diesel.

                B.   Have a discussion on what object
has wheels and an axle. Have
children name and list things
in their lives that have wheels.

ASSIGNMENT: Have pupils list objects and bring
in pictures of objects that have
wheels. (A bulletin board will be
constructed from the pictures.) Tell
them to ask their friends, brothers
and sisters, parents, and relatives.
Look in newspapers, comic books,
magazines, and books for ideas and
pictures. Tell them to look at
objects in and around the house and
on T.V. Get suggestions from the
class also. Give them the weekend
to collect the material.

TRAINING AIDS: Large wooden boxes, wagons, dowel
rods, and wheels. (different sizes)
Illustrative pictures depicting
different types and uses of wheels.
The book <u>Wonderful Wheels</u> by
Feenie Ziner.

Format Eight, which follows, is used in the QUEST
(Quality Urban Education for Successful Teaching) Program
at Chicago State University.[12] The format is followed
with a sample unit on Social Studies.

---

[12]Permission to use the lesson plan format was given
by Dr. Lillian Dimitroff, Director of QUEST.

```
DEVELOPMENT OF LESSON PLAN
          FORMAT EIGHT

                    NAME: _____
                    DATE: _____

SUBJECT AND GRADE LEVEL: _____

     Attach work sheet and tests


_____

I.   INSTRUCTIONAL MATERIALS:


_____

II.  BEHAVIORAL OBJECTIVES:


_____

III. MOTIVATION: (describe)              WHEN?


_____

IV.  CONCEPTS AND/OR GENERALIZATIONS: (principles)
     VOCABULARY:                         WHEN?


_____
```

SUBJECT MATTER: VI. PROCEDURES
(Outline or summary)   (include diagrams)
                                A. Introduction:
                                    arousing interest,
                                    overview if you are
                                    starting a unit,
                                    reviewing, pre-
                                    testing, pupil-
                                    teacher planning.
                                B. Work period activities:
                                    1. Presenting and
                                        explaining new
                                        material
                                    2. Demonstrations
                                    3. Conducting class
                                        discussions
                                    4. Study activities
                                        e.g. work sheets
                                    5. Reports
                                    6. Debates
                                    7. Panel discussions
                                    8. Excursions
                                    9. Interviews
                                C. Conclusion:
                                    Summarizing and
                                    relating materials
                                    studied to the work
                                    that follows in the
                                    unit.
                                D. Assignment:
                                    Introduce, explain,
                                    and practice sufficiently
                                    so pupils will understand
                                    what is expected.

435

SAMPLE LESSON PLAN
FORMAT EIGHT

NAME: _____

DATE: __7/21/75__

SUBJECT AND GRADE LEVEL: __Social Studies - Grade 3__

I. INSTRUCTIONAL MATERIALS
   A. <u>Bowars and Barr</u>, pp. 66-70
   B. Diorama of the O'Leary barn and the Chicago community.
   C. Then and Now bulletin board (Chicago in 1871 and Chicago today)

II. BEHAVIORAL OBJECTIVES:
   A. Given instruction on vocabulary and a definite question, pupil can, after reading a passage, state clearly what he has read
   B. Given a clear understanding of responsibility, a committee of four will observe and/or interview occupants of buildings on type of building materials used for one block in each direction from the school building and will report findings to the class

III. MOTIVATION:
   Diorama of the O'Leary barn on DeKoven Street

436

IV. CONCEPTS AND/OR GENERALIZATIONS   VOCABULARY   WHEN?

		VOCABULARY	WHEN?
prairie	Fires are expen-	dawned	Early
grain elevator	sive in life and	overhead	in the
	property	uninvited	period
		kerosene	
		signal	

V. SUBJECT MATTER

A. Starting and spreading of fire

    1. Fire may have been started in O'Leary's barn.

    2. Fire spread

      a. Conditions- unusually hot and dry fall

      b. Wind

      c. Wooden houses and sidewalks

      d. Fire department moved slowly

      e. Loss of life- 250 people

      f. Loss of property

        (1) 100,000 people lost homes

        (2) 20,000 buildings burned to the ground

VI. PROCEDURES

1. Motivation

2. Briefly look at pictures on bulletin board

3. (Concepts and vocabulary will have been written on the chalk board before class.) Pre-teach concepts and vocabulary in context

4. SQ3R technique

5. Teacher starts reading a few paragraphs aloud.

6. Point to vocabulary on board and again define briefly as reading proceeds.

7. Pupils read and briefly state what they have read. Continue vocabulary study as above. Use SQ3R.

8. Silent reading of

(3) Entire center of city was burned

remaining paragraphs. Use same technique.

9. Review: roll call of first row to tell what has been learned about the great Chicago fire.

10. Assignment: (written on board before class)

a. Teacher asks class to read again what they read today to their parents or to an older brother or sister.

b. In class we shall do a short worksheet tomorrow.

c. I'll do an experiment to show whether wood or bricks burn faster. Which do you think will burn first? Be prepared to tell me tomorrow.

```
                                    d.  Start looking
                                        at buildings
                                        in the neigh-
                                        borhood when
                                        you come to
                                        school to see
                                        what you think
                                        they are made of.
                                    e.  One or more
                                        children will
                                        review what the
                                        class is to do
                                        for tomorrow.
```

The following format is a type of summary lesson
plan written in a horizontal pattern. Lesson Plan,
Format Nine is used in the Early Childhood Department
of Chicago State University.[13] It affords the teacher
a brief outline and summary of the lesson in that the
planning is outlined on one page. It can be adopted
to any subject area.

---

[13]Used with the permission of the student teaching
personnel, Chicago State University.

DEVELOPMENT OF LESSON PLAN

FORMAT NINE

NAME: _____ GRADE: _____ TEACHER: _____

DATE: _____ ROOM: _____ SCHOOL: _____

TIME	OBJECTIVES	ACTIVITIES/CONTENT	MATERIALS/REFERENCE	EVALUATION

LESSON: Study of Parallelism GRADE: 10 TEACHER: S. Jones

DATE: 7-28-75 ROOM: 222 SCHOOL: Robert E. Lee High School

TIME	OBJECTIVES	ACTIVITIES/CONTENT	MATERIALS/REFERENCES	EVALUATION
Mon. 10:30– 11:10	1. The student will learn two theorems resulting from the study of parallelism. 2. The student will be able to prove one of the two theorems involving parallelism.	CONTENT: Theorem 1: The sum of the interior angles of a triangle is $180°$. Theorem 2: Given a right triangle with sides of length a and b and hypotenuse of length c, then $a^2 + b^2 = c^2$. (Pythagorean Theorem.) ACTIVITIES: 1. Prove Theorem 2 for the class using President Garfield's proof. 2. Ask students to try to find another configuration similar to Garfield's with	MATERIALS Chalkboard, picture of President Garfield, chalk, ruler. REFERENCES Johnson, D.A., and Green, W.H. The Pythagorean Theorem. St. Louis: Webster Publishing Co., 1960. Ballard, William R. Geometry. Phila-delphia: W. B. Saunders, 1970.	1. Students put their versions of proofs into notebooks. 2. References are recommended for the students who need or wish further ideas regarding the two theorems. 3. Select several students to demonstrate the proofs on the blackboard.

which they can prove
Theorem 2.

3. Draw the figure
used to prove
Theorem 1.

4. Class suggests steps
in the proof of Theorem 1.

Figure Theorem 1

A   E
_____
B   C   BC

Given AE and ABC, show
$m(\angle A) + m(\angle B) + m(\angle C) = 180°$

Figure Theorem 2 (Garfield)

Proof

Area =

$\frac{1}{2}(a+b)(a+b) = \frac{1}{2}ab + \frac{1}{2}c^2 + \frac{1}{2}ab$

$a^2 + 2ab + b^2 = 2ab + c^2$

$a^2 + b^2 = c^2$

FORMAT NINE

LESSON: Photography
DATE: 7-28-75

GRADE: 12th
ROOM: 217

TEACHER: Stephen C. Wilson
SCHOOL: Mayer High School

TIME	OBJECTIVES	ACTIVITIES/CONTENT	MATERIALS/REFERENCE	EVALUATION
Mon. 11:00- 11:45	General: The students must learn how to mix the solutions for developing film. Specific: Given a list of instructions, the students will mix all four solutions properly for film developing. Specific: At the conclusion of the lesson each student will demonstrate to the teacher that he	1. The teacher will demonstrate how to mix the solutions properly. 2. He will do this one at a time-devel- oper, stop bath, fixer, and show how to obtain the proper water temperature. 3. Emphasize the temperature control when showing stu- dents. 4. Each student will then show to the teacher how to mix	1. Four trays 2. Developer (Part A & part B) 3. Stop bath 4. Fixer 5. Running water at 68°. 6. Graduates 7. Stirring rods 8. Eastman Kodak reference books	1. Observe students mixing the solutions for developing films. 2. Have sev- eral students explain pro- cedures to others. 3. Ask stu- dents questions on a random basis about the process of solution mixing.

443

these solutions.
5. Make sure the
students are accurate
within 1 degree of
the desired
temperature.

can mix the
solutions properly
and be within 1
degree of the
desired temper-
ature for the
solutions.

Format Ten is a slightly different version of
Format Nine. It includes a section on behavioral outcomes in the three domains -- cognitive, affective,
and psychomotor (concepts, values, and skills).

DEVELOPMENT OF LESSON PLAN

FORMAT TEN

DATE: _____ GRADE: _____ ROOM: _____ TEACHER: _____ SCHOOL: _____

TIME	SUBJECT MATTER BREAKDOWN IN TOPICS	SUGGESTED ACTIVITIES FOR CHILDREN TO perform	EXPECTED OUTCOMES IN CHANGED PUPIL BEHAVIOR			EVALUATION
			CONCEPTS, FACTS OR GENERALIZATIONS TO BE LEARNED	SKILL PERFORMANCES TO BE DEVELOPED	DEVELOPMENTAL VALUES TO BE ACQUIRED	

446

SAMPLE LESSON PLAN

FORMAT TEN

DATE: 10/7/75   GRADE: 3rd   ROOM: 102   TEACHER: Mrs. M. Smith   SCHOOL: Bryant

TIME	SUBJECT MATTER BREAKDOWN IN TOPICS	SUGGESTED ACTIVITIES FOR CHILDREN TO PERFORM	EXPECTED OUTCOMES IN CHANGED PUPIL BEHAVIOR			EVALUATION
			CONCEPTS, FACTS OR GENERALIZATIONS TO BE LEARNED	SKILL PERFORMANCES TO BE DEVELOPED	DEVELOPMENTAL VALUES TO BE ACQUIRED	
Mon. 9:00- 9:55	1. Demonstrate a pulley.	1. Read story by Meyer, Jerome S.: Machines. Cleveland, Ohio, Collins-World, 1972. (Gr 4-6).	1. To be able to recognize a pulley	1. To develop skill in making and naming a pulley	1. To appreciate the contributions and help of others	1. The class enjoyed the movie and were thrilled about going outside to look at the flagpole.
	2. Know the parts of a pulley.	2. Show film Simple Machines: Wheels and Axles.	2. To know what a pulley is used for	2. To develop small motor muscles	2. To understand how to work with other children	
	3. Give and show examples of a pulley.	3. Show model of a pulley. Ask class if they recognize anything about this simple machine. It has a wheel and axle.	3. To know where pulleys can be used	3. To develop skills in drawing and writing	3. To be cooperative in group activities	2. They were able to understand the function of the pulley.
	4. Show how the pulley helps man in his work.	4. Demonstrate how a pulley works.	4. To understand how pulleys help man in his work	4. To be able to demonstrate how a pulley operates	4. To appreciate that the pulley saves man work	
	5. Demonstrate how to make a pulley.	5. Have children look around the room to see if they can find other pulleys in the classroom.				3. They seemed to have some difficulty in understanding that the pulley reverses the direction of the pull.
	MATERIALS	6. Have class look at home for examples of pulleys. Suggest looking at draw drapes and shades.				
	1. Model of a pulley	7. Take children outside to see how the pulley on the flagpole is used to raise and lower the flag.				4. Discussed the activities and construction of pulleys with the children.
	2. String, spools, and pencils.	8. Let each child experiment with the example of the pulley. Ask what happens to the object on one end of the rope when the other side of the rope is pulled down. Let rope slip back up through their fingers and ask what happens to the object.				
	3. Hellman, Hal: Lever and the Pulley. Philadelphia, M. Evans, 1971. (Gr 2-6)	9. Have each child make his own pulley by using a pencil, spool, and a piece of string with a small object at the end.				

447

The foregoing formats and sample lesson plans are examples of how teachers can organize daily curriculum and teaching. They serve three fundamental purposes:

The lesson plan gives the instructional program direction, continuity, and substance: in short it helps keep the teacher prepared and organized. The second purpose is the need for teaching flexibility: An effective teacher adapts the lesson to the students. Keene points out that:

> Different classes, because of varying abilities and interests, cannot maintain the same schedule. The pace of a class would influence your term plan, but after the first month you should revise it completely into a more realistic program.[14]

The third purpose is that of evaluation by supervisors; administrators are using lesson plans as the criteria to measure teacher competence and effectiveness. It is much easier to peruse a stack of lesson plans than to make actual classroom visits. Supervisors vary in their opinion as to which is the best format. Some supervisors favor a certain pattern of lesson plan organization. Others are simply satisfied that the teacher have a lesson plan organized on paper. Perhaps the best rule is to let the lesson plan format fit the needs of the instructional program. On this subject Delany states:

> The thoughts and processes involved in the formulation of the lesson plan may be achieved in several different ways, according to the individual teacher's personality and

---

[14]Keene, Melvin. *Beginning Secondary School Teacher's Guide*. New York: Harper & Row, 1969, p. 41.

experience. As a teacher grows to professional
maturity he should permit increased latitude in
matters pertaining to the formally written
lesson plan. No thinking educator can deny
that there is only one real acid test for a
lesson plan, and that test is the effectiveness
of the plan in developing and facilitating
classroom instruction.[15]

The reader has been taken through the process of
organizing and writing lesson plans. Use of any of the
formats with the associated sample daily lesson plans
the reader should have few problems in developing
own lesson plans. Review Chapter II on the formulation
objectives and activities, and Chapter III and IV for
categorization of activities. Also see Chapter II
additional behavioral verbs needed in the formulation
objectives and activities. Review the bibliography
tion on Lesson Plans for additional references for
son plan writing and reference to sample lesson plans
other subject areas.

[15]Delaney, Arthur A. "Lesson Plans - Means and Ends."
aring House, 36:297, 1962.

APPENDIX

Appendix A:
  Bibliography:
    Books and articles on how to construct Units and
    Lesson Plans

    Free resource materials and teaching aids

Appendix B:
  Typical Course of Study: Kindergarten -- Grade Twelve

BIBLIOGRAPHY

BOOKS ON HOW TO CONSTRUCT UNITS AND LESSON PLANS

Alberty, Harold. _Reorganizing the High-School Curriculum_,
    revised ed. New York: Macmillan, 1953.

Aubrey, Ruth H. (Ed.) _Selected Free Materials for
    Classroom Teachers_. Palo Alto: Fearon, revised
    biannually.

Beck, Walter H., Walter Cook, and Nolan Kearney. _Curric-
    ulum in the Modern Elementary School_, 2nd ed.
    Englewood Cliffs: P-H, 1960, pp. 203-219.

Beauchamp, George A. _Basic Dimensions of Elementary
    Method_. Boston: Allyn, 1959.

Biddick, Mildred L. _The Preparation and Use of Source
    Units_. New York: Progressive Education Associated,
    1940.

Bigge, Morris L. _Learning Theories for Teachers_.
    New York: Har-Row, 1964, p. 366.

Billett, Roy O. _Fundamentals of Secondary-School
    Teaching--With Emphasis on the Unit Method_. Boston:
    Houghton, 1940.

Blair, Glen M. et al. _Educational Psychology_, revised ed.
    New York: Macmillan, 1962.

Bloom, Benjamin S. (Ed.) et al. _Taxonomy of Educational
    Objectives: The Classification of Educational Goals,
    Handbook I: Cognitive Domain_. New York: Longmans,
    Ltd., 1956.

Blough, Glenn O. et al. _Elementary School Science and
    How to Teach It_. New York: Dryden, 1958, pp. 564-591.

Blount, Nathan S., and Herbert J. Kausmeier. _Teaching in the Secondary School_, 3rd ed. New York: Har-Row, 1968.

Bossing, Nelson L. _Teaching in the Secondary Schools_. Boston: Houghton, 1952.

Boston, Robert E. _How to Write and Use Performance Objectives to Individualize Instruction_. Vol. 2. _How to Write Performance Objectives_. Englewood Cliffs: Educ Tech Pubns, 1972.

Brown, James W., Richard B. Lewis, and Fred F. Harcleroad. _AV Instruction: Media and Methods_, 3rd ed. New York: McGraw-Hill, 1969.

Bruner, Jerome S. _The Process of Education_. Cambridge, Mass.: Harvard U Pr, 1960.

Burr, James B., Lowry W. Harding, and Leland Jacobs. _Student Teaching in the Elementary School_, 2nd ed. New York: Appleton, 1958.

Callahan, Sterling. _Successful Teaching in the Secondary Schools_. Chicago: Scott F, 1966.

Carter, William L., Carl W. Hansen, and Margaret G. McKim. _Learning to Teach in the Secondary School_. New York: Macmillan, 1962.

Caswell, Hollis L., and Doak S. Cambell. _Curriculum Development_. New York: Am Bk, 1935.

Caswell, Hollis L., and Arthur W. Foshay. _Education in the Elementary School_. New York: Am Bk, 1957.

Charter, W. W. _Curriculum Construction_. New York: Macmillan, 1923.

Clark, Leonard H., and Irving S. Starr. _Secondary School Teaching Methods_. New York: Macmillan, 1959.

Clements, Millard H., William R. Fiedler, and Robert B. Tabachnik. _Social Study in Elementary School_. Indianapolis: Bobbs-Merrill, 1963.

452

Douglass, Malcolm. *Social Studies in the Elementary School*. Philadelphia: Lippincott, 1967, pp. 600-610.

Dunfee, Maxine, and Helen Sagl. *Social Studies Through Problem Solving*. New York: HR&W, 1966.

Faunce, R. C., and C. Munshaw. *Teaching and Learning in Secondary Schools*. Belmont: Wadsworth Pub, 1964.

Ferster, C. B., and Mary C. Perrott. *Behavioral Principles*. New York: Appleton, 1968.

Fitzgerald, James A., and Patricia G. Fitzgerald. *Methods and Curricula in Elementary Education*. Milwaukee: Bruce Pub Co, 1955, pp. 276-400.

Flannagan, John C., Robert F. Mager, and William M. Shanner. *Language Arts Behavioral Objectives*. *Mathematics Behavioral Objectives*. *Science Behavioral Objectives*. *Social Studies Behavioral Objectives*. California: Westinghouse Learning Press, 1971.

Freedman, F. B., and E. L. Berg. *Classroom Teachers Guide to Audio-Visual Material*. New York: Chilton Co., 1961, pp. 134-209.

Gagne', Robert M. *The Conditions of Learning*. New York: HR&W, 1965.

Gates, Arthur et al. *Educational Psychology*, 3rd ed. New York: Macmillan, 1948.

Glennon, Vincent J. *Teaching Arithmetic in the Modern School*. New York: Syracuse U Pr, 1955.

Gilbaugh, John W. *How to Organize and Teach Units of Work*. Palo Alto: Fearon, 1957.

Goetting, M. L. *Teaching in the Secondary School*. New York: P-H, 1946.

Grambs, Jean D., William J. Iverson, and Franklin K. Patterson. *Modern Methods in Secondary Schools*, revised ed. New York: HR&W, 1958.

Gronlund, Norman E. Measurement and Evaluation in Teaching. New York: Macmillan, 1965.

Gwynn, Minor J. Curriculum Principles and Social Trends, 3rd ed. New York: Macmillan, 1960.

Hafner, Lawrence E., and Jolly B. Hayden. Patterns of Teaching Reading in the Elementary School. New York: Macmillan, 1972, pp. 319-342.

Hanna, Lavone A., Gladys L. Potter, and Neva Hagaman. Unit Teaching in the Elementary School. New York: HR&W, 1955.

Harap, Henry. Social Living in the Curriculum. Nashville: Georgia Peabody College for Teachers, 1952, pp. 25-35.

Herber, H. H. Teaching Reading in Content Areas. Englewood Cliffs: P-H, 1970.

Herbert, John. A System for Analyzing Lessons. New York: Teach Col, 1967.

Herrick, Virgil E. et al. The Elementary School. Englewood Cliffs, P-H, 1956, p. 474.

Hildreth, Gertrude. Child Growth Through Education. New York: Ronald, 1948.

Houston, Robert W., Frank H. Blackington, and Horton C. Southworth. Professional Growth Through Student Teaching. Columbus: Merrill, 1965.

Hurley, B. D. Curriculum for Elementary School Children. New York: Ronald, 1957.

Inlow, G. M. Maturity in High School Teaching. Englewood Cliffs: P-H, 1963.

Jarolimek, John Social Studies in Elementary Education. New York: Macmillan, 1967, p. 464.

Jarvis, Oscar T., and Lutian R. Wootton. The Transitional Elementary School and Its Curriculum. Dubuque: Brown W C, 1966.

Johnson, Earl S. Theory and Practice of the Social Studies. New York: Macmillan, 1956, pp. 201-214.

Jones, Arthur L. _Principles of Unit Construction_.
    New York: McGraw-Hill, 1939.

Kambly, Paul E. and John E. Suttle. _Teaching Elementary
    School Science: Methods and Resources_. New York:
    Ronald, 1963, pp. 125-397.

Karlin, R. K. _Teaching Reading in High School_.
    Indianapolis: Bobbs-Merrill, 1964.

Kenworth, Leonard S. _Introducing Children to the World_.
    New York: Har-Row, pp. 209-264.

Kibler, Robert J., Larry L. Barker, and David T. Miles.
    Behavioral Objectives and Instruction. Boston:
    Allyn, 1971.

Kinder, James S. _Audio-Visual Materials and Techniques_.
    New York: Am Bk, 1959.

Kinder, James S. _Using Audio-Visual Materials in
    Education_. New York: Am Bk, 1965.

Klausmeier, Herbert J. _Principles and Practices of
    Secondary School Teaching_. New York: Har-Row,
    1953, pp. 140-165.

Klausmeier, Herbert J., Katharine Dresden, and Helen C.
    Davis. _Teaching in the Elementary School_. New York:
    Har-Row, 1956.

Klausmeier, Herbert J., and Richard E. Ripple. _Learning
    and Human Abilities_. New York: Har-Row, 1971,
    pp. 117-141.

Krathwohl, David R., Benjamin S. Bloom, and Bertram B.
    Masia. _The Classification of Educational Objectives_.
    Handbook II: Affective Domain. New York: McKay,
    1964.

Lazarus, A., and R. Knudson. _Selected Objectives for the
    English Language Arts: Grades 7-12_. Boston:
    Houghton, 1967.

Leese, Joseph, Kenneth Frasure, and Johnson Mauritz Jr.
    The Teacher in Curriculum Making. New York: Har-Row
    1961.

455

Leonard, Paul J. *Developing the Secondary School Curriculum*. New York: Rinehart, 1953.

Lindvall, C. M. (Ed.) *Defining Educational Objectives*. Pittsburgh: U of Pittsburgh Pr, 1964.

Lueck, William R. et al. *Effective Secondary Education*. Minneapolis: Burgess, 1968, pp. 88-115.

McKean, Robert. *Principles and Methods in Secondary Education*. Columbus: Merrill, 1962.

Macomber, Freeman G. *Principles of Teaching in the Elementary School*. New York: Am Bk, 1954, pp. 44-143.

Mager, Robert R. *Preparing Objectives for Programmed Instruction*. San Francisco: Fearon, 1962.

Mehl, Maria, Hubert H. Mills, and Harl R. Douglas. *Teaching in the Elementary School*. New York: Ronald, 1958, pp. 153-196.

Melvin, Gordon A. *The Activity Program*. New York: John Day, 1936.

Melvin, Gordon A. *General Methods of Teachings*. New York: McGraw-Hill, 1952.

Merritt, Edith P. *Working with Children in Social Studies*. California: Wadsworth Pub, 1961, pp. 77-108.

Michaelis, John U. *Social Studies for Children in a Democracy*. 2nd ed. Englewood Cliffs: P-H, 1960, pp. 129-157.

Michaelis, John U., and Enoch Dumas. *The Student Teacher in the Elementary School*, 2nd ed. Englewood Cliffs: P-H, 1960, pp. 79-116.

Miller, Franklin A. et al. *Planning Student Activities*. Englewood Cliffs: P-H, 1956.

Mills, H. H., and H. R. Douglas. *Teaching in High School*. New York: Ronald, 1957.

Morrison, Henry C. "The Practice of Teaching in the Secondary School," in John DeBoer (Ed.) et al. *Secondary Education - A Testbook of Readings*. Boston: Allyn, 1966, pp. 210-232.

lson, Ira I. "Large Units as a Basis for Course
    Organization," in Harl R. Douglas (Ed.) The High
    School Curriculum. 3rd ed. New York: Ronald, 1964.

rbovig, Marcella H. Unit Planning: A Model for
    Curriculum Development. Worthington, CA: Jones,
    1970.

ar, Gertrude. Freedom to Live and Learn. Philadelphia:
    Franklin Pub, 1948, pp. 159-170.

lsen, Merle M. (Ed.) Modern Methods in Elementary
    Education. New York: HR&W, 1959.

iva, Peter F. The Secondary School Today. Cleveland:
    World Pub, 1967.

iver, Albert I. Curriculum Improvement. New York:
    Dodd, 1965.

to, Henry J. Social Education in the Elementary
    Schools. New York: Rinehart, 1956, pp. 429-434.

to, Henry J., Hazel Floyd, and Margaret Rouse.
    Principles of Elementary Education. revised ed.
    New York: Rinehart, 1955.

rrodin, Alex F. (Ed.) The Student Teacher's Reader:
    A Collection of Readings. Chicago: Rand, 1966.

terson, Dorothy G. The Elementary School Teacher.
    New York: Appleton, 1964, pp. 79-281.

erce, Paul R., and Raymond R. Wallace. The Unit of
    Learning in the Chicago Public Schools. Chicago:
    Board of Education, 1954, pp. 57-60.

wer, Edward J. Education for American Democracy.
    New York: McGraw-Hill, 1958.

unds, Ralph L., and Robert L. Garretson. Principles
    of Modern Education. New York: Macmillan, 1967,
    pp. 175-262.

eston, Ralph C. Teaching Social Studies in the
    Elementary Schools. New York: HR&W, 1958, pp. 75-99.

Quillen, James I., and Lavone A. Hanna. Education for
   Social Competence. 2nd ed. Chicago: Scott F,
   1961, pp. 197-234.
Ragan, William B. Modern Elementary Curriculum. New York:
   Dryden, 1953.
Ragan, William B., John H. Wilson, and Tillman J. Ragan.
   Teaching in the Elementary School. New York:
   HR&W, 1972, pp. 78-81.
Robertson, Wanda. An Evaluation of the Culture Unit
   Method of Social Education. New York: Teach Col,
   1950.
Rucker, Ray W. Curriculum Development in the Elementary
   School. New York: Har-Row, 1960, pp. 62-81.
Sanders, Norris. Classroom Questions, What Kinds?
   New York: Har-Row, 1966.
Saylor, Galen J., and William M. Alexander. Curriculum
   Planning for Better Teaching and Learning. New York:
   HR&W, 1954, pp. 399-425.
Schorling, Raleigh, and Max G. Wingo. Elementary School
   Student Teaching. New York: McGraw-Hill, 1949.
Shankman, Florence V., and Robert Kranyik. How to Teach
   Reference Skills. New York: P-H, 1964.
Skinner, B. F. The Technology of Teaching. New York:
   Appleton, 1968.
Skinner, Charles E. (Ed.) Educational Psychology. 4th
   ed. Englewood Cliffs: P-H, 1959, p. 755.
Smith, Joseph R. Teaching a Unit in Astronomy. New York:
   Vantage, 1958.
Smith, Othanel B., William O. Stanley, and Harlan J.
   Shores. Fundamentals of Curriculum Development.
   New York: Har Brace World, 1950.
Sowards, Wesley G., and Mary-Margaret Scobey. The Changing
   Curriculum and the Elementary Teacher. Belmont:
   Wadsworth Pub, 1968, pp. 357-369.

pears, Harold. *Curriculum Planning Through In-Service Programs*. Englewood Cliffs: P-H, 1957, pp. 59-61.

pears, Harold. *Some Principles of Teaching*. New York: P-H, 1949, pp. 25-52.

teeves, F. L. *Fundamentals of Teaching in Secondary Schools*. New York: Odyssey Pr, 1962.

teeves, F. L. *Readings in the Methods of Education*. New York: Odyssey Pr, 1964.

tendler, Celia B. *Teaching in the Elementary School*. New York: Har Brace World, 1958, pp. 76-97.

aba, Hilda. *Curriculum Development Theory and Practice*. New York: Har-Brace World, pp. 194-210.

anruther, Edgar M. *Clinical Experiences in Teaching for the Student Teacher or Intern*. New York: Dodd, 1967.

herman, Viola. *A Good School Day*. New York: Tech Col, 1950.

hralls, Zoe A. *Methods of Teaching Geography*. New York: Appleton, 1958, pp. 236-254.

iegs, Ernest W., and Frank G. Adams. *Teaching the Social Studies*. New York: Gin, 1959, pp. 485-547.

ooze, Ruth A., and Beatrice P. Krone. *Literature and Music as Resources for Social Studies*. Englewood Cliffs: P-H, 1955, pp. 457-478.

ripato, Elinor M. *How to Build Your Own Unit of Study*. Chicago: Ency Brit Inc, 1949.

ristison, Francis et al. *Instructional Units in Handwoodwork*. Bruce Pub Co, 1955.

row, William Clark. *Educational Psychology*. 2nd ed. Boston: Houghton, 1950, pp. 761-777.

yler, Ralph W. *Basic Principles of Curriculum and Instruction*. Chicago: U of Chicago Pr, 1971.

eatch, J. *Readings in Elementary School*. New York: Ronald, 1966.

Walbesser, Robert. Constructing Behavioral Objectives. College Park: U of Md Lib Serv, 1967.

Whitney, David C. The First Book of Facts and How to Find Them. New York: Watts, 1966.

Wiles, Kimball. Teaching for Better Schools. 2nd ed. New York: P-H, 1959, pp. 120-138.

Wingo, Max G., and R. Schorling. Elementary School Student Teaching. New York: McGraw-Hill, pp. 126-129.

Winslow, Leon L. The Integrated School Art Program. New York: McGraw-Hill, 1949, pp. 209-249.

Woodruff, Asahel. The Psychology of Teaching. New York: Longmans, Ltd, 1951.

Wrightstone, J. W. Appraisal of Newer Elementary School Practices. New York: Teach Col, 1938.

PERIODICALS ON HOW TO CONSTRUCT UNITS AND LESSON PLANS

Alwin, V. Planning a year of units. Engl J, 45:334-340, 1956.

Anderzhon, M. L., and J. George. Teacher preparation for planning a unit. J Geog, 63:35-36, 1964.

Annarino, A. A. IIP; individualized instruction in physical education. JOHPER, 44:20-23, 1973.

Arnstine, D. G. Programmed instruction and unit teaching. H Sch J, 47:194-200, 1964.

Baker, G. E. How to become a better teacher. Ind Arts, 61:20, 1972.

Barton, George Jr. The derivation and clarification of objectives. J Educ Res, 41:624-639, 1948.

Berry, E. Unit Process. Educ Forum, 27:357-366, 1963.

Besvinick, Sidney. An effective daily lesson plan. Clearing H, 34:431-433, 1960.

Blackburn, J. Learning activity approach to unit teaching. H Sch J, 47:201-209, 1964.

Bornhorst, I. J. Making sense of our senses; unit.
    Teacher, 91:62, 1974.

Bosham, H. J., and R. J. Doris. New teaching vitality
    from lesson planning. Improv Col & Univ Teach,
    15:130-132, 1967.

Bryant, N. Jr., and H. A. Anderson. Effects of perfor-
    mance objectives on achievement. J Res Sci Teach,
    9(4)369-375, 1972.

Burns, Paul C. A re-examination of aspects of unit
    teaching in the elementary school. Peabody J Educ,
    40:31-39, 1962.

Butzow, J. W. Jr., and L. W. Linz. Model for determining
    the objectives of science education. Sci & Educ,
    57:15-18, 1973.

Chase, J. B. Jr., and J. L. Howard. Changing concepts
    of unit teaching. H Sch J, 47:180-187, 1964.

Cohen, R. D. Instructional priorities for development
    of science curricula. Sci & Educ, 56:477-485, 1972.

Coronata, Sister R. S. M. Using the unit method.
    Cath Sch J, 53:117-118, 1953.

Crosswhite, E. J. Implications for teaching and planning.
    Nat Council Teach Math Yrbk, 33:313-336, 1970.

Davis, R. Writing behavioral objectives. JOHPER,
    44:47-49, 1973.

Day, M. S. Affective and cognitive educational goals
    and behavior in mental retardates. Educ Horiz,
    50:207-211, 1972.

Delaney, A. A. Lesson plans; means or ends? Clearing H,
    36:295-297, 1962.

Del Popolo. Re-definition of the unit. Peabody J Educ,
    43:280-284, 1966.

DeRoche, E. F. Lesson plan approach. Cath Sch J,
    66:39-40, 1966.

DiVincenzo, R. M. Measurement-science: an elementary program in math-science curriculum development. Sch Sci & Math, 73:444-452, 1973.

Donovan, G. E. Two unusual faculty meetings. H Sch J, 43:48-53, 1961.

Draper, E. M., and G. Gardner. How to construct a resource unit. Clearing H, 26:267-270, 1952.

Durnin, R. G. Secrets of successful unit planning. Grade Teacher, 83:92, 1965.

Ediger, M. Developing resource units. Sch & Com, 56:23, 1969.

Ediger, M. Development of teaching units. Sch & Com, 60:23, 1974.

Edwards, C. H. Behavioral objectives: an updating. Contemp Educ, 45:23-26, 1973.

Elliott, A. V. P. For the young teacher; how to plan a lesson. Engl Lang Tech, 19:176-179, 1965.

Etten, J. F. Lesson planning for the inner city. Education, 87:347-353, 1967.

Fabiano, G. J. Unit approach in college teaching. Col & Univ J, 10:87-90, 1962.

Fitzpatrick, W. J. Unit approach for teaching. Clearing H, 37:352, 1963.

Fleck, H. Guidelines to planning. Prac Forecast, 10:13, 1964.

Freedman, L. J. Lesson plans for the substitute teacher. H Points, 43:67-70, 1961.

Freeman, M. H. Performance goals in high school accounting. Bus Educ Forum, 27:14-16, 1972.

Friedman, K. C. Using curriculum guides. Education, 82:215-217, 1961.

Friedman, N. Toward college English in high school: appropriate teaching methods. H Points, 48:19-23, 1966.

461 a

Gerhard, Muriel. How to write a unit. Grade Teacher, 84:123-124, 1967.

Glowatski, E. A. Behavioral objectives for geography facilitate communication and increase test performance. J Geog, 72:36-44, 1973.

Godfrey, L. L. Take a subject, any subject and individualize with learning stations. Teacher, 91:59-62, 1973.

Grant, Dorothy A. Refocus on lesson planning. Teach Col Rec, 68:503-508, 1967.

Graves, W. H. Selecting work units for the disadvantaged. Instr, 78:96, 1969.

Gray, K. Thinking abilities as objectives in curriculum development. Educ R, 24:237-250, 1972.

Gross, S. et al. Behavioral objectives in reading skills program, grades 4-8. Read Teach, 27:782-789, 1974.

Hastings, G. R. Independent learning based on behavioral objectives. J Educ Res, 65:411-416, 1972.

Henry, G. H. Unit Method: the new logic meets the old. Engl J, 56:401-406, 1967.

Hoeber, B. B. To plan, or not to plan, Tex Outl, 49:30-31, 1965.

Hook, Sidney, and Charles F. Madden. There is more than one way to teach. Sat R, 47:48-51, 1964.

Hoover, K. H., and Helene M. Hoover. Lesson planning a key to effective teaching. Clearing H, 82:41-44, 1967.

Ingram, V. W. Why not dinosaurs? Teacher, 91:72, 1973.

Johnson, R. B. Use of objectives in teacher education. Improv Col & Univ Teach, 20:164-167, 1972.

Katz, P. M. Master lesson plans aid substitute teachers. Chicago Sch J, 46:73-74, 1964.

Keedy, M. L. Mathematics in junior high school. Educ Lead, 17:176-181, 1959.

Kline, D. F. Developing resource units. Education, 84:221-225, 1963.

Kohl, H. Nothing to do. Grade Teacher, 88:6, 1970.

Koran, J. Jr., and J. T. Wilson. Research on objectives for high-school biology. Am Biol Teach, 35:151-154, 1973.

Krathwohl, David R. Stating objectives appropriately for program, for curriculum and for instructional materials development. J Teach Educ, 16:83-92, 1965.

Laing, R. A., and J. C. Peterson. Assignments: yesterday, today, and tomorrow: today: area of rectangles and triangles. Math Teach, 66:508-518, 1973.

LaGrand, L. E. Physical educator behavioral objectives in student-teacher relationships. Phys Educ, 29:198-199, 1972.

Lapp, D. K. Can elementary teachers write behavioral objectives. J Educ, 155:31-44, 1973.

Leadon, D. Adjusting lesson plans to improve classroom effectiveness. Bus Educ Forum, 19:11-12, 1964.

Lindman, M. R., and G. P. Grimes. Development and use of behavioral objectives in student teaching. Art Educ, 26:11-15, 1973.

Liveritte, R. H. Getting clear about behavioral objectives. Engl J, 63:46-52, 1974.

Lowell, J. A. Unit learning concept. Jun Col J, 42:24-27, 1971.

Mann, H. Conducting instruction requires planning. Teach Excep Child, 3:87-91, 1971.

Mannello, G. Resource unit versus instructional system. Educ Forum, 35:83-91, 1970.

Marani, J. V. Problem-centered learning. Education, 84:231-234, 1963.

Maves, P. B. Setting objectives for Christian education. Spectrum, 48:4-7, 1972.

Cormack, A. J. Behavioral objectives for science methods courses: a humanistic approach. Sci Educ, 57:55-64, 1973.

LeRoy, R. S. Lesson planning with a purpose. Bus Educ Forum, 21:17-18, 1967.

Neil, J. D. Using instructional objectives to make schools better. NASSP Bull, 56:71-76, 1972.

Phil, Walter E. The teaching unit: what makes it tick? Clearing H, 38:70-73, 1963.

lograno, V. J. Evaluating affective objectives in physical education. Phys Educ, 31:8-12, 1974.

rsand, J. How to plan a lesson. H Points, 47:5-26, 1965.

les, D. T. Affective priorities and educational objectives. Educ Tech, 12:33-35, 1972.

noszon, E. et al. What is the modern lesson like? Soviet Educ, 10:3-6, 1968.

rton, R. K. Flight plan. Improv Col & Univ Teach, 15:4, 1967.

essig, R. H. Bridging the gap between textbook teaching and unit teaching. Social Stud, 54:43-47, 1963.

riel, Gerhard. How to write a unit. Grade Teacher, 84:123-124, 1967.

sso, B. B. Micro resource units aid substitute teachers. Educ Lead, 27:825-826, 1970.

ppi, A. T. Why behavioral objectives? Social Stud, 64:56-59, 1973.

wcombe, P. J. Performance objectives for the first semester of a high school introductory speech communication course. Todays Speech, 20:49-54, 1972.

Brien, T. C. New goals for mathematics education. Childh Educ, 50:214-216, 1974.

Ojemann, R. H. Self-guidance and the use of prepared
    lists of objectives. El Sch J, 73:269-278, 1973.
Peters, D. F. Technique of planning a lesson. Ind Arts,
    21:19-20, 1962.
Phillips, Jack. Instructional media and the curriculum.
    Educ Tech, 7:17-18, 1967.
Polidoro, J. R. Affective domain: the forgotten
    behavioral objective of physical education. Phys
    Educ, 30:136-138,
Poulson, J. et al. Unit plan: the promise of an adminis-
    trative design. Clearing H, 46:535-539, 1972.
Power, T. V. In search of objectives for introductory
    courses in English law. Voc Aspect Educ, 24:123-131,
    1972.
Resource-based learning; symposium. Forum, 16:7-17, 1973.
Riggsby, Ernest D. Instructional media: essential
    element in teacher preparation? Educ Tech, 7:18-19,
    1967.
Roach, S. F. Teacher lesson plans. Sch Mgt, 6:26, 1962.
Sanacore, J. On-going evaluation of behavioral objectives
    and individualized reading instruction. El Engl,
    50:465-468, 1973.
Satlow, I. D. Long-range planning in bookkeeping.
    J Bsns Ed, 38:234-236, 1963.
Sengstock, W. Utilization of staff personnel in a summer
    program to improve instruction in special classes
    for the mentally retarded. H Sch J, 47:247-252, 1964.
Shane, H. G., and R. B. McQuigg. Unit teaching and the
    integration of knowledge. H Sch J, 47:188-193, 1964.
Shannon, J. D. Selecting bookkeeping learning activities.
    Bus Educ Forum, 27:18-20, 1972.
Shockley, J. M. Jr. Needed: behavioral objectives in
    physical education. JOHPER, 44:44-46, 1973.

465

hrader, H. Should we require lesson plans? <u>Education</u>,
    <u>51</u>:202, 1963.

hrake, H. L., and C. H. Troupe. Should teachers hand
    in lesson plans? <u>Instr</u>, <u>75</u>:21, 1966.

humate, N. M. Writing behavioral objectives. <u>Peabody
    J Educ</u>, <u>51</u>:101-106, 1974.

imons, H. D. Behavioral objectives: a false hope for
    education. <u>Educ Digest</u>, <u>38</u>:14-16, 1973.

lack, Charles W. The politics of educational objectives.
    <u>Educ Tech</u>, <u>7</u>(14):1-6, 1967.

tarr, R. J., and W. H. Jones. Behavioral objectives
    in bookkeeping. <u>Sch & Com</u>, <u>60</u>:13-14, 1973.

tutte, J. J. Educational objectives provide two-way
    communication in beginning shorthand class. <u>Bus
    Educ Forum</u>, <u>27</u>:25, 1972.

hiagarajan, S. Good objectives and bad: a checklist
    for behavioral objectives. <u>Educ Tech</u>, <u>13</u>:23-28,
    1973.

hompson, R. A. Take a longer look: tips on planning
    a reading unit. <u>Read Teach</u>, <u>27</u>:156-158, 1973.

insley, D. C. et al. Cognitive objectives in process-
    oriented and content-oriented secondary social
    studies programs. <u>Educ Lead</u>, <u>30</u>:245-248, 1972.

rojcak, D. A. Designing a strategy for long-term
    instruction. <u>Sch Sci & Math</u>, <u>72</u>:811-816, 1972.

uckman, B. W. Four-domain taxonomy for classifying
    educational tasks and objectives. <u>Educ Tech</u>,
    <u>12</u>:36-38, 1972.

nit planning. <u>H Sch J</u>, <u>47</u>:180-222, 1964.

agner, G. What schools are doing: developing resource
    units. <u>Education</u>, <u>83</u>:251-253, 1962.

agner, G. What schools are doing; unit teaching in the
    secondary education. <u>Education</u>, <u>85</u>:508-510, 1965.

agner, S. K. Head start for new teachers. <u>Pa Sch J</u>,
    <u>115</u>:7-9, 1966.

Walbesser, H. H., and H. L. Carter. Behavioral objectives.
      Nat Council Teach Math Yrbk, 35:52-103, 1973.
Walter, J. K. Guide for teaching the blind; lesson plan
      for operation of a drill press. Ind Arts & Voc
      Educ, 56:55-56, 1967.
Watson, L. W. Stating broad goals of mathematics
      education. Sch Sci & Math, 72:535-538, 1972.
Wight, A. B. Beyond behavioral objectives. Educ Tech,
      12:9-14, 1972.
Wilson, G. M. Looking critically at unit teaching.
      Instr, 72:93-94, 1963.
Witherow, M. Recapture those training capsules. Bus
      Educ World, 43:17, 1963.
Zahorik, J. A. Effect of planning on teaching. El Sch J,
      71:143-151, 1970.

FREE RESOURCE MATERIALS

Ausbrey, Ruth H. Selected Free Materials for Classroom
    Teachers. Palo Alto, Calif: Fearon Publishers,
    1965.
Shain, Rovert L. and Murray Polner. Where to Get and
    How to Use Free and Inexpensive Teaching Aids.
    New York: Teachers Practical Press Inc., 1963.
Pepe, Thomas J. Free and Inexpensive Educational Aids.
    New York: Dover Publications Inc., 1966.
Brown, James W., Richard B. Lewis, Fred F. Harcleroad.
    AV Instruction Media & Methods. New York: McGraw-
    Hill Book Co., 1969, p. 597-611.
Free and Inexpensive Learning Materials. Nashville,
    Tenn: Division of Surveys and Field Services,
    George Peabody College for Teachers, 1966-67.
Educators Guide to Free and Inexpensive Materials.
    Randolph, Wisconsin:

SAMPLE UNITS AND LESSON PLANS

Primary Level: Grades K-3

Albera, T. E. Yes; kindergartners can learn from a
newspaper unit. Grade Teacher, 84:30, 1967.

Ainslie, D. Dairy unit at the primary level. Instr,
71:50-52, 1962.

Ainslie, D. Primary pupils can learn to use the library.
Instr, 72:49, 1962.

Ainslie, D. What's in the post office for second grade?
Instr, 71:51, 1961.

Annalissa, Sister Mary. Eskimo social study. Cath
Sch J, 65:33-34, 1965.

Bacon, Philip. North: an easier way to teach directions.
Grade Teacher, 65:38-39, 1964.

Beard, V. It's autumn. Instr, 73:32-34, 1963.

Bland, S. S. Planning a teaching unit for the primary
grades: looking at animals. Sci & Child,
9:21-24, 1972.

Blanchard, H. B. Doll festival. Instr, 71:42, 1962.

Bortniker, C. Well-planned luncheon for Mother's Day.
Grade Teacher, 82:37, 1965.

Buegler, R. Study of the British isles. Va J Ed,
55:26-27, 1961

Clark, G. C. To celebrate October 18, take a trip to
Alaska. Instr, 77:40-41, 1967.

Craun, J. L. First-grade bakers learn from a pumpkin
pie. Instr, 74:49, 1964.

Darrin, G. L. Food store. Grade Teacher, 79:56-57, 1961.

Deacon, D. Roadside stand. Instr, 74:41, 1964.

Denny, M. C. Chicago meets San Juan. Instr, 76:38, 1967.

Denny, M. C. First-grade economics based on division of labor. Instr, 76:67, 1967.

dePietro, J. Pretend trip brings real results. Instr, 76:31, 1966.

Donovan, R. Run, run, run, as fast as you can. Instr, 73:38, 1963.

Don't run into trouble! playground unit. School Safety, 4:23-27, 1968.

Friedman, N. C. Safety to and from school. Grade Teacher, 79:21, 1962.

Fuller, G. Hawaiian holiday. Instr, 73:33, 1963.

Gorham, M. B. School is many things. Instr, 76:38, 1966.

Gray, M. F. Greatest show on earth. Instr, 76:28, 1967.

Hall, K. Come to the zoo. Instr, 74:18-19, 1965.

Hansen, L. E. Science unit on birds. Mont Education, 44:20-21, 1968.

Harmon, A. How nature changes from season to season. Grade Teacher, 82:96-97, 1964.

Harris, M., and R. Parsons. Wonderful world of reading. Grade Teacher, 81:35, 1964.

Higgins, E. J. Launching a luncheon; study of county industries. Instr, 73:45, 1964.

Hoeber, B. Let's teach Texas: a unit on Texas for the second grade. Tex Outl, 48:20-21, 1964.

Hostetter, E. H. Geometry in the kindergarten. Instr, 73:18, 1964.

Huntsinger, P., and G. Buroker. Let's play tepee. Grade Teacher, 85:124-127, 1967.

Jacobson, I. Fire fighters: primary unit for fire prevention week. Instr, 81:128, 1971.

Jacobson, I. Wind. Instr, 77:32, 1968.

Jevdet, M. N. Studying real work and workers. Instr, 82:118-119, 1973.

Karplus, R., and H. S. Thier. Science curriculum
    improvement study. Instr, 74:43-84, 1965.
Kleinert, M. Relating nutrition and science. Instr,
    74:36, 1965.
Leonard, N. A. Water problem. Instr, 72:49, 1963.
Life-giving secrets of little seeds. Grade Teacher,
    84:101, 1967.
Listen to both; school bus unit. School Safety, 4:24-
    29, 1968.
Marks, G. L. Calender. Grade Teacher, 80:45, 1962.
McGregor, M. T. Why do we have Thanksgiving day? Instr,
    73:32, 1963.
Mecham, M. Sweet topic; the sugar beet. Instr,
    76:31, 1966.
Miller, M. E. Kindergarteners learn about being
    American. Instr, 77:50, 1968.
Moore, M. Pilgrims. Grade Teacher, 80:49, 1962.
Muente, G. Grains that feed us. Instr, 73:66, 1963.
Muente, G. Where do we get our seeds? Instr, 77:30, 1968.
Polizzotti, G. Breakfast party. Education, 81:559-
    562, 1961.
Rasmussen, J. Catching up with our shadows. Instr,
    73:49, 1963.
Rasmussen, J. Watch your manners. Instr, 74:119, 1965.
Roodenburg, E. Christmas in space. Instr, 73:30, 1963.
Shuman, S. N. Get ready for winter season. Instr,
    71:48, 1961.
Slane, M. G. Maple syrup in the second grade. Instr,
    79:133-134, 1970.
Smith, M. K. Our hearts replaced valentines. Instr,
    77:92-94, 1968.
Smith, M. K. E. Use apples for an early fall project.
    Instr, 79:130-132, 1969.
Snyder, D. K. February, a month of meaning. Grade
    Teacher, 81:32, 1964.

enzel, E. J. It's cowboy day in Denver. <u>Instr</u>,
    <u>76</u>:26, 1967.

ylor, T. Unit on conservation. <u>Grade Teacher</u>, <u>82</u>:
    36-40, 1964.

n Lieu, R. M. Unit on milk. <u>Grade Teacher</u>, <u>81</u>:50,
    1964.

enop, F. L. Children in other countries. <u>Instr</u>,
    <u>74</u>:69,

kely, H. Making apple jelly. <u>Instr</u>, 73:61, 1963.

lson, H. Brush after lunch. <u>Instr</u>, <u>77</u>:52, 1968.

nemiller, G. M. How pets can teach a lot about
    people. <u>Grade Teacher</u>, <u>82</u>:24-26, 1965.

Intermediate Level: Grades 4-6

ams, R. S. Compass cross country. <u>JOHPER</u>, <u>36</u>:30,
    1965.

rast, C. Teach them to read between the lines. <u>Grade</u>
    <u>Teacher</u>, <u>85</u>:72-74, 1967.

derzhon, M. L. Five Pacific states. <u>Grade Teacher</u>,
    <u>80</u>:42-43, 1963.

derzhon, M. L. From here to there. <u>Grade Teacher</u>,
    <u>80</u>:34-35, 1963.

derzhon, M. L. Seasons of the sun. <u>Grade Teacher</u>,
    <u>80</u>:64-65, 1962.

derzhon, M. L. Writing our own map language. <u>Grade</u>
    <u>Teacher</u>, <u>80</u>:32-33, 1962.

tonilia, Sister Mary. Bring Christ to people through
    the commandments. <u>Cath Sch J</u>, <u>66</u>:36-37, 1966.

bor day planting leads to study unit about trees.
    <u>Grade Teacher</u>, <u>84</u>:47-49, 1967.

thier, M. M. Fifth graders explore ways to make paper.
    <u>Instr</u>, <u>77</u>:90, 1968.

Bacon, P., and A. A. Delaney. Canada neighbor to the
      north. Grade Teacher, 80:46-47, 1963.

Baldwin, G. From foot to wing. Instr, 74:59, 1965.

Ballas, D. J. China, yesterday and today. Grade
      Teacher, 81:62-63, 1963.

Ballas, D. J. East Africa. Grade Teacher, 79:60-61,
      1962.

Ballas, D. J. Northern Africa: land and people. Grade
      Teacher, 79:62-63, 1961.

Ballas, D. J. South China: land and livelihood. Grade
      Teacher, 81:38, 1964.

Be a danger detective; teaching unit. School Safety,
      4:26-27, 1969.

Bennett, L. M. Marine life: for fifth grade. Sci &
      Educ, 48:404-418, 1964.

Bermant, R. M., and G. Bermant. Behavior of primates:
      a unit for grades 4 to 6. Am Biol Teach, 33:167-
      171, 1971.

Bernard, Sister Mary. Bring Christmas to life. Cath
      Sch J, 61:29-30, 1961.

Be sure you can see; pedestrian unit. School Safety,
      4:24-25, 1969.

Bikes are like cars, obey the same rules; bicycle teaching
      unit. School Safety, 3:15-18, 1967.

Buckles, M. E. Impact of ancient Rome on our country.
      Instr, 77:116, 1968.

Buckles, M. E. Late spring unit on the birth of Britain.
      Instr, 76:58-59, 1967.

Caldwell, S. We dig. Grade Teacher, 87:128-133, 1970.

Chrysler, D. Studying a state's mammals. Instr,
      78:47, 1968.

Cirelli, J. Freedom in our town. Grade Teacher, 79:26,
      1962.

Clements, G. Thanksgiving meant much to the pilgrims.
      Instr, 71:49, 1961.

onnor, G. P. Notable Negroes: biography unit. <u>Instr</u>, <u>77</u>:85, 1968.

ooper, P. Egypt in antiquity; a sixth grade unit. <u>School Activities</u>, <u>37</u>:10-11, 1965.

oppola, J. N. Colonial times; a way to relive them. <u>Instr</u>, <u>77</u>:30, 1967.

oursey, J. L. Blast off! <u>Grade Teacher</u>, <u>88</u>:130-135, 1970.

Danger, keep out: dangerous play areas unit. <u>School Safety</u>, <u>4</u>:23-27, 1968.

Darrin, G. L. Canada our northern neighbor. <u>Grade Teacher</u>, <u>79</u>:30, 1962.

Darrin, G. L. Lumbering. <u>Grade Teacher</u>, <u>79</u>:30, 1962.

Darrin, G. L. Pioneers and their movements westwards. <u>Grade Teacher</u>, <u>79</u>:44, 1962.

Deibert, G. S. Actual experiences in heritage teaching: folklore. <u>Instr</u>, <u>75</u>:94, 1966.

Delaney, A. A. Witch doctors, barbers, and surgeons. <u>Grade Teacher</u>, <u>80</u>:50, 1963.

Delaney, A. A., and F. W. Korz. Messages across the centuries. <u>Grade Teacher</u>, <u>80</u>:81-82.

Dennis, R. T. Study of Australia. <u>Instr</u>, <u>74</u>:63, 1964.

DeRoche, E. F. Space travel. <u>Grade Teacher</u>, <u>80</u>:64, 1963.

DeRoche, E. F. Unit on light. <u>Grade Teacher</u>, <u>81</u>:41, 1964.

DuFault, M. L. Dental health unit for upper elementary grades. <u>J Sch Health</u>, <u>38</u>:179-184, 1968.

Dunathan, A. T. Forty-five-ton giant in the classroom. <u>Instr</u>, <u>74</u>:46-47, 1964.

Dvorak, R. Westward movement. <u>Grade Teacher</u>, <u>81</u>:60, 1963.

Ediger, M. Upper graders look at modern farming. <u>Instr</u>, <u>80</u>:144-145, 1970.

Ermish, G. Egypt, past and present. *Instr*, 73:50, 1963.

Ermish, G. Life in the sea. *Instr*, 76:138-139, 1966.

Ermish, G. Westward movement. *Instr*, 75:55, 1966.

Evangela, Sister Mary. Integrated unit on Brazil.
    Cath Sch J, 64:58, 1964.

Fire! follow your teacher: emergency preparedness
    teaching unit. *School Safety*, 3:13-14, 1967.

Fletcher, P. F. Composition unit for grade five.
    El Engl, 44:148-151, 1967.

Fowler, T. W. Lumber. *Grade Teacher*, 79:49, 1962.

Goldstein, I. Pets in the classroom. *Instr*, 73:34, 1963.

Grossman, G. B. Harbor and coastguard visits. *Instr*,
    72:49, 1963.

Guns are dumb, leave them alone; firearm teaching unit.
    School Safety, 2:15-18, 1966.

Haebig, J. Feathers from our friends. *Grade Teacher*,
    79:64, 1961.

Halverbout, A. M. Communication. *Instr*, 69:54, 1959.

Harris, A. E. Growing seeds. *Va Journal of Education*,
    59:18-19, 1966.

Highlights of the Civil war. *Grade Teacher*, 79:70, 1961.

Hill, W. Planning for instruction; designs for social
    studies resource units. *Nat Council Social Stud Yrbk*,
    32:262-270, 1962.

Hilton, J. Bees are interesting insects. *Instr*, 73:70,
    1964.

Hitt, W. Concepts of citizenship. *Instr*, 74:121, 1965.

Hoffman, N. How to bring science alive in your classroom.
    Grade Teacher, 85:104-106, 1968.

Hutzelman, L. Children of the world. *Grade Teacher*,
    77:64-65, 1959.

Innes, I. Let's bake a unit cake! *Grade Teacher*,
    80:46, 1962.

James, Sister Mary. Lesson plan on Japan. Cath Sch J, 65:62, 1965.

Jasnoch, L. Classroom jam session is more than yum! Grade Teacher, 84:40, 1967.

Joire, M. D. Thanksgiving; team teaching style. Instr, 77:134-135, 1967.

Joseph, Sister Francis. Trip to Switzerland. Cath Sch J, 66:63-64, 1966.

Joseph, Sister Francis. Unit on biography. Cath Sch J, 67:72-74, 1967.

Juhas, L. Nutrition = physical growth + mental growth. Instr, 76:34-35, 1966.

Keeps you up if the boat goes down. School Safety, 2: 15-16, 1967.

Krueger, M. G. Putting social lightning into lesson plans. J Teach Educ, 23:186-188, 1972.

Labrecque, C. Art in the classroom; children around the world, art taken from UNICEF cards. Grade Teacher, 85:10, 1967.

Learn to float. School Safety, 2:13-14, 1967.

Lemley, L. M. Our Pennsylvania. Pa Sch J, 110:56-57, 1961.

Lindgren, E. S. January: time to begin. Grade Teacher, 81:24, 1964.

Lock in safety; safe passenger teaching unit. School Safety, 2:12-14, 1966.

Long, L. Our America. Grade Teacher, 79:46, 1961.

Look left, look right, look back before crossing; visual pedestrian unit. School Safety, 2:15-18, 1967.

Look out if he's not there; teaching unit. School Safety, 3:15-18, 1968.

MacDermand, E. Water life. Instr, 71:44, 1962.

MacRae, L. K. Conservation. Grade Teacher, 79:59, 1961.

Maher, A. C. Constructing an experience unit: how we
    use arithmetic in the daily newspaper. Grade
    Teacher, 80:56-57, 1962.
Mallet, L. E. Teaching math with a mail-order catalog.
    Grade Teacher, 83:57-58, 1965.
Mangine, R. A. Dramatic approach in social studies.
    Instr, 72:117, 1962.
Mantz, G. Mental health unit for fourth and fifth
    grades. J Sch Health, 39:658-661, 1969.
Martin, M. M. Importance of food. Instr, 72:51, 1962.
McAulay, J. D. Fourteen units on our American heritage.
    Instr, 75:34-37, 1966.
McGovern, M. Steel and where it begins. Instr, 76:
    82-83, 1966.
Mertz, N. J. Indian life. Instr, 74:120, 1965.
Murphy, M. I. Dinosaurs. Grade Teacher, 80:41, 1962.
Naerten, N. It's about time. Instr, 82:90-91, 1973.
Needham, D. Pollution: a teaching and action program.
    Grade Teacher, 88:24-33, 1970.
Nelson, J. L. Concept unit in the social studies.
    Social Stud, 56:46-48, 1965.
Never swim alone; teaching unit. School Safety, 3:13-
    14, 1968.
Not for play, stay away; dangerous objects teaching unit.
    School Safety, 3:15-17, 1967.
Nuspl, J. J. Story of Tetonia, Wyoming. Grade Teacher,
    88:70-75, 1971.
O'Grady, J. Clip-out, ready-to-use-unit in the language
    arts. Grade Teacher, 84:125-128, 1967.
Ohnmacht, W. A. Colonial America. Instr, 73:47, 1964.
Oliver, Donald W. Unit concept in social studies: a
    re-examination. Sch R, 66:204-217, 1958.
Orleans, J. B. Recitation period in mathematics.
    H Points, 46:53-58, 1964.

Pick up, don't trip up; teaching unit. <u>School Safety</u>,
    <u>3</u>:13-14, 1968.

Puffer, L., and K. H. Puffer. Forests are more than
    trees. <u>Instr</u>, <u>73</u>:28, 1964.

Road signs are your signs of life; bike unit. <u>School
    Safety</u>, <u>4</u>:24-25, 1968.

Sando, R. G. Montana in the Great West. <u>Grade Teacher</u>,
    <u>79</u>:45, 1962.

Sawyer, A. W. Mammoth cave. <u>Instr</u>, <u>71</u>:52, 1962.

Schreiber, L. Christmas curriculum. <u>Sch & Com</u>, <u>52</u>:14,
    1965.

Schreur, W. There's more than news in the newspaper.
    <u>Instr</u>, <u>82</u>:84, 1973.

Skeel, D. J. Ancient Egypt. <u>Grade Teacher</u>, <u>81</u>:51, 1963.

Smith, J. Need for math seemed endless. <u>Am Voc J</u>,
    <u>47</u>:50, 1972.

Smith, M. M. Pyramids of Egypt. <u>Instr</u>, <u>74</u>:37, 1965.

Smith, S. R. Fairfield humanities program: up, up, and
    away. <u>El Engl</u>, <u>48</u>:477-481, 1971.

Stamberg, J. So you have a student teacher: lesson on
    molasses. <u>Arts & Activities</u>, <u>63</u>:15-17, 1968.

Stapp, R. V. Planning an art lesson. <u>Arts & Activities</u>,
    <u>61</u>:25, 1967.

Stone, D. M. Discovering how machines make work easier.
    <u>Instr</u>, <u>76</u>:36-37, 1966.

Stewart, M. J. Newspapers; a thinking child's textbook.
    <u>Instr</u>, <u>76</u>:82-83, 1967.

Stiles, G. E. Sign language for fire prevention. <u>Instr</u>,
    <u>71</u>:66, 1961.

Stradling, D. F. Japan. <u>Grade Teacher</u>, <u>81</u>:51, 1964.

Strauss, J., and R. Dufour. Discovering who I am; a
    humanities course for sixth grade students. <u>El Engl</u>,
    <u>47</u>:85-120, 1970.

Swyers, B. J. That little old module-maker, you.
    <u>Grade Teacher</u>, <u>89</u>:4-5, 1972.

Thompson, C. L., and J. L. Parker. Fifth graders view
the work world scene. El Sch Guid & Counsel,
5:281-288, 1971.

VanLieu, R. M. Dairy farming. Grade Teacher, 80:48, 1963.

Veatch, Jeannette. Social studies unit. Instr, 75:31,
1965.

Wagner, B. B. Seas. Grade Teacher, 80:68-69, 1962.

Wait your turn. School Safety, 2:13-14, 1967.

Walk on the left, drive on the right. School Safety,
2:14, 1966.

Weber, C. E. India & Pakistan. Grade Teacher, 80:64-65,
1963.

Weber, C. E. Insular southeast Asia. Grade Teacher,
80:54-55, 1963.

Weber, C. E. Let's look at Southeast Asia. Grade
Teacher, 80:60-61, 1962.

Weber, C. E. Peninsula Southeast Asia. Grade Teacher,
80:60-61, 1962.

Werner, G. I. Be smart: teach them not to smoke. Grade
Teacher, 82:52, 1964.

Westlake, P. Communication. Grade Teacher, 76:27, 1959.

Wood, R. W. Ham it up! Grade Teacher, 88:116-118, 1970.

Yost, H. A. Operation face lift. Instr, 75:34-35, 1966.

You buckle up too; safe passenger safety unit. School
Safety, 2:13-14, 1967.

Junior High Level: Grades 7-8

Ballas, D. J. Korea: geography, history, and culture.
Grade Teacher, 81:68-69, 1964.

Barrett, R. E. Nongraded learning units revamp junior
high school. NASSP Bull, 57:85-91, 1973.

ttles, R. E. Understandings of democracy. _Instr_,
      _72_:84, 1963.

a careful camper; teaching unit. _School Safety_,
      _4_:25, 1969.

nder, L. English master units: a design for small
      schools. _Engl J_, _52_:208-210, 1963.

rrin, G. L. Aviation. _Grade Teacher_, _79_:43-44, 1961.

rrin, G. L. Banking knowledge for young Americans.
      Grade Teacher, _80_:46-47, 1962.

rrin, G. L. Life insurance knowledge for young
      Americans. _Grade Teacher_, _80_:54-55, 1963.

y, M. M. Building healthy self-images. _Instr_, _74_:22,
      1965.

Blassie, R. R. Occupational information in the junior
      high school curriculum. _J Sec Ed_, _45_:269-274, 1970.

laney, A. A., and F. W. Korz. From the wheel to the
      electronic brain. _Grade Teacher_, _80_:64-65, 1962.

laney, A. A., and F. W. Korz. Messages across the
      centuries. _Grade Teacher_, _80_:81-82, 1963.

iger, M. Middle East; problem-solving unit on a
      tension area. _Instr_, _78_:104-105, 1969.

iedman, N. Toward college English in the high school:
      appropriate teaching methods. _H Points_, _48_:19-23,
      1966.

odwin, D., and W. Knipe. An experimental unit in
      American history. _NASSP Bull_, _45_:91-96, 1961.

uld, J. Teaching about the election. _Grade Teacher_,
      _86_:127-132, 1968.

ghlights of the Civil War. _Grade Teacher_, _79_:70-71,
      1961.

esch, M. M., and M. M. Nelson. Voices of Africa.
      Clearing H, _39_:303-304, 1965.

novate. Chicago: The Chicago Tribune Company, 1971.

mes, Sister Mary. Sight and sound. _Cath Sch J_, _62_:
      73-75, 1962.

Kavett, H., and P. F. Kavett. Oil = soil + toil.
     Instr, 72:48-49, 1962.
McCafferty, R. C., and G. R. Easterling. Understanding
     heredity. Sch Sci & Math, 67:60-87, 1967.
McCormic, A., and N. Dove. Teaching slang; it's a gas!
     Grade Teacher, 86:114, 1969.
Michael, Sister Mary. Mythological moods. Cath Sch J,
     64:40-43, 1964.
Michael, Sister Grace. Unit on the United Nations.
     Cath Sch J, 66:84-85, 1966.
Mustard, S. C., and E. F. DeRoche. Newspaper as a
     daily textbook. Instr, 74:38, 1965.
Peel, J. C. The ubiquitous unit. Phi Delta Kappan,
     37:119-121, 1955.
Programs for Excellence. Chicago, The Chicago Tribune
     Company, 1970.
Sallberg, R. A. Teach a unit on newspapers in the high
     school English class. Cath Sch J, 69:69-70, 1969.
Sampson, S. C., and H. Sampson. Inside story of a
     newspaper. Instr, 74:60, 1964.
Scioscia, F. D. Physical self; fascinating study.
     Instr, 77:28-29, 1967.
Simon, S. B., and M. Harmin. Year the schools began
     teaching the telephone directory; satire. Nat El
     Prin, 49:14-18, 1970.
Van Ness, D. Getting to know a newspaper. Grade Teacher,
     84:104, 1967.
White, J. All kinds of jobs. Instr, 71:46, 1962.

High School Level: Grades 9-12

Bennett, L. M. Marine biology project of Texas woman's
     university. Sch Sci & Math, 68:723-738, 1967.

Burgdorf, L. P., and I. F. Harney. Challenge of the
city. Instr, 79:100-104, 1970.

Burgdorf, L. P., and I. F. Harney. Highways affect
people's lives. Instr, 79:98-102, 1969.

Clark, J. F. Studying the UN. Instr, 75:34-35, 1965.

Cook, R. H. Different way to teach history. Wis J Ed,
100:6-7, 1968.

Friedman, Norman. Toward English in high school.
H Points, 48:19-23, 1966.

Gorskaia, G. I. Thermatic planning. Soviet Educ,
5:15-18, 1963.

Hackl, L. Honor and fame: a tenth grade unit. Engl J,
52:628-629, 1963.

Halsey, V. R. Jr. American history: a new high school
course. Social Ed, 27:249-252, 1963.

Hardy, C. A. Unit on pollution for secondary English
classes. Education, 92:84-85, 1972.

Harnack, R. S. Commuter based resource units. Educ Lead,
23:239, 1965.

Harnack, R. S. Resource units and the computer.
H Sch J, 51:126-131, 1967.

Henricks, J. R., and T. H. Metos. Amerindians; studying
an important minority group. Instr, 79:98-104, 1970.

Hennis, Jr., and R. Sterling. A broad unit approach to
literature. H Sch J, 45:201-207, 1962.

Hiner, G. W. Valentine unit suggests a unit on self-
awareness. Excep Child, 30:317-319, 1964.

Holden, G. S. Effects of computer based resource units
upon instructional behavior. J Exp Educ, 37:27-30,
1969.

Kaltsounis, T. Bridging the old and new. Instr, 80:
54-55, 1971.

Kaplan, M. A. Functional unit in the English classroom.
H Sch J, 56:108-114, 1972.

Murray, W. L. A unit on graphs. H Sch J, 49:400, 1960.

Nadel, Max. Outline for a lesson plan in poetry appreciation. H Points, 41:60-63, 1959.

Nurnberg, M. Uniform lessons in English. H Points, 44:59-70, 1962.

Olson, C. O. Jr. Secondary school education unit. H Sch J, 52:290-297, 1969.

Powell, M. Unified goals and objectives for clerical office practice. Bus Ed Forum, 27:27-28, 1972.

Pull it snug; safety belt unit. School Safety, 4:23-27, 1969.

Sallberg, R. A. Teach a unit on newspapers in the high school English class. Cath Sch J, 69:69-70, 1969.

Satlow, David I. How do you go about preparing a daily bookkeeping lesson? Bus Ed Forum, 19:21, 1965.

Satlow, David I. Long-range planning in bookkeeping. J Bus Ed, 38:234-236, 1963.

Schasre, J. M. Anatomy for beginners. Instr, 80:104-106, 1970.

Shopping center; an environmental pattern. Instr, 79:62-63, 1969.

Sparks, M. C. Utilization of the resource unit. Bus Ed Forum, 22:23, 1967.

Sutton, I. P. et al. Aquatic ecology unit for ninth grade biology. Sch Sci & Math, 62:315-329, 1962.

Thomashow, B. E. Stock-market unit. Arith Teach, 15:552-556, 1968.

Tinsley, D. C. et al. Cognitive objectives in process-oriented and content-oriented secondary social studies programs. Educ Lead, 30:245-248, 1972.

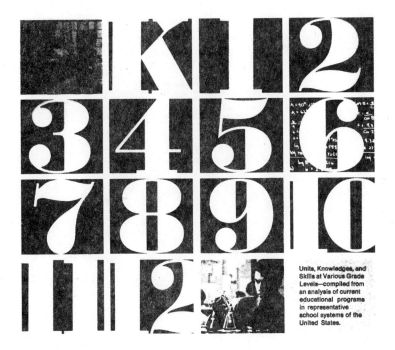

Units, Knowledges, and Skills at Various Grade Levels—compiled from an analysis of current educational programs in representative school systems of the United States.

Typical Course of Study
Kindergarten through Grade 12

By William H. Nault, A.B., M.A., Ed.D.

Executive Vice-President and Editorial Director
Field Enterprises Educational Corporation
Formerly, Director of Instruction, Ridgewood, New Jersey.
Principal, W. K. Kellogg Jr. High School, Battle Creek, Michigan

Typical Course of Study

Kindergarten through Grade 12

This booklet provides an overview of the course of study commonly used in kindergarten through grade twelve. Two major pieces of curriculum research —the *Caswell-Nault Analysis of Courses of Study* and the *Nault-Fischer-Passow Analysis of Courses of Study*—were used extensively in the development of this typical course of study.

The courses of study, curriculum guides, syllabi, and other instructional publications used in these analyses were obtained from a number of sources. A letter to the chief officer of public instruction in each of the fifty states requested curriculum bulletins and guides prepared by the department. These same letters also requested the names of county, city, and other local school systems within each state which had prepared outstanding bulletins. *Curriculum Materials*, the annual publication of the Association for Supervision and Curriculum Development (ASGD), furnished a bibliography of materials exhibited at the annual conference of ASCD. These materials were also made available for the study.

From the numerous guides obtained, the curriculum specialists exercised professional judgment in selecting promising guides for analysis. Among the criteria used in judging the bulletins under consideration were assurances that the courses of study would cover: (a) all major subject areas; (b) the grades kindergarten-twelve; (c) all sections of the country; (d) school units of various size (city, county, state); (e) publication dates of 1965 or later.

GRADE

Typical Course of Study

SOCIAL STUDIES

Meaning of holidays
Role of home and family
Characteristics of home and family
Location of home and school
Diagram of home and school
Relationship between home and school
Relationship of individual to the group
Children in other lands
Why things change
Where things come from
How things change

SCIENCE

Weather and seasons (observations)
Interrelationships of plants and animals
The sun—our principal source of energy
Classification of living things
Simple measurements
How plants are alike and different
Farm animals
Care of pets
Observing animals
Indoor plants
Earth, moon, and stars

LANGUAGE ARTS

Listening to music, poetry, choral reading
Social listening
Listening for correct speech habits and
  word usage
Constructing visual images while listening
Organizing ideas
Relating events and experiences using
  complete sentences

HEALTH and SAFETY

Personal hygiene
Good eating habits
Good clothing habits
Care of teeth
Safety to and from school

ARITHMETIC

Simple counting
One-to-one relationship
Correspondence of quantities
Ordinal-cardinal relationship
Number-numeral relationship
Recognition of basic sets
Elementary geometry (shapes)
Calendar and clock
Denominations of money

GRADE

Typical Course of Study

SOCIAL STUDIES	Citizenship
	Neighborhood helpers
	Our American heritage
	Holidays
	    Christmas
	    Mother's Day
	    Lincoln's Birthday
	    St. Valentine's Day
	    Halloween
	    Thanksgiving
	    Father's Day
	    Washington's Birthday
	    Hanukkah
	Make and read a simple neighborhood map
		School-community
		Homes in other lands
		Farm and Zoo

SCIENCE	Animals and pets
	    Farm animals
	    Zoo and circus animals
	    Woodland animals
	    Common birds
	Where plants live
	Where animals live
	Grouping and classification
	Air and water
	Seeds, bulbs, plants, and flowers
	Day and night
	Sun, moon, stars
	Seasons and weather
		Fire and temperature
		Simple machines

LANGUAGE ARTS	Reading:
	    Phonetic analysis
	    Structural analysis
	    Establishing sight vocabulary
	    Reading informally—names, labels, signs, etc.
	Enunciation and pronunciation
	Simple capitalization and punctuation
	Write name and simple words in manuscript
	Create stories and poems
	Tell favorite stories
	Simple pantomimes and dramatic play
	Use table of contents
		Learn to handle books
		Organize ideas and impressions
		Take part in group discussion

HEALTH and SAFETY	Safety rules to and from school Good eating habits How to dress for weather and activity Exercise and rest Personal hygiene Common cold	
ARITHMETIC	Number line use Place value and numeration Count and write through 99 Simple properties of sets Count by twos to 40 Simple properties of zero Simple number patterns Use of ten as basic unit Concepts of ordinal and cardinal numbers Value of penny, nickel, dime Meaning of inch, foot, yard	Recognize time: clock and calendar Handle ½ and ¼ in appropriate situations Solve simple word problems

GRADE

2

Typical Course of Study

SOCIAL STUDIES

Community services and helpers
Holidays and festivals
    Easter
    Passover
    Christmas
    Hanukkah
Patriotic celebrations
Our food
    Dairy and Bakery
    Garden and Greenhouse
    Markets and Stores
Shelter
Families around the world

Communities in other lands
Interdependence of people

SCIENCE

Animals of our neighborhood
Useful and harmful animals
Birds and insects in winter
Animal babies
How plants and animals get their food
Plant reproduction
How animals protect themselves and their young
Effects of seasons on lives of people, animals,
    and plants
Weather and how it affects our earth
Heat and temperature
The sun
The moon

The earth and sky
Simple constellations
Gravity
Air and atmosphere
Magnets and forces
Exploring space

LANGUAGE ARTS

Write independently in manuscript form
Develop methods of word attack
Simple capitalization and punctuation
Refine manuscript writing
How to study spelling
Listening skills
Give simple book reviews
Compose brief and simple letters
Use table of contents and index of book
Alphabetize through second letter
Read silently for specific purposes
Use and meaning of quotation marks in reading

Develop increased skill in handling books
Organize ideas and impressions
Dramatizations and interpretive or oral reading

EALTH and SAFETY

Know basic food groups
Dental hygiene
Personal cleanliness
Safety in the neighborhood
Communicable diseases
Preventive measures against disease

ARITHMETIC

Decimal numeration system
Addition and subtraction facts through 18
Counting by ones to 999
Reading and writing numbers through 999
Common measures of time, weight, length, liquid,
    and shape
Place value through hundreds
Introduction to multiplication and division
Multiplication properties of zero and one
Telling time and using the calendar
Count by fives to 50

Count by tens to 990
Handling of money (coins)
One-step problem solving
Using ordinal numbers through 10
Using sets and number facts

GRADE

3

Typical Course of Study

SOCIAL STUDIES

Community helpers
History and development of local community
American Indians and pioneers
Shelters of animals and people
Transportation today and yesterday
Communication today and yesterday
Sources of our food
Sources of our clothing
Shelter
Some great Americans
Holidays and folk customs
Flat maps and the globe

SCIENCE

How the face of the earth is changed
Motions of the earth
Earth satellites
Stars and moon
Energy and its sources
Sound
Weather and climate
Rocks and soil
How animals serve man
Plants and animals of the desert
Plants and animals of the sea
Life cycle of animals
Common birds, trees, and flowers

Forest plants
Conservation of plants and animals
Ocean life
Magnets and electricity
Great names in science

LANGUAGE ARTS

Silent reading in increasing amounts and difficulty
Reading prose and poetry aloud
Report experiences orally with accuracy
Write short original stories and poems
Develop methods of word attack
Use period, comma, question mark, apostrophe,
   and quotation marks
Use common contractions, such as "can't,"
   "aren't," and "doesn't"
Develop dictionary skills
Alphabetize through third letter
Begin cursive writing

Spelling
Concept of paragraph
Homonyms

HEALTH and SAFETY

Correct names for various parts of the body
Simple first aid
Proper balance of activities
Prevention and control of diseases
Care of eyes and ears
Health with relation to food, shelter, and clothing
Safety in the community

ARITHMETIC

Numeration systems
Properties of one
100 subtraction facts
Problem solving analysis
Units of measures
Graphs and charts
Two-step problems
55 addition facts and their reverse facts
Basic multiplication facts through the sixes
Division facts corresponding with
   multiplication facts

Distributive property of multiplication
Roman numerals through XII
Reading and writing numbers to 5 places
Simple fractions and equivalents
Count by twos, threes, and fours through 100

489

GRADE

4

Typical Course of Study

SOCIAL STUDIES

History and development of the local state
Relationship of the state to its region, the nation,
    and the world
Geographic or climatic regions of the world
Lands of four seasons
Hot, dry desert lands
Cold lands
Hot lands
Mild lands
Mountainous lands
Types of community life
Uses of the globe

SCIENCE

Measurement systems
Plants and animals of the past
Earth and its history
Balance of nature
Classification systems
Structure of plants
How weather influences physical life
Causes of seasons
Solar system and the universe
Oceans and the hydrosphere
Climate
Rocks and minerals
Plants and seeds

Biological organization
Living in space
Great names in science

LANGUAGE ARTS

Spelling
Silent and oral reading
Choral reading
Listening skills
Simple outlining
Write letters and informal notes
Creative writing
Use of the telephone
Make and accept simple introductions
Develop dictionary skills
Develop encyclopedia skills
Develop skill in locating information

HEALTH and SAFETY

The body and its functions
Care and proper use of the body
Personal and mental hygiene
Principles of digestion
Basic food groups
Good nutrition habits

ARITHMETIC

Numeration systems
Subsets
Reading and writing numbers of 7 digits
Roman numerals through L
Addition—4 numbers of 3 digits each
Multiplication facts through the 10's
Division facts of 4's through 9's
Multiplication by one-, two-, or three-digit numbers
Division with one-digit divisor
Measurement
Meaning of mixed numbers

Find simple averages
Problem solving methods
Simple geometric concepts
Develop ability to compute mentally

490

GRADE

5

Typical Course of Study

SOCIAL STUDIES	Exploration and discovery Establishment of settlements in the New World Colonial life in America Pioneer life in America Westward Movement Industrial and cultural growth Life in the United States and its possessions today Our presidents and famous people Natural resources of the United States Geography of the United States Relationship of the United States with Canada Comparative culture of Canada Fundamental map skills	
SCIENCE	How living things adapt themselves Plants and their food Properties of air Chemical systems Force systems Time and seasons Molds Bacteria Trees Sun Milky Way Great names in science Use and control of electricity	Magnetic fields Latitude and longitude Space and space explorations Conservation Biological adaptations

LANGUAGE ARTS	Spelling
	Silent and oral reading
	Present original plays
	Listening skills
	Parts of sentences
	Kinds of sentences
	Plurals and possessives
	Commonly used homonyms
	Synonyms and antonyms
	Homophones
	Homographs
	Write letters, stories, reports, poems, plays
		Dictionary use for word meaning, analysis,
		  and spelling
		Use of study material: keys, tables, graphs,
		  charts, legends, library file cards, index, table
		  of contents, reference material, maps
		Make two kinds of outlines
		Types of literature

HEALTH and SAFETY	Elementary first aid Community health resources Our water supply Sewage disposal Bicycle and water safety Care of the eyes Dental hygiene	Nutrition and diet Facts about coffee, tea, soft drinks, candy, etc. Germ-bearing insects and pests
ARITHMETIC	Fundamental processes involving whole numbers and common fractions Set of the integers Associative and distributive properties Read and write numbers through millions Common and decimal fractions Numeration systems Nonnegative rational numbers Roman numerals to C Long division concepts Algorism	Simple decimals through hundredths Extension of geometric concepts Tables, graphs, scale drawings Per cent Multiple-step verbal problems

491

GRADE

Typical Course of Study

SOCIAL STUDIES	Lands and peoples of the Western Hemisphere Canada and Mexico Our neighbors in Central America and the West Indies Our neighbors in South America Relationships between nations United Nations Transportation and communication World trade Eurasia and Africa Map reading skills School camping (optional)

SCIENCE	Helpful and harmful insects Improvement of plants and animals Classification of living things Food for growth and energy Microbes Algae and fungi Energy and simple machines Climate and weather Motors and engines Electricity and its uses Simple astronomy Elementary geology Elements of sound	Light and heat Equilibrium systems Atom and nuclear energy Inventions and discoveries Great names in science Space and space travel Conservation

LANGUAGE ARTS	Nonlanguage communication
	Write: letters
	    outlines
	    factual matter (newspaper article, reports)
	    verse (limerick or ballad)
	    creative prose (diary, stories)
	Extend dictionary skills
	Use reference material and indexes
	Types of literature
	Concepts of noun, pronoun, verb, adjective,
	    and adverb
	Work on speech errors and punctuation
		Spelling
		Listening skills
		Reading silently and skimming
		Use roots, prefixes, and suffixes
		Bibliography building
		Organization of a book

HEALTH and SAFETY	Cure and prevention of common diseases Facts on tobacco, alcohol, and narcotics Great men in the field of health Our food supply Safety and first aid Personal appearance Health maintenance

ARITHMETIC	Ancient numeration systems
	Fundamental operations with decimals
	Fundamental operations with compound
	    denominate numbers
	Relationship between common and decimal
	    fractions
	Roman numerals to M
	Multiply and divide common fractions and
	    mixed numbers
	Measures of areas and perimeters
	Metric system
		Operation of powers
		Exponents
		Factoring
		Volume of rectangular solids
		Simple problems in per cent
		Interpret and make bar, line, and picture graphs
		Set of the integers
		Introduction to symbolic logic (Boolean algebra)

GRADE

7

Typical Course of Study

SOCIAL STUDIES	Lands and peoples of the Eastern Hemisphere Prehistoric people Greek and Roman civilizations The Middle Ages Age of Discovery Industrial Age Yesterday and today in the Middle East Yesterday and today in the Far East Yesterday and today in Continental Europe Yesterday and today in Scandinavia Yesterday and today in the British Isles Yesterday and today in Russia Yesterday and today in the Mediterranean Yesterday and today in Africa	World trade and resources Social institutions The family Advanced map reading skills
SCIENCE	Scientific method Scientific classification Bacterial mutations The cell Life cycle of insects Anatomy and physiology Genetics Rocks and soil Minerals Air pressure Atmosphere Conservation Properties and uses of water	Effects of weather and climate Changes and uses of materials Famous scientists and their contributions

LANGUAGE ARTS	Spelling
	Work on reading skills
	Clauses and phrases
	Parts of speech
	Person, number, and gender of nouns
	   and pronouns
	Compound sentences
	Punctuation of conversation
	Plan and produce dramatizations
	Write descriptions, reports, and letters
	Note taking and outlining
	Organization of the library
		Extend research skills—atlases, encyclopedias,
		   magazines
		Refine dictionary skills
		Speech activities
		Listening skills
		Myths and legends
		Types of poetry
		Autobiography
		Biography
		Ballads
		One act plays

HEALTH and SAFETY	Practice of good health habits Good grooming and posture Personality development Effects of stimulants and narcotics Personal and public safety Accident prevention Circulation and respiration	Functions of the body Germ theory Chemotherapy Antibiotics Toxins and antitoxins Immunization
MATHEMATICS	Numeration Properties of nonnegative integers Rational numbers and fractions Three cases of per cent with applications Finite, infinite, and empty sets Continued growth in developing number skills Measurement Areas and volumes of geometric forms Basic geometric concepts Ratio and proportion Elementary business practices	Reading and constructing graphs Development and use of formulas

495

GRADE

8

Typical Course of Study

SOCIAL STUDIES

Our Old World backgrounds
Exploration and discovery
Colonial life
Struggle for independence
United States Constitution and Bill of Rights
Westward Movement
Civil War and Reconstruction
Growth and development of the United States
The United States as a world power
Our American culture
Our economic system
The United States political system
Meaning of democracy
Advanced map reading skills

Choosing a career (optional)

SCIENCE

Scientific method
Science nomenclature
Scientific measurement
Water and its uses
Magnetism and electricity
Composition of the earth
The earth's movement
Weathering and erosion
The ocean
The atmosphere
Weather
The universe
The Milky Way

Space and space travel
Conservation
Contributions of men of science
Astronomy
Heat
Light
Machines
The atom
Chemical changes
Wave energy
Mechanical energy
Electrical energy
Atomic energy

LANGUAGE ARTS

Spelling
Independent reading
Figures of speech
Inductive and deductive reasoning
Advanced dictionary work
Speech activities
Listening activities
Creative dramatics
Extend vocabulary
Biographies of great Americans
American poets and storytellers
Short story

Narrative poetry
Nonfiction
Improving skills in use of basic reference
  material
Kinds of sentences and their essential parts
Functions of sentence elements
Write simple business letters
Study of infinitive, participle, gerund, predicate
  nominative, predicate adjective, direct and
  indirect object

HEALTH and SAFETY

Safety
Sanitation
Mental hygiene
First aid
Grooming
Types and functions of foods
The body's utilization of food

Functions of the body
Community sanitation and health

MATHEMATICS

Maintaining skills in fundamental operations
Application of per cent
Use of fractions and decimals
Simple formulas and equations
Study of insurance, banking, and taxes
Scale drawing
Metric and nonmetric geometry
Polynomials
Powers and roots
Equalities and inequalities
Graph of an equation

Factoring and products
Sets and simple sentences
Numeration systems
Probability statistics
Nonmetric geometry

494

GRADE

9

Typical Course of Study

SOCIAL STUDIES
Basic communities of man
Community government
State government
National government
Political parties and elections
Conservation (including human conservation)
Elementary economics
Labor and management
Taxation
The Constitution
Rights and responsibilities of good citizenship
The United Nations
Foundations of American Democracy

SCIENCE **General Science**
Air and air pressure
Heat and fuels
Weather and climate
Air masses and fronts
Erosion
Nature and uses of light
Water and its uses
Electricity and electronics
Atomic energy
Molecular theory
Earth science
Space and astronomy

Space travel
Metals and plastics
Sound and music
Nature and causes of disease
Health and safety
Nature and uses of chemicals
Simple and complex machines
Transportation and communication
Careers in science

LANGUAGE ARTS
Spelling
Fundamentals of composition
Analyzing poetry
Dramatic poetry
Using poetry anthologies
Language systems
Vocabulary
Grammar
Folklore and myths
Parable and allegory
The novel
Reading the newspaper

Advertising
Structure of a play
Extend research skills
Listening skills
Preparing a speech
Analyzing propaganda
Selecting and using magazines
The unabridged dictionary
Foreign words used in English
Review of the card catalog
Special indexes

MATHEMATICS **General Mathematics**
Mathematical vocabulary
Direct measurement
Banks and banking
Investment
Budgeting
Insurance
Taxation
Graphs and tables
Informal geometry
Elementary algebra
Indirect measurement
Metric system

Algebra
Sets and their relationships
Properties of polynomial forms
Equations
Signed numbers
Fundamental operations

Equations of the first degree
Ratio, proportion, and variation
Relations and functions
Special products and factoring
Fractions and fractional equations
Square roots
Radicals
Quadratic equations
Elements of probability

495

GRADE

10

Typical Course of Study

SOCIAL STUDIES

Prehistoric man
The earliest civilizations
The early Greeks
The Romans
The Middle Ages
The Renaissance
The rise and fall of kings
Birth of modern democracy
The French Revolution
The Industrial Revolution
Nationalism
Imperialism
Science and industry
World War I

Between the World Wars
World War II
The Cold War
The Vietnam War
The search for peace

SCIENCE

Biology

Characteristics of life
Vertebrate life
Mammals and birds
Conservation of human resources
Plant life
Behavior
The scientific method
Disease and disease control
Genetics
Heredity
Biology of man
Microscopic life

Classification
Nutrition and digestion
History of plants and animals
Reproduction and growth
Biology and space travel
Careers in biology

LANGUAGE ARTS

Techniques of writing
History of writing
History of the alphabet
The short story
The novel
Writing short stories
Spelling
Listening skills
Vocabulary
Grammar
Lyric poetry
Sonnet

The essay
American literary heritage
Folklore and ballads
Regional customs, traditions, folkways,
    and language
Geographical dialects
Persuasion and argumentation
Understanding and writing poetry
Writing plays
Extend dictionary skills

MATHEMATICS

Plane Geometry

Sets
Origin and uses of geometry
Simple constructions
Parallel lines
Circles
Polygons
Converse theorems
Inductive reasoning
Nature of proof
Inequalities
Locus
Ratios and proportions
Measurement of geometric figures

Intermediate Algebra

Functional relations
Square roots, surds, radicals
Quadratic equations
Binomial theorem

Imaginary numbers
Exponents and radicals
Logarithms
Progressions
Higher degree equations
Vectors
Determinants

49C

GRADE

11

Typical Course of Study

SOCIAL STUDIES

Age of exploration and discovery
Colonization of America
The new nation is born
The Constitution of the United States
Development of the new nation
Period of nationalism
Sectionalism
Civil War and Reconstruction
The United States as a world power
Between two wars
World War II
The Cold War
The atomic era
Delinquency and crime

Problems of mental health
Urbanization
Public education
Personality problems

SCIENCE

Chemistry

Matter and its behavior
Carbon and its compounds
Formulas and chemical equations
Acids, bases, and salts
Atomic theory
Periodic law
Water and solutions
Oxidation—reduction
The nonmetals
Ionization and ionic solutions
The metals and alloys
Colloids, suspensoids, and emulsoids

Electrochemistry
Equilibrium and kinetics
Nuclear reactions
Radioactivity
Careers in chemistry

LANGUAGE ARTS

American literature
Analysis of plays
Vocabulary development
Grammar
Architecture and sculpture
Mass communication
Music and painting
Propaganda techniques
Spelling
Listening skills
Advertising
Story writing

Editorial writing
Journalistic writing
Proofreading symbols
Use of *Readers' Guide*, etc.
Miscellaneous reference aids
Vocabulary of poetry

MATHEMATICS

Solid Geometry

Lines and planes in space
Dihedral and polyhedral angles
Locus
Polyhedrons
Cylinders and cones
Spheres
Photogrammetry
Slide rule

Trigonometry

Solution of right triangles
Use of tables and interpolation
Measurement of angles
Properties of trigonometric functions
Complex numbers and vectors
Graphs of functions
Solutions of oblique triangles
Logarithms
Identities and equations

General triangle solutions
Slide rule

497

GRADE

12

Typical Course of Study

SOCIAL STUDIES
The democratic ideal
Agriculture in the United States
Urbanization
Conservation
Business and industry in the United States
American party system
Propaganda and public opinion
Democracy vs. Communism
Crime and delinquency
Labor-management relations
Taxation and finance
International relations
International organizations
Distribution and Exchange

Public education
Principles of United States Government
Free enterprise system

SCIENCE
Physics
Mechanics
Heat
Electricity and magnetism
Sound and acoustics
Light and optics
Wave motion
Nuclear Physics
Electronics
Force
Work, energy, and power
Space, time, and motion
Relativity

Solid state physics
Careers in physics

LANGUAGE ARTS
Spelling
Listening skills
Shakespeare
Current periodical literature
Problems of communication
Mass communication
Comparative study of mass media
Radio and television
Literary, social, and political heritage of England
Techniques of acting
Nature of tragedy and comedy
Social and business letters

Write book reviews, précis, essays
Identify verbals
Parliamentary procedures
Bibliography development
World literature
Report writing
Film as an art form

MATHEMATICS
Analytic Geometry*
Coordinates of a point
Slopes of lines
Equations of straight lines and circles
Plotting equations
The conics
Parametric equations
Polar coordinates

Elementary Calculus*
Derivative of a function
Computation of derivatives
Rate of change of a quantity
Maxima and minima
Integrals
Length of curves
Volume and surface areas

Elementary Statistics*
Tabular data
Graphs

Measures of central tendency
Quartiles and percentiles
Measures of dispersion
Simple correlation
Statistical inference

Advanced Algebra
Sets of numbers
Binomial theorem
Progressions
Complex numbers
Theory of equations
Permutations
Functions and their graphs
Combinations
Probability
Determinants
Inequalities
Matrix algebra
Mathematical induction
The derivative (optional)

*Not typical, but increasing in popularity

498